And Bid Him Sing

And Bid Him Sing

Essays in Literature
and Cultural Domination

Vernon February

LONDON AND NEW YORK

First published 1988 by
Kegan Paul Internation Limited

Published 2019 by Routledge
2 Park Square, Milton Park, Abingdon, Oxon OX14 4RN
52 Vanderbilt Avenue, New York, NY 10017

First issued in paperback 2019

Routledge is an imprint of the Taylor & Francis Group, an informa business

Copyright © 1988 Vernon February

All rights reserved. No part of this book may be reprinted or reproduced or utilised in any form or by any electronic, mechanical, or other means, now known or hereafter invented, including photocopying and recording, or in any information storage or retrieval system, without permission in writing from the publishers.

Notice:
Product or corporate names may be trademarks or registered trademarks, and are used only for identification and explanation without intent to infringe.

Distributed by Associated Book Publishers (UK) Ltd.

ISBN 13: 978-1-138-96351-1 (pbk)
ISBN 13: 978-0-7103-0278-6 (hbk)

Acknowledgements

I owe my insights in this book, *And Bid Him Sing*, to several people who influenced my life. It is a tribute to the late Professor A. C. Jordan who taught me the beauties of Xhosa at the University of Cape Town. Jordan's lessons have been more than a shield to me during my years of exile; those lessons are a vindication of the Xhosa proverb he taught me many years ago: *Isiziba siviwa ngodondolo*, literally, the bottom of a pool is reached with a long enough stick; figuratively, we'll get there in the end. In exile, the late Professor Jan Voorhoeve of Leiden University inducted me into the joys and mysteries of creole literature. To these two men, the one African, the other Dutch, I owe an intellectual and spiritual debt.

I am grateful for the many students who, in various parts of the world, were prepared to lend me a willing ear.

I am thankful to Mrs Miriam Bleekrode who typed large parts of this manuscript.

The publication of this book would not have been possible without the generous financial assistance provided by Novib, the Dutch organization for international aid and development. I am indebted to the Board of Directors of Novib. More specifically, I would like to single out the General Secretary of Novib, Dr Sjef Theunis, for a special word of praise. He was not only prepared to listen to me but also personally championed my course.

I also want to thank Doctorandus Jona Bos from the Ministry of Foreign Affairs who, like his illustrious countryman, Douwes Dekker (Multatuli), is a civil servant with 'a heart for the cause'.

Above all, I would like to dedicate this book, *And Bid Him Sing*, to the one person who shares my insights, Esther; she it is who keeps on reminding me that 'where there is light, there is *simcha*'.

Vernon A. February,
Amsterdam/Leiden
1986

Contents

Preface ix

Introduction xi

1. The Imbongi, the Scop and the Skald 1

2. From Peau Noire to Po' White 25

3. Sipho Sepamla – The Soweto I Love 43

4. Cape of Torments 47

5. Incarceration and Creation 55

6. Ilizwi LikaJakobi Kodwa Isandla Sika-Esau 67

7. Asingeni – We Shall not Enter 101

8. Trefossa – Posthumous Homage to a Creole Poet 119

9. Boesi Sa Tek' Mi Baka – Let the Bush Receive Me Once Again 131

10. From the Green Antilles 163

11. Only Connect – E. M. Forster's *A Passage to India* and Multatuli's *Max Havelaar* 187

Index 203

Preface

This collection of essays, talks and reviews covers a remarkable range of subject matter, knowledge and expertise, organized under a strong controlling viewpoint. Dr February combines political and social concern – what is loosely called 'commitment' – with the deep grounding of a scholar and researcher who has himself, in South Africa, experienced at first hand those conditions whereby culture and knowledge are abused to serve the ends of a dominant group. In 'Incarceration and Creation' he says, 'In our times, writers are called upon to be committed, and if one surveys the world scene, it is almost impossible to remain aloof.' There is no escaping, in over half these pieces, the pervasive political significance of language 'to such an extent', February observes, that honest research is sometimes wellnigh impossible, though not, one adds, impossible for him. Research here subtly links the history of the Afrikaner's freedom struggle – against British imperialism – with that, in their turn, of the Africans' Soweto protest of 1976.

The most authoritative and impressive of these essays probe the very roots of the colonialist's rationalization of this assumption of absolute power, notably, the relentlessly analytical 'Ilizwi LikaJakobi Kodwa Isandla Sika-Esau', based on a sound typology of the process of conquest, deculturation and deracination. In 'Asingeni', as in 'Ilizwi . . .', scholarship lays bare the civilized pretensions of apartheid, an ideology forged to legitimize power. One recalls the Nazi and Soviet abuses of language to conceal or distort, not reveal, truth; in the language of National Socialism *volk* is a word reserved for the Chosen People.

February's revealing essays on the careers of two Surinamese writers, Trefossa and Cairo, whose work is hedged about by the

Preface

linguistic chances of 'colonialism and its consequences' (Cairo) and confined to a minuscule Dutch readership, give fresh glimpses into the fragmented world of those writers excluded from a larger awareness by the 'consequences'.

Time and again February draws attention to the ironic colonial inheritance, that the colonized person is 'often coerced into writing and expressing himself in the language of the colonizer' ('From the Green Antilles'). But, as Salman Rushdie has said, it is in this language that 'the Empire strikes back' and, as February notes, many third-world writers have adopted, as their prototype, Shakespeare's despised Caliban who tells his colonial overlord, Prospero:

> You taught me language, and my profit on't
> Is, I know how to curse.

Not that February curses, his tone is even; mostly he lets the rich material speak, though occasionally he allows himself a leavening wit: 'Note, whenever the possessive is used [as in the whites' approving "Our native"], the said "native" is in grave danger.' ('From Peau Noire to Po' White'). There is a teasing invention in 'Ilizwi . . .' of the first 'linguistic confrontation' between 'two robust, ruddy-faced, big-boned Dutchmen' and the Khoi – later, in the same essay, we learn that even the English qualify as 'Bantu' . . .

Overall, *And Bid Him Sing* is a serious and timely body of work, a humane critic's substantial contribution to the writer's saving cause of 'truth', for which Solzhenitsyn spoke passionately in his Nobel Prize Lecture; we are constantly reminded, in the words February quotes from Frank Martinus Arion, that 'writing with the wrong pen . . . can cost you your soul.'

Michael Thorpe

Introduction

And Bid Him Sing[1] consists of a series of lectures, first delivered at various institutes of higher learning in Africa, Europe and the United States of America between 1971 and 1985. These essays all reflect my involvement with African literature and culture and, in a wider sense, my deep interest in colonial processes. It is no accident that the lines of the Afro-American poet, Countee Cullen, serve as the title of this book for those lines contain that singular marvel of the man of colour who, against tremendous historical and sociological forces, has managed to salvage something of his past to give expression to his suffering and alienation and his zest for living in a creative manner.

In a sense, then, these essays are also commentaries on cultural imperialism. Some of these critical and creative exercises, presented here, deal specifically with Dutch colonialism. This is not so surprising since it is often forgotten that the Dutch colonial Empire made its influence felt in the East Indies, in the Cape, in West Africa and also in the Dutch Antilles and Surinam. These essays are, therefore, a reflection of the African and the colonial experience as found in literature and as perceived in Africa. They also reflect the diaspora via the 'middle passage' man.

The first essay deals with praise poetry in African societies, more specifically, within South Africa. Most of the South African literary

[1] 'Yet Do I Marvel' by Countee Cullen, *The Poetry of the Negro (1746-1970)* (ed. Langston Hughes & Arna Bontemps), Doubleday, New York, 1970, p. 233.
The last lines read:

> Yet do I marvel at this curious thing
> To make a poet black, and bid him sing!

Introduction

scene is controlled by naked discrimination and apartheid. Thus, much that passes for creativity in that part of Africa often seems to be in reaction to the white man's domination and destruction. The African cosmological world and the great poetic tradition in Nguni suffers as a result of a larger struggle for freedom. The process of coming to grips with one's own cultural and literary tradition is, to my mind, as much a part of the struggle for freedom. The prime exponent of this is Mazisi Kunene. The first essay deals with the phenomenon of praise poetry in comparative vein; what better mode, as contrast, than the oral literature of Anglo-Saxon and Norse societies?

The second article is about stereotypes, dealt with more extensively in my book, *Mind Your Colour* (1981). The difference in this article, however, is that references are made in greater detail to this phenomenon in other cultures in which oppression is rife. This puts the question of stereotypes in a wider perspective, other than the narrow apartheid context.

Two essays are devoted to language. This question of language in societies of oppression or colonialism periodically demands the attention of scholar-linguists, men of literature and, sometimes, scholars from the social sciences. In South Africa, honest discussion is often obstructed by the fact of race. Thus, the country is often projected as bilingual, the two official languages being English and Afrikaans. The issue of Bantu languages as a means of creative expression is complicated by the fact that the South African government has always tried to use Bantu languages for its own sinister purposes. Thus, a psychological attitude towards a Bantu-language policy, foisted on to the oppressed by the rulers, was a logical outflow.

Bantu languages were, therefore, either the preserve of Bantu-language experts, more interested in tone, for example, than the literary man. The South African poet, Mazisi Kunene, is a welcome departure from this trend. 'Ilizwi . . . ('The Voice of Jacob but the Hand of Esau') is about the variegated aspect of language inside South Africa. Thus, references are not only made to the historical context in which languages were used in the country, but are also set against the background of the socio-political scene. Attempts are made to see the Khoisan languages in proper perspective; the detailed reference to a Bantu language is to a Nguni language, Xhosa, spoken in the Cape Province. Afrikaans is referred to, as is the variety which

Introduction

exists in the urban areas, namely Flytaal (Flaaitaal), described very well by the young South African Dennis Makhudu in his MA thesis in America in 1984.

The second article on the language question is specifically about Afrikaans and the reasons why students used, as their slogan in 1976, *Asingeni* We Shall Not Enter (the classrooms). The article shows what can happen when language is abused by the ruler and opposed by the subjected.

'Cape of Torment' is a review of a book by the historian Robert Ross in which the horror of slavery, as it obtained at the Cape, is poignantly and painfully laid bare.

'The Soweto I Love' gives an impression of the South African poet and novelist, Sipho Sepamla, and his 'God's-Eye vision' of a microcosmos set against the violent backdrop of the greater apartheid macrocosmos. His poetry is a good example of his attempt to survive. The concluding articles cover the diaspora and the colonial territory.

No one will dispute the importance of a discussion of creole languages and creole literature within the context of African languages and literature or, at least, with reference to Africa.

The essay on Trefossa is an indication of what can happen when the language debate is resolved among the colonized; it is also a demonstration of the coming of age of a creole language. Secondly, it is a decided contribution to what is now sometimes referred to as 'third world' literature.

Hall (1966) and other linguists all stress the fact that a creole language must have had its origin in a pidgin language. We learn that 'a pidgin language originates in a situation in which no communication is possible in any of the existing mother tongues'. In these circumstances people try to communicate in one of the available languages (usually the language of the power-groups), although they have no opportunity to acquire a good command of it. A reduced, simplified language arises that is only used in restricted situations: in trading, in the market, in the factory, on the plantation or in the army. In all other situations the mother tongue is still used (*Creole Drum*, 1975, p. 273) In the same book Hall states, p. 284:

> A creole language develops from a pidgin as it becomes the native tongue of a group. If people speaking different tongues begin to intermarry and form a single community (as was the

Introduction

case for example when slaves of different origins were brought together on a plantation), and if a particular pidgin is the common language of this community, it will become the mother tongue of the children of mixed-language marriages and eventually of the whole community (though not of the group who do not intermarry with others such as the white settlers). As soon as this pidgin becomes the native language of a group it must be used in many more situations than when it was only a contact language between people who had their own native languages and we may thus assume that it undergoes a process of expansion to meet the new demands on it ... with the promotion of a pidgin to creole status the pidgin ceases to exist.

There is reason to believe that this language (the Surinamese Creole) had a Portuguese pidgin origin and was creolised in contact with English. Surinam Creole (also called Negro-English) is clearly an English-based Creole.

In the case of Surinam we know that the slaves came from various ethnic backgrounds; this did not mean that they had no means of communication with one another. The existence of an Afro-Portuguese pidgin on the coast during the sixteenth century has been amply documented and 'we may assume that the Africans from different ethnic backgrounds made use of this language acquired at home, in the slave depots, or in the ships'. (*Creole Drum*, p. 3)

The first reference to Surinamese creole is in 1693. The language did not have such an easy passage in Surinam. Creoles were initially against the use of a language which, to their mind, only served to stress their *negroness*. Products of plantation slavery, they were the dupes of the Dutch policy of assimilation which taught them that the Dutch language was the best means of communication. This attitude of 'socialized ambivalence' is, of course, not peculiar to the Surinamese Creole and was also one of the features of the creolized in the Dutch Antilles.

It was left to Creoles like Papa Koenders in the early 1940s and the poet Trefossa in the fifties, as also the lawyer Eddy Bruma and the linguist Hein Eersel, to begin the process of demythologization, thus restoring creole to its rightful place within Surinamese society. This task has now been taken over by Edgar Cairo. Frank Martinus Arion fulfils a similar role within the Antilles. He is not only well known for his novels and poetry in the Netherlands but also for his comments

Introduction

and articles on the Papiamento language. In an unpublished paper, The Antillean Jorge Labadie writes: 'Papiamento is a creole tonal language, spoken by some 250,000 people, the majority of which live on the Leeward islands of Aruba, Bonaire and Curaçao, otherwise known as the ABC-islands.' (Amsterdam, 1984)

The Antilles have produced several writers who wrote in Papiamento but who received only limited recognition in their own part of the world. Of these Antillean writers the most prominent were Willem Kroon (1886–1949), with his *Giambo Bieuw ta Bolbe na Wea* (Old Love Does Not Die), Nicolás Piña (1921–67), who wrote in Dutch, Spanish and Papiamento, with a distinct preference for the latter, and Rosario, who is known for his *E rais ku no ke muri* (The Root Won't Die Out).

The Antillean R. G. Römer, in his article 'The Language Situation in the Netherlands Antilles' (1977), writes:

> Papiamento is now the mother tongue on all three islands (i.e. Aruba, Bonaire and Curaçao), a language which derives its basic vocabulary not from Dutch but from Portuguese and Spanish, while the grammatical structures show parallels with the other so-called 'mixed-languages' in the Caribbean, irrespective of the fact whether colonisation took place by the English, Dutch or French.

Römer points out that the stigma generally attached to creole languages in the Caribbean was understandable in historical terms because creole was generally the means of communication of the 'have-nots' in the society. With reference to Papiamento, however, a slightly different pattern occurred on the Leeward islands. This favourable treatment was, according to him, due to the fact that on the Leeward islands there were two 'prestige-groups, the West-Indies Company group and the Sephardic Jews who spoke mutually unintelligible languages'. Here then, according to Römer, Papiamento would have operated as the lingua franca.

Edgar Cairo and Frank Martinus Arion are both historically and politically involved with their African past. They write from their respective backgrounds with passion about Africa and, ironically or bitingly, about their Dutch colonial background. As such their creative works are a welcome addition to third-world literature, although the latter term is, in itself, in serious need of examination in view of the colonial experience.

Introduction

The final essay is a comparative evaluation of E. M. Forster's novel, *A Passage to India*, and the Dutchman Eduard Douwes Dekker's (Multatuli) novel, *Max Havelaar*. The Dutch have left their imprint in South Africa, the west coast of Africa (Ghana), the East Indies and in the Antilles and Surinam. The English colonial influence is still clearly visible in the East, the Caribbean, in large parts of West Africa and in South Africa. The colonial heritage hovers like a ghost over the lives of many a colonized man or woman. The poor are still poor and the great mass still beyond art.

And Bid Him Sing is an attempt to come to grips with the African experience, in particular, and the colonial experience in general. It is about the effects of subjugation on the creative processes. For, in the words of the Surinam Creole poet, Michael Slory:

> Only together
> Can we come to terms
> With that which nibbles at our souls.

Or, in his own language, Sranan Tongo:

> Makandra nomo
> un sa brasa den dangra
> di tergi wi kra.

1

The Imbongi, the Scop and the Skald

African, Anglo-Saxon and Old Norse Oral Poetry

Africa is blessed with a written and an unwritten (oral) literary tradition. These two traditions exist side by side and influence each other. For a long time, scholars have only emphasized the written tradition which, by implication, stood for civilization, a highly developed technological society and progress. In terms of such an approach, Africa was easily classifiable as backward. The oral tradition meant a low standard of development and a less civilized people.

When, in the twentieth century, Europe did decide to pay attention to African writers, they were mainly those writers who, during and after the process of decolonization, started publishing their novels, short stories and poems in the languages of their former colonizers. Whatever information one had about Africa came to us via the missionaries (or the missionary turned linguist – sometimes only the linguist), the anthropologist and the traveller. These accounts were not devoid of Eurocentrism and exoticism.

Ruth Finnegan (1970) and other scholars have clearly defined and identified some of the characteristics of the oral tradition. As the name already implies this is a literature which is not committed to paper and comes into its own when performed. Performer and performance cannot be seen in isolation. Finnegan comments:

> ...the connection between transmission and very existence is a much more intimate one, and questions about the means of actual communication are of the first importance – without its oral realization and direct rendition by singer or speaker, an unwritten literary piece cannot easily be said to have any continued or independent existence at all. In this respect the parallel is less to written literature than to music and dance; for these two art forms in the last analysis are actualized in and through their performance and, furthermore, in a sense depend on repeated performances for their continued existence.[1]

Finnegan stresses further that 'every category of relationship between poet and audience can be found... in one context or another'.[2]

The oral poet will be found at royal courts, as (formerly) in Rwanda, where he was rewarded and welcomed as a professional. He can be involved in pastoral farming or even be an itinerant performer. His poetry can be uncomplicated and in praise of a favourite cow or hill, in the case of the Nguni. Praise poetry may have assumed a different shape as the community passed through different stages. Thus, from uncomplicated praises, praise poetry during the highly centralized kingdom of Shaka (1787–1828),[3] the great Zulu King, was even composed in stanza form.

As in Africa, the oral poet in Anglo-Saxon and old Norse societies also featured prominently. Some of the features relating to the African oral poet will also be applicable to the *scop* and the *skald*. Here, we attempt to explore the similarities between the oral poets in these three respective oral societies.

The Anglo-Saxon scop fulfilled an important function at courts as an itinerant poet and here, too, one would find almost every type of relationship existing between the poet and his audience. The scop and the skald are found in social contexts reminiscent of those at times in Africa. An attempt will be made to identify these parallels in terms of the following:

a. The function and importance of praises;
b. The meaning of praises;
c. The manner of delivery (recitation);
d. The role and importance of the praiser.

For the sake of clarity, the emphasis will be on the praise poet and praise poetry in South Africa. This will be limited further to the Nguni-speaking peoples, mostly Zulu and Xhosa. Evidence of oral poetry in Anglo-Saxon and Skaldic literature is widely documented. The Anglo-Saxon poems which are singled out are those well known to students of English literature, namely, the epic *Beowulf*, *Widsith* (Far-away), *Deor's Lament*, *The Seafarer* and *The Wanderer*. The Nguni examples were culled from the research done by eminent South African scholars, including A. C. Jordan, G. P. Lestrade, E. W. Grant, B. Vilakazi and T. Cope. The Skaldic examples are from private notes and from Hallberg, Campbell, Koegel, Turville-Petre and others.

The Importance of Oral Poetry – the Nguni

Ruth Finnegan in her *Oral Literature in Africa* (1970) gave a very perceptive account of the genre as one encounters it on the African continent. She refers to the importance of praises in Zulu and Sotho societies, traces the relationship between the poet and his sponsors and deals with the question of patronage.

She inducts us into the court poetry of the Rwanda of Burundi. Quoting from several sources, she reveals this fascinating African genre to us in a very illuminating manner:

> In the highly centralized traditional kingdom of Ruanda, the Royal poets had their own association and were officially recognized as holding a privileged position within the state. They were in charge of the delivery and preservation of the dynastic poems whose main object was to exalt the king and other members of the royal line. This was only one branch among the three main types of Rwanda poetry (dynastic, military, and pastoral) which corresponded to the three pivots of their society (king, warrior, and cattle).[4]

We know from Cope's *Zibongo, Zulu Praise-Poems* (1968) that praises were very important to the Zulu:

> Praises play an important part in Zulu social life. The parents

give their children praises, children of the same age group (*intanga*) give one another praises, and young men of the same age-set (*ibutho*) or regiment (*impi*), the official enrollment of all the same age groups, give one another praises according to the code of conduct expected of a warrior.[5]

We also learn from Eileen Krige that 'praises are an important instrument in the educational system. Not only do they act as an incentive to and reward for socially approved actions, but their recital is a reminder to all present what qualities and conduct are considered praise worthy.'[6]

David Livingstone, in 1857, stressed in his *Missionary Travels* the value attached to the composition of praises or *leina*. Yet, in that very same year, the Reverend J. L. Döhne, an American missionary who had worked among the Nguni for over twenty years, erroneously concluded in his *Zulu-Kafir Dictionary* that the 'Zulu-Kafirs' were devoid of any poetic feelings. He continues in the following vein:

> Some have expected to find much poetry among the Zulu-Kafirs, but there is, in fact, none. Poetical language is extremely rare, and we meet with only a few pieces of prose. The Zulu nation is more fond of *ukuhlabelela* i.e.: singing and engages more in 'ukuvuma amagama ezinkosi', i.e. singing the praises of the chiefs, than any other Kafir tribe. . . nothing like poetry or song exists. . . no metre, no rhyme, nothing that interests or soothes the feelings or arrests the passions, – no admiration of the heavenly bodies, or taste for the beauties of creation. We miss the cultivated mind which delights in seizing on these subjects and embodying them in suitable language.[7]

In his book *Izibongo*, Trevor Cope stated:

> Zulu social life provides occasion for self-display and the publicization of praises, but particularly in the practice of the male solo dance (*uku-giya*), which is hardly to dance but to give a bombastic exhibition of oneself: rushing hither and thither, stopping and starting, leaping, twirling and twisting, rattling spear against shield, glaring ferociously towards an imaginary enemy, all to the accompaniment of one's praises shouted by one's fellows and sometimes by oneself.[8]

Males were given such opportunities when they were courting their sweethearts, whenever there were public celebrations, for example, marriage ceremonies and activities before they went to battle. Praises also formed part of initiation rites, of the various stages towards adulthood undergone by an individual in a clan.

The Function of Praises – Nguni

Trevor Cope observes in *Izibongo* that the

> function of praise poems arises from the function of praises in general, which is to bring about uniformity to the approved modes of behaviour. In addition to displaying the good conduct expected of the common man, a chief is expected to be generous in his disposal of cattle and land to deserving subjects, and in his provision of food, especially meat and beer, to his visitors and tribesmen when in council or in ceremony.[9]

Cope continues that, where necessary, the praise poem is expected to give 'an accurate account of the chief's personality and actions without which it would not fulfil its function as an agent of conformity to the approved patterns'.

The praise poem can thus be the vehicle whereby transgressions or acts of cruelty are exposed – in short, social criticism can be levelled at those who deviate from socially approved norms. Thus, for example, the conduct of Nangelizwe, chief of the Thembu, who was notorious for his cruelty, is symbolically and very subtly condemned in a praise poem. He is personified as the eagle who swoops down on defenceless birds (in this case the dove).

> See how the doves flutter and huddle
> dismayed at the sight of the eagle
> Woe to the dove that has no wings.[10]

Mazisi Kunene observes of Magolwane, Shaka's court poet:

> The symbols he chose were not only aimed at strong parallel

qualities but also the fusion of related qualities. In his epic, he combined both analysis and synthesis so that his stanzas not only introduced and treated the subject, but also contained philosophical conclusions and summaries.[11]

The Meaning of the Word Praiser – Nguni

The word 'praiser' has the following meaning according to scholars: the verb *bonga* means '(a) thank (as when given something), (b) admire, speak in high tones of, use emotional language and (c) give clan name or kinship term'.[12]

The word *isibongo* (plural *izibongo*) is derived from the Zulu word, *ukubonga*, whose meaning is wide. It is defined by Bryant as follows: 'To praise, extol, a person or thing. . . The same authority shows two distinct meanings of the derived noun "isibongo". Tribal or clan name; name of praise, given to a young man by his comrades; plural izibongo, – praises of a person, cow or dog, etc. . . .'[13]

The Nature of Praise Poems – Nguni

Praise poems in Nguni have been likened to eulogies, odes and epics. The late Professor Lestrade typified them as a 'type of composition intermediate between the pure, mainly narrative, epic and the pure, mainly apostrophic, ode, bearing a combination of exclamatory narration and laudatory apostrophising'.[14]

The late Professor A. C. Jordan considered it 'perhaps the proudest achievement of Bantu-speaking South Africans'. He further characterized it as 'partly narrative, or partly or wholly descriptive. It abounds in epithets, very much like the Homeric ones, and the language in general is highly figurative'.[15]

The Manner of Recitation (Delivery, Literary Devices) – Nguni

The Nguni praiser

recites the praises at the top of his voice and as fast as possible.

The Imbongi, the Scop and the Skald

These conventions of praise-poem recitation, which is high in pitch, loud in volume, fast in speed, create an emotional excitement in the audience as well as in the praiser himself, whose voice often rises in pitch, volume, and speed as he progresses, and whose movements become more and more exaggerated, for it is also a convention of praise-poem recitation that the praiser never stands still.[16]

The Nguni praiser resorts to an exploitation of repeated rhymes, repetition, assonance, parallelism, rhetorical constructions; his language is extremely rich in imagery.

The Importance of Song – Nguni

Song was, and still is, an important element in the oral tradition. The importance of song in the African context is evident from the following modern example which is illustrative of white-black relations in South Africa. There is more than a hint that the white character is taken for a ride. Apparently, a young and inexperienced white foreman was appointed over some African workers. He immediately forbade them to sing, as was the custom. Whereupon, the working rate dropped tremendously. He soon found himself in the office of his boss who wanted an explanation for this alarming state of affairs. When he told his boss that he had forbidden them to sing, the latter exploded and told him what an idiot he was. He ordered him to allow them to sing once more and, sure enough, the working rate picked up.

Similarly, songs always constituted an essential element in the freedom struggle of the African National Congress in South Africa. Tennyson Makiwane commented in an article:

> By far the most inspiring, however, are the songs the workers have composed as a direct reaction to oppression, the color bar and so on. There is the classic:
>
> > Abelungu ngodem, abelungu ngodem,
> > basibiza ooJim, basibiza ooJim.

And Bid Him Sing

(Be damn the whites, be damn the whites, they call us Jim, they call us Jim.)[17]

There are numerous freedom songs popularized by Miriam Makeba and, more recently, by that marvellous singer, James Madhlope Phillips. Many a European is familiar with 'Unzima Lomthwalo' written by another important figure in South Africa, the Reverend Calata, or the executed freedom fighter, Vuyisile Mini's 'Indod' Mnyama', or his 'Sizabadubula', again through the singing of James Madhlope Phillips.

The Importance of the Mbongi

As in the case of the scop and the skald, the Nguni praiser is the recorder of events, the castigator, the poet laureate and moral guardian of values. The unique position of the imbongi attached to a chief is reflected in his dress, a fantastic costume of feathers, furs and animal tails, as impressive as the apparel of the isangoma (medicine man).

Metaphors – Nguni

Zulu praise poetry is also full of metaphors. Powerful chiefs in Zulu society are described in the following graphic manner:

> *Dingane* is the 'deep silent pool' which has 'powerful force', that is, *iziziba esinzonzo sinzonbele* . . .
> *Mpande* is 'He who stands alone like the sun stands in the sky,' that is, *usima yedwa njengalanga, lona limi lodwa ezinzulwini*. . .
> *Shaka*, mighty warrior, conqueror, nation-builder and Zulu chief, becomes 'the battle axe that overcomes the other axes', i.e. Senzangakhona's sons, that is, *ilemb' eleq' amany' amalembe ngokukhalipha* . . .

The Imbongi, the Scop and the Skald

Senzangakhona, Shaka's father, is described as the 'gate-post of the kraal', that is, *uthi lwempundu*...

Cetshwayo is called, 'a maize plant which grew alone while others grew in a conspiratorial cluster', that is, *ikhaba elimile, lodwa, amany' emil' isixexelegu*.[18]

But it was Shaka, the conqueror and nation-builder who fascinated the creative artist – this chief of whom the singer Miriam Makeba said that he was not the black Napoleon of Africa but Napoleon was the white Shaka of Europe. This Zulu chief was eulogized in many ways, of which the poem which follows is an illustration.

>He is Shaka the unshakable,
>Thunderer-while-sitting, son of Menzi;
>He is the bird that preys on other birds,
>The battle axe that excels all other axes;
>He is the long-strided pursuer, son of Ndaba,
>Who pursued the moon and the sun;
>He is the great hubbub like the rocks of Nkandla
>Where the elephants take shelter
>When the heavens frown.
>'Tis he whose spears resound causing wailing.
>Thus old women shall stay in abandoned homes
>And old men shall drop by the wayside.[19]

The Importance of the Scop

From gnomic verses we know that the scop was as welcome to a chief as jewels were, by way of adornment, to a queen:

>Sinc on cwene
>god scop gumum garniþwerum.[20]

The scop was especially appreciated when he was a widely travelled man. The importance of the art of poetry is clearly illustrated by the life history of Caedmon, now generally regarded as the first poet of note in the English language. Caedmon's initial unhappiness and

And Bid Him Sing

sadness were attributed to his inability to sing and to compose poetry. At the time when Caedmon was alive, it was the custom in the monastery to compose songs when seated at the banquet table (*symble*) and to pass the harp around. Now when the harp approached poor, museless Caedmon, he always got up and sadly left the banquet table. His fate was changed radically when, in a dream, by some heavenly intervention, he was granted the gift of composing songs. The following passage describes the state of mind of the poor, hapless Caedmon before the divine intervention:

Waes hē se mon in weoruldhāde geseted oð ða tīde þe hē waes gelȳfrede yldo, and hē naefre aenig lēoð geleornade: and hē for þon oft in gebēorscipe, þonne þaer waes blisse intinga gedēmed þaet hīe eall sceoldan þurh endebyrdnesse be hearpan singan, þonne hē geseah þā hearpan him nēalaecan, þonne ārās hē for scome from þaem symble, and hām ēode tō his hūse.

This man had lived a secular life till he had reached old age, and he had never learned a song. And so often at the feast when it was decreed for the sake of mirth that each in turn should sing to the accompaniment of the harp, when he saw the harp approaching him, then in shame he rose from the banquet table and went home to his house.[21]

The dramatic change in Caedmon is evident from the following song in praise of God:

    Nū wē sculan herian   heofonrīces Weard
    Metodes mihte   and his mōdgeþonc
    weorc Wuldorfaeder;   swā hē wundra gehwaes
    ēce Dryhten,   ord onstealde.
    Hē aerest gesceōp   eorðan bearnum
    heofon tō hrōfe   hālig Scyppend;
    ða middangeard,   moncynnes Weard,
    ēce Dryhten,   aefter tēode
    fīrum foldan,   Frēa aelmihtig.

It is meet that we worship the Warden of heaven
The might of the Maker, His purpose of mind,
The Glory-Father's work when of all his wonders

He the Eternal God made a beginning.
He first created for the children of the earth
Heaven as a roof, the Holy Creator;
Then Mankind's Ward created the world,
Eternal Monarch, making for men
Land to live on, Almighty Lord![22]

Major Anglo-Saxon Poems

The Anglo-Saxon poems which are of particular importance to us are *Widsith*, *Beowulf*, *Deor's Lament*, *The Seafarer* and *The Wanderer*. *Widsith* was probably composed in the fourth century. The epic poem, *Beowulf*, was composed in the early part of the seventh century.

Subject Matter

Widsith is an account of the experiences of a court singer and his journeys to the court of the Gothic king, Eormanric. Similarly, *Beowulf* affords one a peep into court life. One knows from accounts that the Saxons were reported to have had a higher culture than any other people living between the rivers Oder and Rhine. Their love for poetry is evident from the personal history of Caedmon, related above. We also know that professional Germanic singers first make their appearance among the Anglo-Saxons.

The scop sings of desolate and lonely conditions, as when the mariner is in dire straits in the Anglo-Saxon poem, *The Seafarer*:

> Ne biþ him tō hearpan hyge.
> (His thoughts are not concentrated
> on the harp.)[23]

One of the worst conditions in which the scop can find himself is that of exile. Thus *The Wanderer*, in exile, is now bereft of his many known songs:

And Bid Him Sing

> Flēotendra ferð   nō þaer fela bringeð
> cuðra cwidegiedda.
> (The souls of sailors bringeth not there
> many known songs.)[24]

The scōp sings of joy at the numerous feats of victory as, for example, at Heorot, prior to the intrusion of the monster, Grendel:

> þaer waes hearpan swēg
> swutol sang scopes.
> (There was the sound of the harp and
> the clear song of the scop.)[25]

It is when tragedy strikes in the form of Grendel that song and poetry disappear. They will only return with the defeat of the monster.[26]

The Importance of Song

As in Nguni society, the Anglo-Saxons showed a tremendous appreciation for the art of *singing, recitation* and *dancing*. Professor Anderson, in his study on the Anglo-Saxon scop, commented: 'Numerous allusions in the historic records of the Anglo-Saxons lead us to believe that they were distinguished even among the Germanic peoples by their love of poetry and song.'[27]

Both societies were largely preliterate in the sense that the written word did not play an important role. From Bede's account of Caedmon we know that even simple farm labourers were wont to compose songs and sing them at their meetings. They also used the harp by way of accompaniment. From other sources we know that the harp played a role in

> the lives of nearly ten million Africans ... African societies usually accord special status to both harpist and harp-maker, and rank the instrument itself high in cultural value. Harps and harp-playing are often steeped in symbolism. Harpists can function as historians and genealogists as well as the central figures in religious rituals.[28]

The Imbongi, the Scop and the Skald

The operative words in many of these Anglo-Saxon poems are *singing* and *saying* or, in their Anglo-Saxon equivalents, *singan* and *secgan*, practically interchangeable in early Germanic literature. Thus one reads in *Widsith*:

> For þon ic maeg singan and secgan spell,
> maenan fore mengo in meoduhalle.
> (Therefore I may sing and recite tales before
> the company in the meadhall.)[29]

Similarly, *leoþ*, i.e., song, was used as synonymous with *gyd* which, in turn, was derived from *gyddian*, meaning *to speak*.

Germanic society was fairly conversant with the phenomenon of the professional singer. The earliest reference to such singers is to be found in the works of Tacitus. From historical sources it is clear that the Goths were the first to make use of epic poetry. Kindred groups (tribes) were not loth to adopt their heroic songs. The influence of these songs via the Goths becomes clear from the following observation in *Geschichte der deutsche litteratur*: 'Dafur spricht der Umstand, dass gerade die bedeutendsten und beliebsten Sagestoffe gotische Ursprungs sind: Ermanrich, die Harlunge, Dietrich v. Bern sind gotische Helden.'[30]

Therefore the argument can be advanced that precisely the most significant and most well liked myths are of Gothic origin. Ermanrich, die Harlunge, Dietrich von Bern are Gothic heroes. (transl.)

Literary Devices

The Anglo-Saxon scop exploited alliterative syllables, sang and recited in declamatory fashion. L. F. Anderson comments: 'Firstly the singer was not only a man distinguished by his skill in almost the only art which the Anglo-Saxon cultivated but he was the curator of their literature and of their religious and historical myths . . .'[31]

R. K. Gordon wrote: 'One mark of the style is the comparative absence of similes but the frequency of descriptive phrases, known as kennings, as, for example, when Beowulf's boat is called "the foamy-necked floater".'[32]

The Skald

Likewise, the skald has been accounted for in several ways. None of these explain the term adequately. A skald has variously been taken to mean a poet, a migrant (itinerant) poet, a story-teller. Sometimes he is also referred to as an oracle priest. In old Norse times, the skald was someone who composed his own poems. Sometimes, however, he would also use the poems, sagas and stories of other skalds. He was an entertainer attached to the household of the king or some such important person of substance and wealth. He also travelled and stayed with other households (kings, persons of wealth and fame), for brief periods. In this, then, the skalds resemble the oral poets in Africa and the scop in Anglo-Saxon society. He is present at battles which he records for posterity, is both historian and poet laureate.

The Nature and Subject Matter of Skaldic Poetry

Skaldic poetry was generally of a eulogistic nature and composed in honour of a reigning monarch. The skalds also dealt with mythic-heroic motifs: 'Skaldic verse was addressed chiefly to kings and highly distinguished nobles... Often it was addressed to nobles with a family tradition of patronage of poetry.'[33]

Thus, the death of a favourite son is mourned by Egill Skalla-grindson in 'Sonatorrek' as follows: 'Much does it cost me to move my tongue with the airy weight of song's measure.'[34] Also, 'I used to stand well with the Lord of spears. I trusted him until the giver of victory broke his friendship with me.'

The following Skaldic poetry was quoted by Kolbrunarskald just before the battle of Stiklesand (29 July 1030):[39]

> Daybreak has come, the rooster flaps his wings, it's time for slaves to go to work! Awake, friends! All [King] Adil's best men... I don't wake you up to wine, nor to speech with women, but rather to Hild's [war's] hard play.[35]

Literary Devices and Skaldic Poetry

Two of the poetic devices found in skaldic poetry are the *heiti* and the *kenning*. They both produce effects also observable in Anglo-Saxon and Nguni poetry. As Hallberg commented: 'The art of the skalds... consisted not least of all in the manipulation of the specifically poetic words, the so-called *heiti* and of the *kennings*.'[36]

The kenning, for example, can identify a person not only by his own personal name but also on the basis of his ancestry, or some such other relationship. Baldur is thus referred to as Frigg's son; Odin as Baldur's father.

Similarly, in Nguni, Bhambatha is designated as UmntakaShabase, that is, the son of Shabase. Sometimes a chief is called son of Ndaba, by way of indicating that he is descended from a famous ancestor, for example, Isibhene SikaNdaba, that is, the straight-limbed son of Ndaba.

Skaldic poetry is characterized by a great variety of metres, assonance and intricate alliteration.

Out of the heiti grew the kenning. This is a synonym placed in an unusual context, for example, a man's name *steinn* (meaning a stone) = the heart of the sea (also = stone). The sun of the forehead = the eye; the moon of the brow = the eye; headstem = the nose; outlet = the mouth; ship of the desert = the camel. Thus, the kenning substitutes two or more words for one. In skaldic poetry each word in the kenning might be circumscribed by another kenning. Consequently, one has a string of kennings which, in turn, requires a knowledge of mythology and heroic myths.

The main word in a kenning is called a *stofn*. This is usually followed by a modifier in the genitive case (*kenniorð*) and is used in combination to constitute a compound noun. The word kenning is derived from a verb *kenna*, which means 'characterize or to define'.

As we have seen, the kenning can denote relationship. In its metaphoric use one would find the following examples:

Ship = *brimhengest*, i.e., stallion of the breakers.
Eye = *heafodgim*, i.e., the jewel of the head.
Sea = *brimleid*, i.e., the path of the breakers.
Blood = *hjörlögr*, i.e., the fluid of the swords.

And Bid Him Sing

But a kenning may also point to the activity of a particular character; for instance, a warrior = the feeder of the raven; brandisher of the sword; destroyer of the shield.

In the case of the skalds, one is dealing with a refined artist. The skalds distinguish themselves through the *drapa*, a praise poem without a refrain, and the *flokkr*, a praise poem with a refrain. The latter is generally considered to be of a lesser quality. Here, too, one stumbles upon devices such as alliteration and assonance.

Alliteration in Nguni languages is linked to the fact that such languages are distinguished by their concords. Thus the concord belonging to the noun *people* which, in Nguni is *abantu*, i.e., a noun of class 11 plural, is *ba*. This concord would also determine the form of the verb and the qualificatives.

The Nguni (Xhosa in this case) sentence: 'All people want freedom,' would then be rendered into Xhosa as follows: 'A*b*antu *b*a*funa inkululeko.' Note that the concord *ba* will determine the form of the verb, 'to want', which has, as its stem, the Xhosa *funa*. 'They want' then becomes '*Ba*funa'.

The concord is also reflected in the qualificative, *all*, i.e., *onke* in Xhosa. Together with the concord belonging to the substantive this would become: ba + onke = *bo*nke.

Heroism – the Mbongi, the Scop and the Skald

The Zulu under Shaka, like many of the Germanic tribes, were people who set high store on feats of bravery. Mazisi Kunene and others have indicated that Zulu poetry reached its peak during the reign of Shaka, when small scattered tribes were subjugated and welded into the mighty Zulu nation. Ritter and Omer Cooper have written books on the Zulu, generally regarded as classics.[37] We know that it was Shaka who introduced the short, stabbing spear for close-range combat and who refined the art of combat among the Zulu to such an extent that they are the only African people with the distinction of ever having routed the English – at Isandhlwana in Natal.

This military tradition provided young men with the opportunity of displaying feats of untold bravery and heroism. As Mazisi Kunene observed, the greatest insult one could heap on a chief was to accuse him of being a ruler over women. This did indeed happen to Mpande, the Zulu ruler, who was characterized by the praise-poet Mshongweni in the following rather unflattering manner: 'You are a ruler who rules over women.'[38] In a short introduction to his *Zulu Poems*, Mazisi Kunene admits that 'the best South African poetry is epitomised by the heroic epic'.[39]

Dorothy Whitelock observes of Anglo-Saxon society: 'One of the least Christian features of extant heroic poetry, a feature perhaps inherited from heathen times, is that men seem more concerned with the reputation they will leave behind them than with divine rewards in this world or the next.'[40] This viewpoint is also expressed in *Beowulf*: 'Each of us must experience an end to life in this world; let him who can achieve glory before he dies.'[41]

We find a similar emphasis on honour in the national literature of medieval Iceland. Honour may drive a good man to tragic actions. Insulted honour requires revenge but, out of honour, springs bravery which, in Old Norse, is called *drengskapr*. It is well to say of both the enemy and the friend: he died well spoken of.

The Anglo-Saxon man was loyal to his *lord* and the warrior was expected to die when his lord fell in battle. Survival was an act of shame. Mbogozi, one of Shaka's mainstays, proves to be a Zulu Offa when he dies on the battlefield some eight hundred years later, for his chief, Shaka. Note the similarity of the lines uttered by him with those in *Beowulf*: 'My father, we must all die sooner or later and if my time has come nothing will hold it back. It is far, far better *to die with the joy of battle in the heart* than to pine away with age, or like a sick ox in a kraal. I have lived by the spear and I shall die by it.'[42]

Similarly, at the battle of Maldon in 991 Offa gave his life for his protector and is depicted thus in his heroic fall: 'Quickly Offa was cut down in the fight: Yet he had carried out what he had promised his Lord, when he vowed to his treasure-giver that both would ride home safely into the stronghold, or fall in the army, die of wounds on the battlefield. He lay as befits a thane, close to his Lord.'[43]

Rewards

In all these societies acts of heroism were richly rewarded. In fact, forfeiture of the lord's protection in Anglo-Saxon society led to unforetold miseries. This heart-breaking fact is poignantly portrayed in the poem, *The Wanderer*, when the lord dies: 'All joy has departed. Truly does he know who must forego the advice of his dear Lord.'[44]

As in Nguni society, 'personal allegiance is strengthened by the Lord's generosity, and the poems are full of praises for the Lord who knows how to give freely. He is called "the giver of rings", "the bestower of treasure", "the gold-friend of men"... The minstrels, Widsith and Deor, both received grants of land from their masters.'[45]

As distinct from the *mappum*, i.e., treasure (gold) of Anglo-Saxon society, there was, in the case of the Nguni, *iinkomo*, i.e., cattle. For, in the words of the Xhosa, 'Cattle beget children.' A man who owned lots of cattle was obviously someone of substance and wealth. Moreover, cattle enabled him to pay a high bride-price and have more than one wife. In Anglo-Saxon society it was also not so surprising to learn that, 'the ideal chieftain is one who avails himself of the scop's art, is a connoisseur in song, generous in gifts and who wishes to exalt his fame before his warriors to assert his lordship.'[46]

The Praise Poem in Modern Context

The written tradition in Western societies has almost turned oral poetry into an obsolete art form. In contrast, despite the fact that Africa was colonized by Europeans and forced to incorporate some European traditions in its history, the oral tradition is still very much alive.

The genre is far from extinct in Southern Africa. The absence of wars, the arrival of the white man and his subsequent destruction of the African way of life, also had its effect on art forms. New phrases had to be coined for the new inventions, for example, trains. This was brilliantly solved by means of the explosive ideophone: *xhegwazana phek' iphapha, xhegwazana phek' iphapha*, which meant, 'Grandmother, I want my porridge.' The sounds when made will sound exactly like the sound produced by the steam train.

In 1925 the Xhosa poet, Mqhayi, exploited this genre in welcoming the then Prince of Wales to South Africa. That it had not lost its power as a means of social criticism is evident from the final product. After all, what better mode to indict the dubious British heritage than the praise poem?

> Ah, Britain, Great Britain!
> Great Britain of the endless sunshine!
> She hath conquered the oceans and laid them low;
> She hath drained the little rivers and lapped them dry;
> She hath swept the little nations and wiped them away;
> And now she is making for the open skies.
> She sent us the preacher: she sent us the bottle;
> She sent us the Bible, and barrels of brandy;
> She sent us the breechloader, she sent us the cannon,
> O, Roaring Britain! Which must we embrace?
> You sent us the truth, denied us the truth;
> You sent us life, deprived us of life;
> You sent us light, we sit in dark,
> Shivering, benighted in the bright noon-day sun.[47]

Beowulf and Luthuli, two ostensibly unlinkable names, the one from Europe, the other from Africa, are heroes whose deeds bear testimony to the greatness in man in completely different surroundings. Of Beowulf it was said: 'Beowulf (was), the son of Scyld ... renowned in Scandinavian lands – his repute spread far and wide. So shall a young man bring good to pass with splendid gifts in the father's possession ... In every tribe shall a man prosper by glorious deeds.'[48]

Albert Luthuli, one of the great sons of Africa, was ignominiously treated by the whites in his land of birth, South Africa. He was a chieftain to his people in the narrower and traditional sense of chieftancy and, in the wider sense of the liberatory struggle, in his capacity as the President of the African National Congress of South Africa in the 1950s and sixties.

Alan Paton, the South African novelist, chose the praise poem as the only appropriate form in which to eulogize Albert Luthuli when the Chief, as he was widely known, was awarded the Nobel Prize for Peace in 1961.

> You there Luthuli. They thought your world was small,
> They thought you lived in Groutville.
> Now they discover it's the world you live in.
> You there Luthuli. They took away your name of 'Chief'
> You were apparently not worthy of it.
> Now they discover you are 'Chief' more than ever

> Go in peace Luthuli. May your days be blessed
> Your land cannot exact enough from you.
> Win also for all of us, Luthuli,
> the prize of peace.[49]

All men who achieve practically unattainable heights are smitten by intense loneliness and sadness. Such is the fate of both the epic hero and the martyr. In the Anglo-Saxon poem, 'The Vision of the Cross', a singular tribute is paid to the supreme martyr, Christ, who excels and endures and who, despite the supreme agony he is forced to undergo, sets an example of unselfish dedication for others. In a Germanic understatement the lines read:

> 'reste hē ðaēr maēte weorode.'

Literally, it means, 'He rested there with a small retinue!'[50] Figuratively, it expresses the intense loneliness and suffering of Christ on the Cross and means: 'He rested there alone.'

The imprisoned ANC leader, Nelson Mandela, also showed a willingness to pay the supreme sacrifice in order to achieve freedom for his people when he said, before the court about to sentence him to life imprisonment in 1964, 'It is an ideal which I hope to live for and achieve. But if needs be, it is an ideal for which I am prepared to die.'[51]

Notes

1. *Oral Literature in Africa*, Clarendon Press, Oxford, 1970, p. 2.
2. ibid., p. 82.
3. In a private letter to the author in 1984, Professor Daniel Kunene, the South African writer and scholar in exile, now attached to the University of Wisconsin, commented on Shaka, Tshaka, Chaka/Tjhaka as follows:

    > Regarding the spelling of Chaka/Shaka, it's really quite simple. A Zulu word containing the voiceless palatal *fricative* (phonetic, spelt 'sh' in *both* Zulu and Sesotho), if also existing in Sesotho will, in the latter language, contain a voiceless palatal *affricative* (phonetic t h, spelt 'ch' (Lesotho orthography) and 'tjh' (South African orthography). I might as well mention Xhosa here too because it

behaves like Sesotho in this regard. In Xhosa, however, the spelling is 'tsh'. The result is as follows:

	Zulu	Sesotho	Xhosa
Phonetic		t h	t h
orthographic	sh	ch/tjh	tsh

A good word to illustrate this is the following:

Zulu	Sesotho	Xhosa
-sha	-cha/-tjha	-tsha

which as adjective means 'new', 'young', 'fresh', and as a verb means 'burn', intransitive *in all three languages*. That is why the Zulu king is *uShaka* in Zulu, *Chaka/Tjhaka* in Sesotho, and *uTshaka* in Xhosa.

Daniel Kunene's reply is of great importance, in view of the query in an Afrikaans newspaper as to the spelling of the name Shaka in Afrikaans, just after the start of a special series on the Zulu King on South African television in October 1986. See *Die Burger*, 10 October 1986.

The following is an extract in Afrikaans from *Die Burger* (with English translation).

Chaka, Tsjaka, Sjaka of Shaka?

Hoe spel 'n mens nou eintlik op Afrikaans die naam van die groot Zoeloeleier oor wie gisteraand 'n reeks oor TV 1 begin het? Die titel van die (Engelse) reeks is Shaka Zulu, maar op Afrikaans het hy tot dusver Tsjaka geheet. So staan dit in die Tweetalige Woordeboek van Bosman, van der Merwe en Hiemstra. Dit stem ooreen met 'n alternatiewe Engelse spelling, Chaka. Dit is hoe die eerste blanke reisigers sy naam gespel het. Maar mettertyd het 'Shaka' die oorhand gekry oor 'Chaka'.

In Sotho sou daarvan byvoorbeeld 'Tjhaka' gemaak word. Maar volgens prof. Justus Roux van die departement van Bantoetale aan die Universiteit van Stellenbosch is 'Shaka' die korrekte Zoeloeskryfwyse. Die vraag is nou net of dit op Afrikaans 'Shaka' of 'Sjaka' moet wees. Dr. Leon de Stadler van Stellenbosche departement van Afrikaans meen dat 'Shaka' gebruik kan word. Aangesien die woordelys 'Shangaan' naas 'Sjangaan' en 'Shona' naas 'Sjona' erken, behoort sowel 'Shaka' as 'Sjaka' te deug.

(How should one spell the name of the great Zulu leader in Afrikaans, about whom a series on TV 1 started last night? The title of the (English) series is Shaka Zulu, but in Afrikaans he has hitherto been called Tsjaka. It is noted down in this way in the Dictionary of Bosman, van der Merwe and Hiemstra. It also agrees with the alternative spelling in English, namely, Chaka. This

And Bid Him Sing

is how the first European travellers spelt his name. But in the course of time, 'Shaka' ousted 'Chaka'.
In Sotho, one would, for example, have 'Tjhaka'. But according to Professor Justus Roux of the department of Bantu Languages at Stellenbosch, 'Shaka' is the correct Zulu way of writing. The question now is, whether it should be 'Shaka' or 'Sjaka' in Afrikaans. Dr Leon de Stadler of the Department of Afrikaans at Stellenbosch is of the opinion that 'Shaka' can be used. Since the dictionary lists 'Shangaan' next to 'Sjangaan' and 'Shona' next to 'Sjona', then both 'Shaka' and 'Sjaka' ought to be acceptable.
4. Finnegan, op. cit., p. 87.
5. Trevor Cope, *Izibongo – Zulu Praise Poems*, Oxford University Press, London. 1968, p. 21.
6. See in Cope, op. cit., 1968, p. 21.
7. *Zulu-Kafir Dictionary*, Gregg Press, 1967; see especially the introduction (facsimile of original first published in 1857).
8. Cope. op. cit., p. 21.
9. ibid., p. 31.
10. A. C. Jordan, *Towards an African Literature*, University of California Press, Los Angeles, 1974, 2nd edn, p. 21. First published as a series of articles in *Africa South* (ed. R. Segal), Traditional Poetry II, vol. 2, no. 1 (Oct.–Dec. 1957), p. 105.
11. *Zulu Poems*, André Deutsch, London, 1970, p. 14.
12. B. W. Vilakazi, 'The Conception and Development of Poetry in Zulu', *Bantu Studies*, Witwatersrand University, Johannesburg, vol. 12, 1938, p. 106.
13. Bryant quoted in Rev. E. W. Grant, 'The Izibongo of the Zulu Chiefs', *Bantu Studies*, vol. 3, 1927-9, p. 203.
14. 'Traditional Literature', *The Bantu-Speaking Tribes of South Africa* (ed. I. Schapera), Routledge & Sons, London, 1946, p. 925.
15. Jordan, op. cit., p. 21.
16. Cope, op. cit., pp. 28-9.
17. 'African Work Songs', *An African Treasury* (ed. Langston Hughes), Crown Publishers, New York, 1968, 5th edn, p. 99.
18. Cope, op. cit., 1968, pp. 8, 39, 89.
19. Jordan, op. cit., 1974, 2nd edn, p. 25; see also 'Towards an African Literature' in *Africa South* (ed. R. Segal), vol. 2, no. 1 (Oct.–Dec. 1957), pp. 103-4.
20. See Gnomic Verses, pp. 127-8. Quoted in L. F. Anderson, *The Anglo-Saxon Scop*, Toronto, Toronto University Studies, 1902, p. 12
21. C. T. Onions, *Sweet's Anglo-Saxon Reader in Prose and Verse*, Clarendon Press, Oxford, 1959, 14th edn, p. 42, lines 20-26.
22. ibid., p. 43, lines 41-9.
23. ibid., p. 153, line 144.
24. ibid., p. 149, lines 54-5.
25. For *Beowulf* see C. L. Wrenn (ed.), George G. Harrap & Co., London, 1953, p. 97, lines 89-90.
26. Wrenn, op. cit., p. 122, lines 1063-7.

The Imbongi, the Scop and the Skald

27. L. F. Anderson, *The Anglo-Saxon Scop*, University Studies, Toronto, 1902, p. 12.
28. Susan de Valle, 'Harps African', 1978, unpublished version through kind permission of Professor Lois Anderson of the University of Wisconsin.
29. For *Widsith* see R. K. Gordon, *Anglo-Saxon Poetry*, Dent, London, 1964, p. 68.
30. R. Koegel, *Geschichte der Deutsche Litteratur*, Karl J. Trübner, Strassbourg Verlag, 1894, pp. 134–5.
31. Anderson, op. cit., p. 34.
32. Gordon, op. cit., Introduction.
33. Alistair Campbell, *Skaldic Verse and Anglo-Saxon History*, H.K. Lewis, London, 1970, p. 11.
34. The author's private notes made while taking courses on Norwegian language and literature at Oslo University, 1968.
35. See note 34.
36. P. Hallberg, *The Icelandic Saga* (trans. with an introduction and notes by Paul Schach), University of Nebraska Press, Lincoln, 1962, p. 42.
37. Omer-Cooper, *The Zulu Aftermath*, Longman, London, 1966; E. A. Ritter, *Shaka Zulu: the Rise of the Zulu Empire*, Mentor Books, New York, 1973.
38. Mazisi Kunene, op. cit., p. 13.
39. ibid.
40. *The Beginnings of English Society*, Penguin Books, Harmondsworth, 1962, p. 27.
41. For *Beowulf* see C. L. Wrenn (ed.), p. 130, lines 1383–8.
42. See Ritter, op. cit., p. 314.
43. See Onions, op. cit., pp. 119–20, lines 288–94.
44. For *The Wanderer* see C. T. Onions, op. cit., p. 149, lines 36–8.
45. Anderson, op. cit., p. 42.
46. ibid. p. 22.
47. For Mqhayi see Jordan, op. cit., p. 27.
48. See Gordon, op. cit., p. 3.
49. The *Observer*, 28 October 1961.
50. Onions, op. cit., p. 145, line 69.
51. See Nelson Mandela's speech at the Rivonia trial for high treason held in the Supreme Court, Pretoria, October 1963–June 1964.

Bibliography

Anderson, L.F. (1902): *The Anglo-Saxon Scop* (Toronto, Univ of Toronto).
Campbell, Alistair (1970/71): *Skaldic Verse and Anglo-Saxon History*, London. (H. K. Lewis for Land. Univ. College Studies – M.A. Thesis).
Omer-Cooper (1966): *The Zulu Aftermath* (London, Longmans).

And Bid Him Sing

Cope, Trevor (1968): *Izibongo Zulu Praise Poems* (London, Oxford Univ. Press).
Döhne, J.L. (1967): *Zulu-Kafir Dictionary* (Hants. England, Gregg Press Ltd. fascimile – first printed in 1857).
Finnegan, Ruth (1970): *Oral Literature in Africa* (London, Oxford Univ. Press).
Gordon, R.K. (1964): *Anglo-Saxon Poetry* (London, Everyman, Dent & Sons Ltd.).
Grant, W. (1927/1929): 'The Izibongo of the Zulu Chiefs'. In: *Bantu Studies*, vol. III, 1927–1929 (Johannesburg, Univ. of Witwatersrand Press).
Hallberg, P. (1962): *The Icelandic Saga* (translated with an introduction and notes by Paul Schach), (Lincoln, University of Nebraska Press).
Jordan, A.C. (1974²): *Towards an African Literature* (Los Angeles, University of California Press); first printed in *Africa South* (ed. R. Segal, vol. 2, no. 1, Oct.–Dec. 1957).
Koegel, R. (1894): *Geschichte der Deutsche litteratur* (Stuttgart, Verlag Karl).
Kunene, Mazisi (1970): *Zulu Poems* (London, André Deutsch).
Lestrade, G.P. (1946): 'Traditional Literature'. In: *The Bantu-speaking Tribes of South Africa* (ed. Schapera, London, Routledge & Kegan Paul).
Livingstone, David (1857): *Missionary Travels and Researches in South Africa* (London).
Onions, C.T. (ed) (1959[14]): *Sweet's Anglo-Saxon Reader in Prose and Verse*. (Oxford, Clarendon Press).
Ritter, E.A. (1973): *Shaka Zulu* (New York, Mentor Books (first published G. P. Putnam's Sons, 1955).
Valle, S. de & Vilakazi, B.W. (1938): 'The Conception and the Development of Poetry in Zulu', in: *Bantu Studies*, vol. 12, 1938 (Johannesburg, Univ. of Witwatersrand Press).
Whitelock, D. (1962): *The Beginnings of English Society* (London, Penguin Books).

2

From Peau Noire to Po' White[1]

(With Apologies to Ogden Nash)

One of the direct consequences of colonialism and racism for people of colour is that they invariably become the dupes of a series of rationalizations, whereby the whites (the power-holders) justify their dominant position in society. These rationalizations may range from the historically embedded 'wilde' to the latterday 'happy-go-lucky and innocent children of nature' image. This process is still very apparent in South Africa where race determines one's ascribed role in society. It is, therefore, hardly surprising that the well-known critic and writer, Es'kia Mphahlele, should rail against Joyce Cary's *Mister Johnson* in the following vein:

> I flung away *Mister Johnson* in exasperation when I tried to read it for the first time in South Africa. I had seen too many journalistic caricatures of black people and 'bongo-bongo cartoons', showing Africans with filed teeth and bones stuck in their hair, too many for me to find amusement in Johnson's behaviour always on the verge of farce.[2]

This angry reaction of Mphahlele was – and still is – shared by many a black man and highlights the emergence of the 'new African' who is prepared to hit back. In the old relations, the man of colour was forced into a subservient role through a series of coercive measures. Force was one means of achieving the subjugation of the man of colour. Bartering, often ending in open bribery, stealing of possessions and expropriation of land, was another means.

There is a dialectical relationship between the stereotype and its function. The stereotype is an attempt to define or evaluate people who differ from one's own norms, somatically, culturally or in terms of social institutions, on the basis of a system of beliefs and conceptions, whether proven or unproven, real or imaginary. This, then, would constitute the criteria whereby value judgements about the 'native' are formed.

During the initial phase of exploration and travel the stereotype owed its existence to the fruitful imagination of over-zealous travellers who sent back glorious reports of exotic places, populated with noble savages, such as one finds in the accounts of Henry Smeathman from the Banana Islands:

> Pleasant scenes of vernal beauty, a tropical luxuriance, where fruits and flowers lavish their fragrance together in the same bough! There nature animates every embryo of life; and reigning in vegetable or animal perfection; perpetually glows in wild splendor and uncultivated maturity.[3]

The stereotype made it easier for the conqueror to adopt a set of attitudes towards the 'native' which, to some extent at least, also justified his treatment of the said 'native'. It was, after all, easier to justify the application of a different norm if the other party was classified as a 'native', a savage, a ne'er-do-well, a happy-go-lucky fellow, a drunkard or a comic object.[4] All the characteristics imputed to the 'native' negated the aspirations of the Graeco-Roman Christian tradition.

The stereotype by extension – and probably unconsciously so during the initial phase – was also useful in keeping the colonized in his place. Having determined for him a different norm, it was not so difficult to establish spatial (geographic) and physical (sexual) categories. The portrayal of the man of colour was therefore determined by the manner in which he was subjugated.

The African could then become a docile and submissive type to be bullied at random. At best he was a creation of Edgar Rice Burroughs, or Rider Haggard, a tall and impressive black man who intrigues and owes his existence to a peculiar exploitation of the exotic. He was enshrined in *Bwana Jungle* and appeared in the film as a savage who was fairly happy. He becomes '*our native*' in the mouth of white users. Note, whenever the possessive is used, the said 'native' is in grave danger.

In this respect Ralph Ellison's novel, *The Invisible Man* (1972), is of great interest. Many racial themes are to be found in this profound novel. The black man is insecure, possessionless and an alienated human being. Ellison's Invisible Man starts his sojourn in the Deep South and moves to Harlem where there are greater opportunities. But the problems, instead of disappearing, are only different. Invisible man joins the militant Brotherhood, striving to wipe out some of the social evils confronting the black man. But even the Brotherhood is subject to disintegration.

The black man comes across as a rapist and a cheat. His sole concern is to covet the white man's possessions. Ellison portrays this very clearly in his novel in which the protagonist is first confronted with a scantily clad white woman, dancing in front of him but just beyond his reach. This is 'the quest for white flesh by alienated psyches'.[5] The protagonist is made to crawl in front of a rug, desperately trying to retrieve some money from it. But the rug is electrified and he is frustrated in his attempt to gain access to that other white God, Mammon.

It is against this background that we must view the reaction of the French West African and the Antillean in Paris during the 1930s. Négritude as a cultural and ideological weapon owes its origin to a discovery by the colonized of their own 'self-deception-in-self-definition'. In a sense there is a greater symbolism in the title of Ralph Ellison's book, *The Invisible Man*. On the other hand, the black man was as invisible as ever during the 1930s. At the same time, the black man was busy illuminating his culture and personality as never before during the Harlem Renaissance in America – Harlem was referred to as the black capital of the black world. When Claude McKay, the Jamaican poet, wrote those momentous lines in Harlem, 'If we must die, let it not be like hogs,'[6] he could never have dreamt that Winston Churchill would recite them in the House of Commons, when exhorting his countrymen to oppose Hitler. In France, the Antilleans and West Africans did much to focus attention on the African heritage. Africa became a nostalgic frame of reference, a place of rhythm and dance.

The French colonies in West Africa and the Caribbean were all subject to a system of assimilation. The authorities creamed off the top layer in the colonies, provided them with special schooling and turned these blacks into pseudo-Frenchmen. The indigenous culture of the blacks was suppressed and the colonized were taught to recite that their ancestors were Gauls (or so the school books taught them). French culture and French ways were transmitted through the schools, French expatriates and administrative officials. The special category of blacks created as a result of the policy of assimilation received, in return for their connivance with the colonial overlords, special privileges. They were, for example, exempted from doing special chores. Admittedly, there was a great deal of mistrust on the part of the colonized. Yet, at the same time, the colonial regime was able to count on at least some cooperation from the colonized in the implementation of their schemes. How else could one explain the fairly non-violent decolonization process?

The black elite, created by the French, looked upon Paris as the cultural Valhalla and, naturally, all their dreams were concentrated on seeing Paris one day. Once in the metropolis, these West Africans and Antilleans soon discovered that their black skins precluded them from the normal privileges extended to Frenchmen. The image of France, so carefully nurtured during the years, proved to be a lie. The blacks in France painfully experienced the deflation of the norm in which they had been led to believe.

Their reaction was of a varied nature. In 1932 the Martiniquean student, Etienne Lero, started his *Légitime Défense*, a magazine based on communism and surrealism. The magazine had a short life. Its successor, *l'Etudiant Noir*, appeared in 1934. The aim was to unite the Antillean and West African students. Prime movers were Leopold Sedar Senghor, Aimé Césaire, Birago Diop and Leon Damas. The word 'négritude' was first used by Aimé Césaire in his well-known book, *Cahier d'un retour au pays natal* (1939). The students not only rejected France culturally. They also put to the test some of the old assumptions they had been fed during colonial times. In the words of Coleman, 'A particularly striking feature of the African nationalism has been the literary and cultural revival which has attended it.'[7]

Africa became the focal point for writers from the French Antilles. It became a place of rhythm, of ancestral veneration and a source of creative energy and inspiration. The barbaric and savage image of Africa, so carefully kept alive by whites for centuries, was exposed by the creative artist. It led to a rediscovery of, for example, creole as a means of creative expression. Jean-Paul Sartre, in his introduction to Leopold Sedar Senghor's anthology of Negro-French poetry, *Nouvelle anthologie de la Poesie nègre et Malgache* (1948), said of négritude:

> In choosing to see what he is, he split himself in two and he no longer coincides with himself. Reciprocally, it is because he was already exiled from himself, that he found for himself the duty of expression... One must, however, break through the walls of the culture prison, one must, one day go back to Africa. In this way, the horizontal return to the native land and the vertical return to the brilliant Hades of the negro soul are themes indissolubly linked in the 'vates' of Négritude.

Négritude was, then, the breaking down of this 'culture prison' and, as such, an ideological weapon in the liberation of the black man. Poets used it to express their longing for Africa, to re-evaluate their ancestral home. Others exploited négritude to give vent to their anti-clerical feelings. European culture was rejected and African forms discovered. This rehabilitation of Africa and the black man was also reflected in the writings of Afro-American writers and poets. It is no accident that Langston Hughes should write:

> I am a negro,
> Black as the night is black
> Black as the depths of my Africa...[8]

Harlem in the 1930s was surely the capital of black creative writers from different parts of the world. Ironically, despite the economic recession in the United States at that time, the black man was at his creative best via poetry and prose. Black solidarity is given excellent form in the following poem by Langston Hughes:

> We are related – you and I
> You from the West-Indies
> I from Kentucky
> We are related – you and I
> You from Africa
> I from the States
> We are brothers – you and I.[9]

This process of demythologization was to repeat itself during the late 1950s and early sixties, coinciding with the period of decolonization. The process of casting off the shackles of colonialism inevitably had its effects on the black world at large. Africa, at least, was slowly being rescued from Tarzan. Scholars from various disciplines and with Western training were helping to reshape the image of the new Africa. Legend has it that, when the first Africans from newly independent countries arrived in America to represent their countries as diplomats, their colourful and beautiful African garments and robes, which formed such a striking contrast with the clothes of the Westerners, set the Afro-American mind on fire. Some sources claim that it was Miriam Makeba, the South African singer, who, with her natural hair, influenced Afro-American women into accepting fuzzy hair as aesthetically pleasing. Leaders of the stature of Kwame Nkrumah and Jomo Kenyatta further contributed to the process of demythologization.

In America, the concept of soul did much to provide black people with a sense of pride. Stephen Henderson defined soul as 'all of the unconscious energy of the Black experience ... the primal spiritual energy ... the expression of total personality, drawing its reserve from centuries of suffering and joy'.[10]

While the rest of the black world was giving angry expression to its blackness, the South African black man found himself in an increasingly oppressive situation, culminating in that traumatic and tragic event at Sharpeville in 1960. As during plantation slavery in the West Indies and the Americas, the African in South Africa found, or rather established, certain patterns of survival which are strongly reminiscent of those among Afro-Americans.

All over the black world this defiant note was heard during the 1960s. Thus Mercer Cook and Stephen Henderson observe:

> Taking the white man's language, dislocating his syntax, recharging his words with new strength and sometimes with new meaning before hurling them back in his teeth, while upsetting his self-righteous complacency and clichés, our poets rehabilitate such terms as Africa and blackness, beauty and peace.[11]

From the history of the man of colour, one could so easily and erroneously conclude that he was a willing victim of colonialism, racism and slavery. The patterns of survival among blacks are varied and interesting. Thus Frantz Fanon could write in his *Black Skin, White Masks* (1967): 'The black man has two dimensions. One with his fellows, the other with the white man.'[12] In his very interesting and instructive book, *Black Culture and Consciousness* (1977), Levine quotes a song from the Deep South, sung by Afro-Americans long before Fanon wrote down his message. The song is as follows:

> Got one mind for white folks to see,
> 'Nother for what I know is me,
> He don't know, he don't know my mind.[13]

One of the devices used to satirize whites, to fool white society, was the song. This was (and is) so in Africa, Surinam and the ante-bellum South. In South Africa, where blacks had very few avenues open to express their anger, songs often provided such an outlet (see p. 7). The writer and musician, the late Todd Matshikiza, records in his book, *Chocolates for My Wife* (1961), the reactions of one of his characters when she sees black and white workers working side by side for the first time in London. The only thing they didn't do was sing for, as she observed: 'Singing while you are digging digs the hole deep down.'[14]

In Surinam, the former Dutch colony in Latin America, songs were not only humorous but sometimes directed with venom at the enemy.

> Street concerts in Surinam's capital Paramaribo have been responsible for bitter fights in the past and Surinam is possibly one of the few places in the world where concerts have been repeatedly forbidden by the law. In a government proclamation of 19th November 1928 the so-called *Du societies* (for dance and song) were forbidden in Paramaribo and other parts of the country.[15]

Another genre, the *lobisingi* (love songs) suffered a similar fate in the 1900s. As in the ante-bellum South in America, the slave could not openly criticize his master or the state of affairs on his plantation. Song provided him with the only means of doing so. In Surinam, the way in which Creole women wear their kerchief and the way in which it was (and is) bound around their heads is of great symbolic significance, 'bearing often on social and political issues'.[16]

The black worker in South Africa sings, while swinging his pick axe:

And Bid Him Sing

> Abelungu ngodem, ngodem
> Basibiza ooJim,
> (White man, go to hell, they call us Jim.)[17]

And the white foreman muses in the sun, 'A singing native is a happy native.' The slaves in Surinam lamented on the plantation:

> Te mi masra dede, nowan yobo wani bay mi
> te mi masra dede, nowan masra wani bay mi
> Na bakabaka tan bun masra kan bay mi
> now dede wanwan kan bay mi.

And the 'masra' does not hear the message which says:

> When my master passed away
> no white man wanted me
> When my master passed away
> no master wanted me
> A bad one later did
> now death alone wants me.[18]

In the ante-bellum South the slaves produced the following satirical dig:

> My old Mistis promised me
> Dat when she died, she gwine set me free.
> But she lived so long en got so po
> Dat she lef me diggin wid er garden ho.[19]

Song and dance, then, became the two satirical weapons in the hands of the man and woman of colour finding themselves in a position of extreme subordination.

The black man, like the Jew, ostensibly demeans himself by making jokes at his own expense or that of his group. What GrotJahn says of the Jewish joke is also applicable to that of blacks:

> The Jewish joke constitutes victory by defeat. The persecuted Jew who makes himself the butt of the joke deflects his dangerous hostility away from the persecutors onto himself. The result is not defeat or surrender but victory.[20]

Humour is used as a means of social control. The white man is made to appear ridiculous, despite his ostensibly impregnable position. The black man plays the little negro, just as the Jew plays the little Jew, obsequious in the presence of his superior, going to great lengths to demean himself. But the ultimate effect of such displays is that the man of colour emerges as the superior and not the inferior. In the South African context, Gammatjie, the Malay character, is often seen to fulfil this role. It is not so ironic that one would come across jokes which were well known in the south of the United States and which are also found in a slightly different variation in South Africa. Yet, there are no indications of borrowing. In the South African context, the joke would run as follows: a black man drove through the red lights and was promptly stopped by a white traffic cop. On being asked why he did such a dangerous thing he replied: 'You see Baas, I see white people stopping when the lights are red and driving when they are green. So, I thought, red must be the signal for us to go.' A similar joke is recorded in Levine's book *Black Culture and Consciousness*. The author observes: 'The anger and aggression that had to be swallowed and hidden normally could surface in jokes.'[21]

White ways and attitudes are made fun of through jokes. Some of the stereotypes which the white man so readily and expertly exploits in referring to blacks are reversed at the expense of the white man. It is an indisputable fact that, in the ante-bellum South, blacks on the plantation were wont to imitate dance forms of their masters (for example the waltz), but in such a ridiculous fashion as to give cause for laughter to the whites who observed such antics. They, the whites, failed to realize that such parodies were deliberate and that the blacks were mocking them. White institutions are also satirized. What Levine then observes of the Afro-American is equally applicable to blacks elsewhere: 'The critical thrust of Negro humor was aimed inward as well as outward, at blacks as well as whites.'[22]

In the Caribbean and American context Anansi, the Spider, brought over with the slaves, is of tremendous symbolic significance. It is no accident that Anansi survived the middle passage to re-emerge on the plantations in the ante-bellum South as Brer Rabbit and, in Surinam and the Antilles, under his own name, Anansi. Anansi, the Spider, who outwits his opponents, is often seen as the slave who, in the tightly woven, structured and constricting plantation system, managed to outwit his superior, the white man. As such, Anansi becomes the black man who survives by means of guile, cunning and wit. Nothing is sacrosanct and he will stop at nothing to achieve his aim. Anansi is the answer to the wickedness of the plantation system. He is the picaresque folk hero who survives the ravages of white destruction.

The black man, as already pointed out, has many ways of surviving. As the slave saying from South Carolina puts it so aptly: 'De Buckruh (whites) hab scheme, and de nigger hab trick, en ebery time de buckruh scheme once de nigger trick twice.'[23]

The black man has learnt to build up his own system of symbols whereby he manages to throw white society into confusion. The intricate and varied way in which Afro-Americans sometimes shake hands comes to mind. There are even deliberate attempts to change a particular handshake when whites try to catch on. Blacks have also developed their own forms of attire. Afro haircuts and dashikis are now openly sported in the United States.

The Rastafarians and reggae have further contributed to the emergence of new cultural forms among young blacks. Blacks have also developed their own forms of language. In the Dutch context Edgar Cairo, the Surinamese writer, is one of the main exponents of this trend. While one might quibble about the orthography, the language used in Cairo's articles, poems and novels is, at least, an attempt to recognize the fullness of the black Surinamese experience. Again Levine shows tremendous perspicacity when he observes: 'Living in the midst of a hostile and repressive white society, black people found in language an important means of promoting and maintaining a sense of group unity and cohesion.'[24]

Whites all over the world were assured of a large and interested audience who looked after their children, dished up their food, observed them when they were sad or happy, even copied their manners, but who laughed behind their backs at times. And the whites were blissfully unaware of all this. Blacks used the stereotypes whites had of them and held them up to scorn and ridicule. The man of colour was in the throes of liberating himself from the white world, a process started in the 1930s, gaining momentum in the 1950s and coinciding with the period of decolonization. It is no accident that much writing should be initially in reaction to the white world.

One of the ways of maintaining sanity was through the inversion of the stereotype. This made it possible for the blacks to re-establish a different order in which they emerged as victors. Stereotypes, as we have seen, are strongest in areas where there are unequal power

From Peau Noire to Po' White

relations. Since the image of the white man is largely created by himself, the stereotypes which emerge will also logically reflect the historical white-black relations. Thus, I have tentatively tried to identify several situations in which the novelist or the short-story writer would proceed to portray the white man as stereotype. These categories are, to my mind, the following:

1. violent, brutal, the predator;
2. the sexual pervert, the 'quest for black flesh' by alienated psyches;
3. aesthetic downgrading of the whites, the dumb and ugly white man as opposed to the proud and beautiful black man;
4. humour as a means of social control, for example, cultural comparisons ridiculing the white world; the white man falls foul of socio-linguistic idiom of the black world.

On the basis of white-black relations, it is not so difficult to abstract the image of the cruel white man whose only form of creativity and creation is destruction. André Brink, the South African novelist, allows one of his characters to say in comic vein by way of justifying his presence in Africa: 'No, I only came to start a little vegetable garden.' Not surprisingly, therefore, within situations of oppression, black authors see whites as cruel, monstrous and inhuman beasts, bereft of all human feelings. They either have steely blue eyes or penetrating stares (mostly both). They are also invariably policemen. The image of blue as a symbol of cruelty is as well established as that of black as a symbol of evil for whites. Even the late Alex La Guma, the South African novelist whose compassion for people was well known, cannot prevent the characters in his novel, *A Walk in the Night*,[25] from being trigger-happy policemen with steely blue eyes. His main white character, Raalt, is a policemen and a predator with an insatiable thirst for blood: '... Raalt's smile was a crooked grimace, ugly as a razor slash. He shifted his grey-dust eyes on the dark-skinned man ...'

A little further one reads: 'Under the lowered lids the eyes were hard and flat and as shiny as cartridge shells...' One is never allowed to forget Raalt's 'grey-dust eyes' as he lifts his right hand to strike 'the olive-skinned man across the mouth...' Raalt, the policeman, shoots Willieboy, a coloured youth, senselessly. When challenged by his fearful partner his 'eyes were hard and grey like two rough pebbles in the dark'. Even Raalt's language has a similar violence, lexical items which define him only in terms of his violent nature. His speech is liberally strewn with the following words whenever he comes across 'Coloureds': bedonered (crazy), bliksem (miscreant), donder (wretch), hotnot (hottentot).

A similar pattern is found in the novel *Wild Conquest* by Peter Abrahams. The main characters, Kasper and Koos Jansen, are hardened people who, in the words of Koos, live by the following rules: 'Shoot first and speak afterwards. It's a good old Boer rule...Our forebears who had to fight the Kaffirs knew just how good it was.'[26] Ger Villiers, a major character in another novel of Abrahams, *The Path of Thunder*, is also defined in terms of the violence he unleashes on his helpless victims. He is a violent person who kept his victims in an 'obsequious attitude by extreme penalties of fear and violence'.[27]

This violence also pervades the novel by the Afro-American, Richard Wright. His main character in *Native Son*, bigger Thomas, is reduced to inarticulacy and fear in the presence of whites. 'In the world that bigger Thomas knows, the whole process of life hinges on . . . color designations. White human beings in America symbolize generally wealth and power. Black human beings equate poverty and misery in most cases.'[28] Novels by Afro-American and Anglo-American (WASP – White Anglo-Saxon Protestant) writers share this with their South African counterparts: a preoccupation with race and colour.

It is also no accident that the sexual theme is so often exploited. White women who are involved with black men are, as Claude Wauthier puts it, 'Desdemona[s] [who] come to a tragic end'.[29] Chester Himes makes fun of this in his book, *If He Hollers, Let Him Go*, in which the white girl, Madge, afraid of being caught with a black lover, resorts to the standard stereotyped trick by shouting, when she sees the white man approaching, 'Help me! Help me! My God, help me! Some white man, help me! I'm being raped!'[30] At the same time Himes falls in the same trap by downgrading her aesthetically by describing her as a 'big overpainted strumpet with her eyes as wild as Oklahoma'.

The white man is aesthetically downgraded by way of compensation for the years of denigration suffered by black people. He becomes ugly, non-sexual, even effeminate, a Raalt who constantly suspects his wife of cuckolding him, a Villiers who can only beat people into submission, the white man in Ralph Ellison's book, *The*

Invisible Man, who derives pleasure out of seeing the black man who had raped his own daughter.

Minorities are often forced to play out comic roles in order to retain their sanity. The black clown often hides more from the white man than he reveals. The black writer exploits cultural comparisons in such a manner that the very tenets of white society look ridiculous. The Camerounian novelist, Ferdinand Oyono, used this technique in his two novels *Houseboy* (1966) and *The Old Man and the Medal* (1967). In the first novel the houseboy discovers a condom under madame's bed. Since he had never seen one, he went to the omniscient cook for advice. This leads to a tremendous amount of hilarity and affords the author a chance to poke fun at the French expatriates and officials in Africa.

> 'But tell me . . . these little bags made of rubber . . . musn't the houseboy . . .' I was not allowed to finish. His face which a moment before had been so solemn was split from side to side by enormous peals of laughter.[31]

Oyono sustains this scene for almost two pages. Through his sputtering the cook eventually explains: 'To do things properly. . . They put it on, like a hat or a pair of gloves. . . ', said the cook in an off-hand knowing manner, mocking his innocence.

In the second novel, *The Old Man and the Medal*, old Meka had been awarded a medal by the French government for giving four of his sons to die for the mother country. In this episode Oyono holds the French to scorn in superb fashion. One of the characters maintains, towards the end, that Meka should have received his medal wearing only a *bila*. 'I-I-say, he should wear a bila . . . because if he did . . . the Chief of the whites . . . have to bend down and pin the medal on on his bila!' The laughter burst with the violence of boiling water breaking out.[32] *Bila*, according to an African colleague, comes closer to a penis shield than a loin-cloth.

Similar techniques are employed in Afro-American folklore. The following example is from the year 1866:

> 'Now children, you don't think white people are better than you because they have straight hair and white faces?'
> 'No Sir.'
> 'No, they are not better, but they are different, they possess

great power, they formed this great government, they control this vast country ... Now what makes them different from you?'
'MONEY.' (Unanimous shout)
'Yes, but what enabled them to obtain it?'
'Got it off us, stole it off we all.'[33]

In demythologizing the white world, the black man often forged his own language, his own symbolism. Often it took the form of playing with socio-linguistic patterns. It is a deliberate exploitation of an idiom which is calculated not only to confuse but also to ridicule. One of the best illustrations of this type of behaviour is found in the Afro-American, David Bradley's novel, *South Street* (1975). A white man knocked down a black alley cat in Harlem and then had the nerve to enter a bar where he boldly informed the astounded blacks that he had just knocked down a cat. Now anyone familiar with Afro-American idiom knows that the word *black cat* had a completely different connotation for the blacks in that bar. They immediately assumed that this white man, this 'honkey' as they would have it, had knocked down one of their own and was now so brazen as to ask them for help in removing the body. The atmosphere was decidedly hostile and our innocent white man came close to being lynched. When the blacks discovered that he was referring to a real cat, they left him alone, amazed at the ways of whites who would make such a fuss over nothing.

Cultural comparisons have led to anti-clericalism and extreme rejection of white culture. They range from Césaire's 'Hurrah for those who have not invented anything'[34] to the more irreverent 'Surprise Jesus Joseph Mary, that we grabbed the missionary by the beard.'[35]

In conclusion I would like to recall a story by Malinowski in his foreword to *The Savage Hits Back* (1966) by Julius Lips:

> Yet I remember talking to an old cannibal who from missionary and administrator had heard news of the Great War raging then in Europe. What he was most curious to know was how we Europeans managed to eat such enormous quantities of human flesh such as the casualties of a battle seem to imply. When I told him indignantly that Europeans did not eat their slain foes, he looked at me with real horror and asked what sort of barbarians we were to kill without any real object.[36]

From Peau Noire to Po' White

The SAVAGE, to borrow from Lips, HITS BACK with impunity and a smile.

Notes

1. This is a revised version of an article which first appeared in Robert Ross (ed.), *Racism and Colonialism: Essays on Ideology and Social Structure*, Martinus Nijhoff, The Hague, 1982, pp. 181-97.
2. *The African Image*, Faber & Faber, London, 1962, p. 161.
3. See J.C. Lettsom (ed.), *The Works of John Fothergill M.D.*, London, 1784, p. 577 quoted in Philip Curtin, *The Image of Africa*, Madison, University of Wisconsin Press, 1964, p. 60.
4. See V.A. February, *Mind Your Colour*, Kegan Paul Int., London, 1981, pp. 23-30.
5. See Frantz Fanon, *Black Skin, White Masks*, Grove Press, New York, 1968, 5th edn, p. 81.
6. James Weldon Johnson (ed.), *A Book of American Negro Poetry*, Harcourt, Brace and World, New York, 1959 p. 168.
7. J. Coleman, 'Nationalism in Tropical Africa', P.J.M. McEwan & R.B. Sutcliffe, *The Study of Africa*, Methuen, London, 1965, p. 166.
8. Langston Hughes cited in Langston G. Hughes: 'The Twenties: Harlem and Its Négritude', *Africa Forum*, volume 1, number 4/spring, 1966, p. 17. New York, published and distributed for the American Society of African Culture (AMSAC) by Publications Development Corporation.
9. See Colin Legum, *Panafricanism*, London, Pall Mall Press 1962, p. 16.
10. Mercer Cook & Stephen Henderson, *The Militant Black Writer in Africa and the United States*, Wisconsin University Press, Madison, 1969, p. 124.
11. ibid., Foreword, p. VIII.
12. Grove Press, New York, 1967, p. 17.
13. Oxford University Press, London, 1977, Preface, XIII.
14. Hodder & Stoughton, London, 1961, p. 67.
15. J. Voorhoeve & U. Lichtveld (eds.), *Creole Drum* (trans. V.A. February), Yale University Press, New Haven, 1975, p. 15.
16. ibid.
17. Tennyson Makiwane, 'African Work Songs', *An African Treasury* (ed. Langston Hughes), Crown Publishers, New York, 1968, p. 99.
18. Voorhoeve & Lichtveld, op. cit., pp. 28-9.
19. Levine, op. cit., p. 13.
20. See Anton Zijderveld, *Sociologie van de Zotheid*, Boom, Meppel, 1971, p. 154.
21. Levine, op. cit., p. 317.

And Bid Him Sing

22. ibid., p. 321.
23. ibid., p. 81.
24. ibid., p. 153.
25. *A Walk in the Night and Other Stories*, Heinemann, London, 1967, pp. 41, 42, 87. La Guma died towards the end of 1985 while serving as a representative of the African National Congress (ANC) in Havana, Cuba.
26. Anchor Books, New York, 1971, p. 51.
27. V. A. February, op. cit., p. 151.
28. See *The Negro Novelist 1940–1950*, The Citadel Press, New York, 1970, p. 60.
29. Claude Wauthier, *The Literature and Thought of Modern Africa*, Praeger, New York, 1967, p. 197 (translated from the French by Shirley Kay).
30. Double Day, New York, 1946, pp. 150–52, 219.
31. Heinemann, London, 1969, pp. 100–102.
32. Heinemann, London, 1969, pp. 165–6.
33. Levine, op. cit., 1977, p. 124.
34. See G. R. Coulthard, *Race and Colour in Caribbean Literature*, Oxford University Press, London, 1962, p. 59.
35. ibid., p. 51.
36. Julius Lips, *The Savage Hits Back*, (trans. V. Benson,) University Books, New York, 1966, p. VII.

Bibliography

1. Abrahams, Peter (1952): *The Path of Thunder*, London, Faber & Faber (first published Harper, New York, 1948).
2. Abrahams, Peter (1971): *Wild Conquest*, New York, Anchor Books (first published Harper, New York, 1950).
3. Bradley, David (1977): *South Street*, New York, Signet Classic (first published in 1975).
4. Cary, Joyce (1952): *Mister Johnson*, London, Mermaid Books (first published in 1939).
5. Césaire, Aimé (1969): *Return to my Native Land*, London, Heinemann (first published in French under title: *Cahiers d'un retour au pays natal* (Paris, 1939)).
6. Cook, Mercer & Stephen Henderson (1969): *The Militant Black Writer in Africa and the United States*, Madison, Wisconsin University Press.
7. Coulthard, G. R. (1962): *Race and Colour in Caribbean Literature*, London, Oxford University Press.
8. Curtin, Philip (1964): *The Image of Africa*, Madison, Wisconsin University Press.

9. Ellison, Ralph (1972): *Invisible Man*, New York, Random House.
10. Fanon, Frantz (1967): *Black Skin White Masks*, New York, Grove Press (first published as *Peau Noire Masques Blancs*, Paris, 1952).
11. February, V.A. (1981): *Mind Your Colour*, London, Kegan Paul Int.
12. Harris, Wilson (1971): 'The Native Phenomenon', Denmark, Aarhus.
13. Himes, Chester (1946): *If He Hollers, Let Him Go*, New York, Double Day & Company.
14. Hughes, Carl Milton (1970): *The Negro Novelist 1940–1950*, New York, Citadel Press.
15. La Guma, Alex (1967): *A Walk in the Night and other Stories*, London, Heinemann.
16. Levine, Lawrence W. (1977): *Black Culture and Black Consciousness*, London, Oxford University Press.
17. Lips, Julius (1966): *The Savage Hits Back*, New York, University Books, transl. Victor Benson.
18. Matshikiza, Todd (1961): *Chocolates for my Wife*, London, Hodder & Stoughton.
19. Wright, Richard (1940): *Native Son*, New York, Harper.

3

Sipho Sepamla – The Soweto I Love[1]

Soweto, acronym for South Western Township, is an oft-found word in the Western press ever since the 'slaying of the innocents' in June 1976. Although a non-African word it seems to have acquired an African connotation, even linguistically one suspects. Few people outside the political and sociological context of South Africa would know the true meaning of Soweto. Through the years it has come to mean several things. To the black inhabitants of Soweto it stands for ghetto township, dehumanization, oppression, institutionalized violence and – since June 1976 – the wanton shooting of children. But there is also a heroic tinge to the word. As with all places of poverty, it is home to the dispossessed of the world.

Several South African poets in exile and at home found inspiration in the tragic events at Soweto. Daniel Kunene exploits the word in its total socio-linguistic and political sense in his poem called 'Soweto'; the effect is traumatic. James Matthews, who lives in South Africa, sees Soweto as the beacon which lights the way to freedom. Lewis Nkosi's *Children of Soweto* is an angry indictment and a cry of anguish. Even some breakaway members of the African musical group, Ipi Tombi, decided to call themselves Soweto Sounds. Thus, even black South African artists have pounced on the 'cult value' of Soweto in Western countries.

Sipho Sepamla's collection, *The Soweto I Love*, is particularly interesting because his is an inside, one would almost hope 'God's-eye-view', of the black struggle, suffering and hopes for the future. It is no accident that a simple tabulation of the words used in his poems (with their meanings) would invariably connect with fear, anger, stench and humiliation. Thus I counted the following words which all link up one way or the other with the concept of fear: *terror, fleeing, cowed, scared, alarm, frantic, scare, cowardly, hounded, panic, scurry and scuttle, tremble.* These words find their complements in others, such as *scavenger, rodents, stench and smell of death, pain of humiliation, storm raging* and *choking dust.*

This imagery defines Sepamla's landscape and society which is consumed with fear, hatred and predators. Upon first reading his poetry, one tends to think of it as simple and naïve. A critic at Wisconsin made a similar observation of Daniel Kunene's poem 'Soweto'. A second and more thorough scrutiny teaches that the simplicity is singularly deceptive and hides a deeper, more profound meaning. The terror of Sepamla's South African landscape is poignantly portrayed precisely through this simplicity of language, the at times inverted sentence structure which further creates the impression of an awkwardness with the English language. Only when he abandons his special style, however, does he really sound awkward as, for example, in the poem 'I Saw This Morning' in which the very direct 'he was crippled by' and 'he was wheeling round his teacher', jar. This simplicity, coupled with a staccato English and fairyesque quality – the Big Bad Wolf image – is hauntingly portrayed in 'A Child Dies'. His poem 'Like a Hippo' must, at first glance, appear to the Western reader as the work of a child. This impression quickly gives way to an understanding of the greater symbolism in the poem – again deceptively simple – similar to oral stories with a tremendous sting in the tail. The Hippo becomes the State = Afrikanerdom = apartheid.

Sepamla had, hitherto, avoided writing 'poetry conscripted for the victims'. Like the Afro-American artist the poet in South Africa can, to a large extent, function as a 'guerilla fighter who can talk Black English and ignore accepted aesthetics'. There is, after all, the fundamental realization that, while the language of the black artist in South Africa is Western, his idiom is definitely non-Western.

The poet's anger is contained with poise and does not spill over into a bitterness, a vituperation. He seldom allows himself a comic ironic stance yet, when he does exploit humour as a device, the effect is visibly felt as, for example, in 'Shop Assistant'; this evokes images of another South African poet, Adam Small, writing in Afrikaans, who lampoons white women in 'Oppie parara' ('On the Parade').

Sepamla's 'Civilization Aha' falls short of the reference to 'Western syphilization' by the Afro-American poet, Jon Eckles. Although oral in tone at times, Sepamla's poetry draws its strength from the urban proletariat environment which spawned him, the poet. Despite the fact that Soweto has, in the words of the poet, 'made of mourning a way of life', he can still say 'I love you Soweto,' thus recalling Can Themba's affection for that other cheap black reservoir of labour which defined the landscape of black writers two decades ago, namely, Sophia Town. Of the gulf between white and black, Sepamla can write:

> Go measure the distance from Cape Town to Pretoria
> you'll never know how far I stand from you.[2]

Yet he can still find the strength and the moral courage to conclude, in all humility, a quality in which white South Africa is totally deficient:

> but a wish of mine remains
> peace at all times with all men.

This moving collection is another affirmation of the Afro-American Nikki Giovanni's belief that 'There is no difference between the warrior, the poet and the people.'

Notes

1. First published in *African Literature Today* (ed. E. D. Jones), no. 10, Heinemann, London, 1979, pp. 256-8; also included in *Soweto Poetry* (ed. Michael Chapman), McGraw Hill, Johannesburg, 1982.
2. See the poem *A Wish* by Sipho Sepamla in his anthology; *The Soweto I Love*, London, Rex Collings with David Phillip, Cape Town 1977, p. 53.

4

Cape of Torments

Cape of No Hope – a Review[1]

Books on slavery do not make for pleasant reading. They fascinate and send tremors down the spine, very much like an encounter with the green mamba in Africa. Here one finds the sum total of man's inhumanity to man. The South African novelist, Es'kia Mphahlele, once wrote that if you kill a man, created in the image of God, you can never wash off the blood. Books on slavery are generally written by whites and with good reason. They, after all, are the descendants of the creators of this Western tradition of slavery. Not surprisingly, therefore, whites are possibly more zealous in their attempts to 'wash off the blood'.

Robert Ross is an English-born historian who specializes in South African history and is currently attached to Leiden University. He has several articles on history to his credit, a book, *Adam Kok's Griquas* (1976), and now he has written an important and moving book on slavery at the Cape, significantly called *Cape of Torments* (1983).[2]

Slavery as a subject has not attracted much attention inside, let alone outside, South Africa. When the word is used nowadays, it is generally meant to refer to the system of apartheid inside South Africa. In school books, the subject was generally glossed over or written from such a white point of view (and then only cursorily), that it never merited much attention. Victor de Kock has written on slavery, a reasonably well-known book called *Those in Bondage* (1950). Anna Boëseken's *Slaves and Free Blacks at the Cape, 1658-1700*, was published in 1977. Hengherr made slavery the subject of his MA thesis in 1953. There is a study by I. Edwards, entitled *Towards Emancipation: a Study in African Slavery* (1942). R. C. H. Shell published *The Impact of the Cape Slave Trade and Its Population on Demography* ... (1979).

Other references are to be found in numerous South African history textbooks. Many of these interpretations or accounts are coloured by the ethnic origin and ideas of the 'white' historian in question. The dispossessed also expressed their views, notably members of the Non-European Unity Movement, but mostly in publications catering for the intelligentsia of the dispossessed in and around Cape Town. Ironically, the one history that was (and according to informants, still is) widely used, namely, *Three Hundred Years* by Mnguni (1952), was written by a member of the Unity Movement who, although from a traditionally enslaved people (the Jews), was classified in terms of South African taxonomy as white.

The 'coloureds', as the descendants of the slaves at the Cape, have largely ignored this tragic period in their history for some very obvious reasons. In the post-slavery period, the emphasis was on assimilation, that is, becoming as white as possible in order to advance within South Africa. A dupe of South African historical forces, the 'coloureds' found themselves in such a spiral that forced them into a process of 'self-deception in self-definition'. Slavery, the highest form of degradation endured by human beings, did not lend itself to any form of myth-making amongst the 'coloureds'. The 'coloured' response was a form of amnesia. Similarly, the whites and, in particular, the Afrikaner, preferred amnesia to a detailed analysis of slavery at the Cape.

In the Cape, then, there was no literary tradition of romantic, wild and passionate slave novels in the Mandingo vein, or reminiscent of those written by Edgar Mittelholzer (see *The Kaywana* trilogy) until the Afrikaner André Brink appeared on the scene to fill this literary hiatus. *An Instant in the Wind* (1976) and *Houd-Den-Bek* (1983) are masterpieces of slave eroticism in the best North American and Caribbean vein. *Houd-Den-Bek*, his latest novel, is based on a slave uprising, excellently described by Robert Ross in his book, *Cape of Torments*.

Cape of Torments

Slavery at the Cape was as cruel as anywhere in the New World. Robert Ross has written a harrowing account of slavery at the Cape, based on actual accounts and court records. This, to my mind, has never been done before, or never so systematically. Ross states that his approach is descriptive although, sensitive historian that he is, he would be the first to concede that mere descriptions involve interpretations or, at least, lend themselves to interpretations. Ross is too conscious of his task as an historian – probing as he does in the historical minefield of South Africa – to fool himself into thinking of the historian only as an objective observer.

In his article, 'The Teaching of South African History in Schools' (February 1983, pp. 96–112), the late Willem van Schoor, a prominent member of the Non-European Unity Movement, spells out the problem in no uncertain terms. He maintains that there are two distinct types of historian in South Africa. Referring to the first type, the so-called liberals, found generally among university professors and lecturers, he says:

> Their work is characterised by wide scientific research and a wealth of useful factual evidence . . . But, however commendable and laudable as this may be, their work is nevertheless open to severe criticism, and this because of an intellectual dishonesty, which manifests itself in their would-be 'objectivity'. Through this 'objectivity' they claim to be 'fair' and 'just' to all sides, to oppressors and oppressed, exploiters and exploited. But it is precisely by means of this 'objectivity' that they commit the unpardonable sin of treating the forces of progress and reaction on the same basis.

According to van Schoor, the 'second type of "historian" are the petty pedlars of potted history, the crude, dishonest blockheads, whose cheap textbooks are crammed with the crudest and most disgraceful stock of lies and distortions'. These are the ones who:

1. whitewash white domination;
2. justify the cruel extermination, subjugation, exploitation and oppression of the subject races;
3. vilify and degrade the oppressed races and deny them their rightful place in the history of South Africa.

Cape of Torments, in the typology of Willem van Schoor (and also

And Bid Him Sing

to my mind), is an honest attempt 'to look at history as the living reflection of the development of the productive forces and property relations'. The study of history is, after all, about human relations, the cultural and social lives of human beings. It tells us about that society in the past, how it developed and about the people (named or otherwise) who played an active role in it. Largely, *Cape of Torments* is about those nameless characters in South African history. To his credit, Robert Ross has managed to rescue some of them from anonymity. Regrettably, because of the nature of slave society, not many names are left. But Leander Bougis, the leader of the Hanglip maroon community, is rescued from anonymity and assigned an almost Robin Hood place in South African history – no mean feat.

The central question in *Cape of Torments* is, of course, the pattern of revolt among the slaves against their inhuman treatment at the Cape and the reason for the absence of any form of combined rebellion. The book is composed of commentaries on various aspects of slavery and the slave community, rather than inter-connecting characters. Ross starts off with a fairly detailed introduction in which he reveals, in no uncertain terms, his attitude towards slavery and the slave system at the Cape. It was cruel in the extreme.

> The government of the Dutch East India Company was concerned to keep the monopoly of force in its own hands...
> [p. 2] For more serious offences they were subject to a legal system that exacted punishments of the utmost barbarity...
> When the victim was the slave's masters, the condemned man would be impaled on a stake, driven up his anus and left to die. If he were lucky, he would become unconscious in two days... [p. 3]

In his introductory chapter, Ross reveals himself as a historian who writes objectively, yet not dispassionately, about slavery, someone capable of placing his work about the past firmly in the present. Thus, he reminds us, the beautiful seventeenth-century Cape Dutch gable houses, masterpieces of architecture, were 'built by slaves and with proceeds of the exploitation of slave labour ... Beautiful they may be, but neither they nor the society that built them can be the object of romanticism. The petals of the protea are as poisonous as those of the magnolia.' (p. 2)

Cape of Torments

Cape of Torments is concerned with resistance rather than acquiescence – the ways by which slaves tried to improve their lot. Ross is particularly concerned about the absence of any combined rebellion amongst the slaves at the Cape.

Relying on Eugene Genovese's eight conditions as a sine qua non for rebellion among slave communities in the New World, Ross concludes that only one was present, namely, foreign-born slaves decisively outnumbering the Creoles. For the rest, the small sizes of the slave communities, the scattered farms and the few slaves on them, the control of the master, the general absence of a community, all these factors contributed to the absence of a culture of resistance. Rebellion took the form of individual efforts. At the Cape there was no Berbice or Toussaint l'Ouverture, although the leader of the rebellion at Hanglip, Leander Bougis, certainly had all the makings of a folk hero.

Ross describes in detail the life of the slaves at the Cape, their areas of origin (Indonesian islands, Bengal, South India, Sri Lanka, Madagascar and the East African coast). He gives a harrowing account of the problems of existence encountered by slaves at the Cape, the cruelty of institutionalized justice or barbarity. He vividly recreates Cape slave life and gives an indication of the language situation in the eighteenth century, the main languages being Dutch, Malay and Portuguese creole. On Afrikaans he states emphatically: 'Afrikaans, then, is a language created out of the interaction of slaves (and Khoisan) with Europeans. In this sense, too, it is a paradigm for the construction of slave culture.' (p. 15)

In his discussion of the structure of domination, Robert Ross seems to shift the guilt onto the *mandoor* (driver) and the *knegten* (servants), thus seeming to appear as an apologist for the master. He, of all people, must surely know that the master shared full responsibility for the system of institutionalized violence and barbarity at the Cape during slavery. In fact, Ross, true to himself and never forgetting the parallel with the modern system of oppression inside South Africa, constantly reminds us of it: 'Then, as now, the sjambok, a hippopotamus hide whip was the symbol of white baasskap in South Africa.' (p. 33)

His remarks on the interaction between slaves and the Khoisan is characterized by the same sensitivity which he has shown throughout the book.

He manoeuvres through this veritable minefield with skill and diplomacy, revealing how the slaves fled and found refuge with the San, how they were sometimes betrayed to white masters and even taken back by the Khoi, and how all this could not prevent some form of sleeping together between slaves and Khoi, which, in turn, led to greater tension. But, Ross concludes 'despite such tensions, the very similar positions of slaves and Khoi in respect to White exploitation slowly led to an increasing accommodation between them'. (p. 47) Nowhere is slavery at the Cape so clearly revealed than in 'the pattern of individual, uncoordinated resistance ... the realisation that they had no hope of turning the whole of Cape society upside down through combined rebellion'. (p. 117)

Ross deals with the relationship between sailors and slaves, an important element in the efforts of slaves to escape on the ships which touched at the Cape periodically. He gives a similar vivid account of slave – Xhosa relationships. It testifies to the power of the author that one is assailed with a feeling of revulsion in reading his account of slavery at the Cape. The Dutch in the Netherlands have much to answer for.

His most interesting chapter is on Leander Bougis and Hanglip. This is also evident in his style. Hanglip and its slave rebel community may not have been Berbice; yet, it had all the elements of romance, rebellion, resistance against injustice, the yearning for freedom, violence in extreme forms. Robert Ross has certainly rescued Leander Bougis from obscurity, without trying to turn him into a folk hero for the 'coloureds' or a sex partner in André Brink style for some lost white woman in South Africa. His description of the slave rebellion led by Galant (turned into a novel by Brink: *Houd-Den-Bek*) is excellent.

This is the most vivid account of slavery at the Cape that I have ever come across. The book has an interesting appendix, a very useful bibliography and excellent footnotes. This work merits close study and constant reading. It is an important record of slavery and slave rebellions at the Cape. At the same time it is also an indictment of early South African society. As such, *Cape of Torments* is a good piece of resistance literature.

Ross does not hesitate to draw comparisons between the past system of oppression and the present system of apartheid. As an historian, he reminds his fellow historians 'to keep matters in perspective, never to let them escape from the context in which they occurred. At the Cape of Good Hope that context was exceedingly

unpleasant for the majority of those who lived there, the slaves and, increasingly the Khoisan'. (pp. 9-10)
That context is still exceedingly unpleasant for the dispossessed.

Notes

1. First published in *Azania Worker*, London, vol. 1, no. 2/3, Summer 1984, pp. 35-6.
2. Routledge & Kegan Paul, London, 1983.

5

Incarceration and Creation[1]

I think it was Kenyatta[2] who remarked that prison for the African formed a necessary extension of his education during the colonial period. Writers who have had the courage to strike a blow for freedom have felt the wrath of the dictator. And their threnodies of hope and despair revealed systems of unfreedom in no uncertain terms. In our times writers are called upon to be committed and, if one surveys the world scene, it is almost impossible to remain aloof.

Mention Pasternak[3] and everybody will recall the anthracite-eyed performance of Omar Sharif in *Dr Zhivago*. Say Daniel and Sinyavski and Russia watchers in the West will bristle with indignation. Both these writers had dared to call upon the creative powers of the imagination to promulgate what they considered to be a blow for freedom under a dictatorial regime. Drop the name Solzhenitsyn and the words Nobel prize winner and unfree Russia are readily supplied. Speak of Alex La Guma, Arthur Nortje and Dennis Brutus[4] and blank silence or rank ignorance follow, with the exception of a few 'Africa-watchers' and 'lovers' of the Commonwealth.

While not denying the creative writers' unfreedom in Russia, one has just a sneaking suspicion that the West, with its fear of Communism, is ready to applaud and recognize any crack in the red wall. Michael Shayer expressed beautifully this hypocritic syndrome in a poem, read at the Commonwealth Poetry Conference in England in 1965, when he wrote:

And Bid Him Sing

> It is allright you bastards
> when some Russian
> or a New York Jew
>
> shouts out in poetry
> then, you think it colourful
> you even print translations (poor-ones)
> in your bloody newspapers

In many parts of the world writers have spoken out on behalf of the dispossessed or the enslaved when times and circumstances demanded such actions. Outstanding examples of writers who can be associated with revolutions or revolutionary causes are Garcia Lorca who, inevitably, received the highest accolade of being murdered by the Fascists in Spain and the poet Botev who fought with Levsky[5] for Bulgaria's freedom. In Greece the name Theodorakis comes to mind. In South Africa one recalls Dennis Brutus, La Guma, Lewis Nkosi[6] and others, who all fell foul of the apartheid regime.

Jean-Paul Sartre, in a lecture 'La Résponsabilité de l'Écrivain', delivered at the Sorbonne on the occasion of the first general meeting of Unesco, 1 November 1946, expressed one or two ideas which are of fundamental importance to the writer living in an atmosphere of unfreedom.

> Dostoevsky has said: Every man is responsible to everyone for everything. This statement becomes truer from day to day. As national collectivism becomes more and more part of human collectivism, as every individual becomes more and more part of the national community, we may say that each of us becomes more and more responsible, more and more widely responsible.[7]

For Sartre the artist who propagates art for art's sake has no place in our times. He states in no uncertain terms:

> Thus, art for art's sake derives from the comfortable observation that the writer, not being in harmony with his own class or indeed with any other, cannot help anyone. Hence, the theory that the writer is irresponsible, that is, free to create and create in innocence.

Nor is it, in his view, enough to appeal to freedom without desiring any real changes:

> To appeal to freedom without a desire to change anything only in order that liberty may take its pleasure in the presence of a beautiful work of art, is what is creating art for art's sake.

Sartre realizes that the power-holders may at times exploit the writer and use his creativity for their own nefarious purposes. Thus he very strongly warns:

> The bourgeois is delighted to pay a writer to vent his anger against its philistinism, its lack of taste and intelligence, when such wrath might have been directed on oppression which would be far more inconvenient.

For: 'What we must avoid, we writers, is that our responsibility changes into guilt, so that in fifty years it may be said of us: 'They saw the greatest world catastrophe coming and they kept silent.'

In South Africa the Federasie vir Afrikaanse Kultuur[8] seems to hover like a moralizing deterrent over the iconoclasts while, in Russia, the Party apparently fulfils this role. That the writer can become a potent force in the freedom struggle is beyond dispute. But, at that point of vociferous action, he or she will also experience the full wrath of the totalitarian regime. Hence the books under discussion here will all be by writers who are now in exile or dead.

Dennis Brutus falls under the statutory classification, 'coloured', in South Africa. I say statutory, for all attempts to turn this hybrid class into a so-called separate nation has failed. The term itself is largely inspired by racist thinking in South Africa and is rightly rejected by sane and politically conscious South Africans. Opposed to the apartheid regime in the land of his birth, Brutus soon became involved in politics and eventually fell foul of the law. Escaping from South Africa to Lourenço Marques, he was detained on the border and sent back to face trial. While trying to escape he was shot.

Brutus recovered and spent two years on Robben Island. After his term of imprisonment he left South Africa for England where he continued his activities as the leader of SANROC, i.e., the South African Non-Racial Olympic Committee. Ardent sportsman himself, he pursued his pursuers in the one field he knew would hit them hardest. And his efforts have not remained unrewarded.

And Bid Him Sing

Letters to Martha are poems which record his experiences and feelings as a prisoner on Robben Island. As is the custom in South Africa Brutus was banned on release from prison. This not only severely restricted his freedom of movement but, worse still, made it impossible for him to publish anything. Brutus, therefore, wrote these poems as letters to his sister-in-law, Martha. The *Guardian*, in reviewing the work, wrote: '... in the deft simplicity of the first part of the book, he has grace and penetration, unmatched even by Solzhenitsyn ...' This is high praise indeed and for anyone unfamiliar with the poet's work, possibly a bit surprising. Yet, before referring to poems in *Letters to Martha*, it would be in the interest of all poetry-lovers and those concerned with freedom to refer to an earlier anthology, *Sirens, Knuckles and Boots* (1963).

Daniel Abasiekong, writing in *Transition* in 1965, said: 'It is natural that a South African poet with an open sensibility should react to the horny police regime that operates in his country.'[9] It is impossible for the artist in South Africa to escape the suffocating laws which regulate people's lives. Afrikaans writers formed an exception for a very long time. Now, however, there are indications that even the Afrikaans writer can no longer ignore the black presence or the oppressive circumstances surrounding the lives of blacks in general. Protest-writing at its worst can, of course, be appalling. It can so easily develop into tracts or pamphlets. Rightly does Stephen Spender warn against 'poetry conscripted for the victims'. Brutus sees himself as a troubadour, traversing all his land:

> A troubadour, I traverse all my land exploring
> her wide flung parts with zest
> no mistress-favour has adorned my breast
> only the shadow of an arrow-band.[10]

The poet himself conceives of a good poem as one in which 'we are conscious of a rich variegated experience which sums up the whole in a complex intellectually satisfying emotion'. Generally, one could state that, at the point of creating a poem and in the end product itself, there is an element of irrationality. This irrational element has led the poet to be regarded as the mouthpiece of another power, inside or outside, a God, a demon, an unconscious or subconscious power. Although writing of music, Browning seems to have referred to that magical element when he wrote: 'And I know not if, save in

Incarceration and Creation

this, such a gift be allowed to man. That out of three sounds, he frames not a fourth sound, but a star.'

One could simply define the poet as a maker of good verse, a definition which would not exclude the irrational element. For good verse is unique. To the general public, the poet is a person impelled by emotions, possibly instincts, the inhabitant of a dream world. The whole creative process may be described as a process of rationality in a state of possession. It is natural that poets tend to regard the poem's content and vision of reality as more important than the form itself.

The poet knows that Mallarmé utters half a truth when he avers that a person does not create verses from thoughts but from words. The poet plays for high stakes by attempting to give eternal form to his insight into truth. Dennis Brutus uses the system of political oppression in his poetry in such a way that the reader is given an insight into what constitutes truthful values to him. Understandably, for the South African artist, there can be no truth as long as the vast majority of the South African population is oppressed. Brutus is capable of portraying the unfreedom and oppression inside South Africa in imagery which needs no explanation:

> Under *jackboots* our *bones* and *spirits crunch*
> forced into sweat-tear sodden slush
> now glow-lipped by this sudden touch
> Sun-stripped perhaps, our bows may later sing
> or spell out some *malignant nemesis*
> *Sharpevilled to spearpoints* for revenging.[11]

In *Letters to Martha* the reader is confronted with the experiences of the poet while a political prisoner. One is immediately struck by the simple, almost staccato, language whereby the sickening realization of the oppressive circumstances inside South Africa is further demonstrated.

> One learns quite soon
> that nails and screws
> and other sizeable bits of metal
> must be handed in;
> and seeing them shaped and sharpened
> one is chilled, appalled
> to see how vicious it can be
> this simple, useful bit of steel:

>   and when these knives suddenly flash
>   – produced perhaps from some disciplined anus –
>   one grasps at once the steel-bright horror
>   in the morning air.
>   and how soft and vulnerable is naked flesh.[12]

In the claustrophobic microcosmos of prison, sexual assault and violence frequently occur. Intermittently, there are flashes of longing for a bit of blue sky and more *lebensraum*:

>   I remember rising one night
>   after midnight
>   and moving
>   through an impulse of loneliness
>   to try and find the stars.
>   And through the haze
>   the battens of fluorescents made
>   I saw pinpricks of white
>   I thought were stars.[13]

He was brusquely reminded of rude reality, *anxious boots, machine-gun posts*, and the memory of the *brusque inquiry* lingering *longer than the stars*. Towards the end he says:

>   I have lashed them
>   The marks of my scars
>   lie deep in their psyche.

In his poetry, Brutus makes it crystal clear that he sees no difference between the poet and the warrior. In a sense, he reaffirms the statement by Jean-Paul Sartre who sees the role of the writer in the following terms:

> Yet, in the name of ethical values, he must demand plainly and above all else – for otherwise he is an oppressor or a trickster – the liberation of all oppressed people, proletarians, Jews, Negroes, colonial subjects, occupied countries and so on.[14]

Ruth First was neither poet nor novelist, but a person renowned for her political writings. Her insight into political problems is profound. In her *One Hundred and Seventeen Days* (1965), the reader is confronted with her prison experiences. The book is an indictment against the system of apartheid.

More moving even than her personal psychological problems is her portrayal of people who have fallen foul of the South African regime and its gaolers. One shudders at the story of 'Look Smart' who met his death at the hand of his gaolers. Perhaps one should look upon these political asides and detours as a tribute to the strength and magnanimity of the authoress who, in no way, seeks to over-emphasize her own role. Nowhere is her indictment of the system stronger than in those few pages on 'Look Smart', the man who was tortured to death in his cell. Her references to other political prisoners recall a line from Brutus's *Letters to Martha*, 'those who endure much more and endure . . .'

Other testimonies only add to the litany of oppression. One of the detainees writes: 'My thoughts were occupied with trivialities. . . I burst very easily into laughter, my mind seems befuddled. . .'[15] Another lamented: 'I flung myself on the mat and started to cry bitterly. . . The thought of another ninety days was too much.'

An interesting facet of prison literature is the way in which the victim afterwards manages to portray the captors or wardens – small but necessary cogs in the wheel of oppression – with humour and empathy. By using this device of pity, the victim emerges as the victor and the captor is revealed as a sad miscreant. Moral strength triumphs over brute ignorance.

Pringle, the first English South African poet, uses this device to portray the slave owner as pitiable in the early nineteenth century. Ruth First also uses this technique to show how white people inside South Africa, who blindly execute commands in the name of racial purity, are the victims, not the victors. Her characterization of the two white female warders is priceless:

> I identified the wardresses by the sound of them long before I saw them. Female voices, Raucous. Shrill. Pained. Competent ('I know my job. I don't lose control but don't think you can get the better of me'). In time Raucous and Shrill personalized into the two ugly sisters among the wardresses. Raucous was stupid as a stone, and as deaf. She knew by rote the mechanical duties of a wardress. . .[16]

And Bid Him Sing

The other wardress Shrill 'had a face like an underdone crumpled crumpet, with eyes as expressive as a fish moth's'. Pained 'was a handsome Wagnerian blonde, with long elongated hands, but feet crippled by bunions. Her aches and twinges might have been an excuse for her long-suffering voice and expression, and for her treatment of all prisoners as inveterate nuisances . . .'

Incarceration inevitably involves a reorientation in the life patterns of the individual. Reading through gaol diaries one cannot but have a feeling that a mild epidemic of Bible-philia and conversion-phobia reigns supreme in Western prisons. Callous and bizarre is the account of Ruth First's release and immediate re-arrest, an apparently stock part of the special branch repertoire:

> In the charge office I was sickly silent and tight-lipped. Not till later in the month did I confront Nel with, 'I thought you said you were releasing me?' to hear his Jesuitical prevarication. 'I did release you. I didn't re-arrest you.'[17]

One Hundred and Seventeen Days is the record of an individual's struggle to endure. Her general concern transcends her own personal suffering. And therein lies the strength of the book and the indictment.

The Jail Diary of Albie Sachs is, like that of Ruth First, a moving account of his imprisonment. Here, too, imprisonment is exploited to demonstrate the ignominy of the South African political and social situation. It is an absorbingly human diary in which the reader meets Sachs the person, is confronted with his ideas, fears, weaknesses and strength. Here, more than in First's diary, the reader is forced to identify with the main character. The author himself is an advocate who had defended political prisoners inside South Africa on many occasions. Now, ironically, he found himself placed beyond the very same rule of law in which he had so firmly believed.

From the inception he established a basic rule not to answer any questions. The urge to communicate was, however, strong and overwhelming at times. One of the most impressive and moving parts of the diary is to be found in chapter two, entitled Diary of Love. In his loneliness he hears someone whistling the 'Going Home' theme from Dvorak's *New World Symphony*. This leads him to communicate with some other, unknown prisoner.

Incarceration and Creation

It is in the early afternoon and I am lying in a stupor on my mat when suddenly I become aware of familiar music. The notes are very very distant, as though floating in from another planet. I can barely follow the melody. It is a faint whistling that I hear, as silvery and tenuous as a wind-blown spider thread. This is not the jolly music of a policeman. The melody, rich and sad and far away, is repeated. I can make it out! It is the 'Going Home' theme from the *New World Symphony*. I jump up and listen attentively. Someone is whistling out so that all the prisoners can hear . . . I wait for the long plaintive notes to stop, and then start whistling at my door. The notes soar out high and loud. Faintly, distantly, the response comes, line by line, we whistle.[18]

There are beautiful, almost child-like, passages of the advocate outwitting his captors. He, for example, takes his comb into his cell, which is forbidden, he salivates at the prospect of cleaning it, the flush of the toilet becomes sheer music to him in his confinement. In the end, the reader is almost tempted to give vent to the same, unbridled joy of the author when he is freed: 'I am free!'

All these writers have, to use a term by Pasternak, 'borne witness' to the horror of apartheid to South Africa. Yet, the ultimate note is not one of despair only. In the words of the Bulgarian poet, Khristo Botev, who fought with Levsky for the freedom of Bulgaria:

> Do not weep mother, nor sorrow
> that I have become a haidut,
> a haidut, mother, a rebel . . .[19]

Notes

1. First published in *Kroniek van Afrika*, Afrika Studiecentrum, Leiden, vol. 11, no. 3, 1971, pp 201–8.
2. Jomo Kenyatta (1890–1978) was the leader of the Mau Mau rebellion against the English in Kenya and the first Prime Minister of an independent Kenya. Together with Kwame Nkrumah of Ghana he did most to free Africa from colonialism. He is the author of *Facing Mount Kenya* (1938, 1953 2nd edn).

And Bid Him Sing

3. Boris Pasternak is the author of *Dr Zhivago* and was a dissident Russian writer; Omar Sharif played a leading role in the film of Pasternak's novel.
4. Alex La Guma (1925-85) was a leading South African writer and novelist; see *A Walk in the Night* (1962); *And a Threefold Cord* (1964); *The Stone Country* (1967) et al. He died in Cuba while stationed as the representative of the African National Congress (ANC). La Guma was a treason trialist and very active in the struggle for liberation.
   Dennis Brutus, poet and freedom fighter, became well known through the following anthologies: *Sirens, Knuckles and Boots* (1963); *Letters to Martha* (1968).
   Arthur Nortje, one of the finest poets from South Africa, died in exile; see *Dead Roots* (1974).
5. Vasili Levsky, Bulgaria's national hero, led the struggle for freedom against the five-century-old occupation by the Turks of his country. This was during the 1870s; see, especially, Mercia MacDermott, *The Apostle of Freedom*, London, 1967.
   Botev was a poet who fought with Levsky.
6. Lewis Nkosi is a noted literary critic and novelist. He wrote *Home and Exile* (1965), *Tasks and Masks* (1981), *Mating Birds* (1986).
7. For Jean-Paul Sartre see *The Creative Vision* (eds. H. Block & H. Salinger), Grove Press, New York, 1960, p. 165.
8. FAK = Die Federasie van Afrikaanse Kultuurvereniginge, a cultural organization started in 1929 as part of the process of building an Afrikaner identity and encouraging Afrikaner nationalism.
9. 'Poetry Pure and Applied', *Transition*, vol. 5, no. 23 Kampala, 1965, pp. 45-8.
10. *A Simple Lust*, Heinemann, London, 1973, p. 2.
11. *Sirens, Knuckles and Boots*, Mbari, Nigeria, 1963.
12. *Letters to Martha*, Heinemann, London, 1968, p. 3.
13. Brutus, *A Simple Lust*, p. 67.
14. See H. Block & H. Salinger, op. cit., p. 181.
15. Ruth First, *One Hundred and Seventeen Days*, Penguin Books, Harmondsworth, 1965, p. 109. She was killed by a parcel bomb in Mozambique in 1982.
16. ibid., p. 28.
17. ibid., p. 107.
18. Harvill Press, London, p. 20.
19. See Mercia MacDermott, *The Apostle of Freedom*, Allen & Unwin, London, 1967, p. 148.

Bibliography

1. Brutus, Dennis (1963): *Sirens, Knuckles and Boots*, (Nigeria, Mbari).

2. First, Ruth (1965): *One Hundred and Seventeen Days* (Harmondsworth, England, Penguin Books).
3. MacDermott, Mercia (1967): *The Apostle of Freedom* (London, George Allen & Unwin).
4. Sachs, Albie (1966): *The Jail Diary* (London, Harvill Press).

6

Ilizwi LikaJakobi Kodwa Isandla Sika-Esau

The Voice of Jacob but the Hand of Esau

During the years 1957 to 1959 the celebrated Nguni scholar, Dr A. C. Jordan, author of the novel *Ingqumbo Yeminyanya* (Wrath of the Ancestors, 1954), and a well-known political figure in the Cape, using the pseudonym of V. Rylate,[1] were involved in a series of polemics on the language question inside South Africa. These articles were all published in the *Educational Journal* of the Teachers' League of South Africa, a body which catered mostly for the needs of those referred to in South Africa as 'coloured'.

In the very first article Rylate wrote, of language in general:

> By its very nature the language question reaches beyond the frontiers, but not beyond the horizons of education. Its backdrop is not the classroom but the nation, whether as subject, school or official medium. Language itself is a means of communication and of production and, as such, is always a social and sometimes a political instrument. The language question in South Africa does not arise out of the relative intrinsic merits, the 'carrying power' of this language or that, but out of a unique as well as typical matrix of social conditions. These have to be examined concretely and

historically in order to reveal the mainsprings of the role of South Africa languages in the antagonistic processes of oppression and liberation.[2]

Very often South Africa is treated as if it is only a country of white people who determine the historical processes and project the cultural image of the inhabitants. The cosmological world of the majority (over twenty million) is largely ignored or exploited in such a manner as to conform only to the ideological world, created by invaders from overseas. South Africa then is lifted out of the context of Africa and transformed into a special case, a land and a people set apart from the rest of the African continent. African scholars who have, hitherto, attempted to work within their own cosmological world have experienced great difficulties because, invariably, their products have been used and exploited to justify the *ethnos* theories designed by the architects of apartheid to justify the division of the country into multi-national, ethnic states.

In this context the multi-national character of the country, the ethnic identity and the different ethnic cultures, based on language classification, customs and norms within the apartheid nexus of the invaders, is emphasized. No attempt is made to see South Africa as an integral part of Africa, to view the struggle of the oppressed as part of the overall struggle against domination and colonialism. It is against this background that I would like to trace the position in which the African finds himself as a result of conquest. My typology would resemble the pattern shown in Fig. 1.

The first stage in the diagram represents the 'vestiges of legend and enigmatic proportions' and is essential in the reconstruction of the original situation. These are what the Guyanese novelist, Wilson Harris, calls, 'the forgotten perspectives which ... may provide a personal scale of imagination or as far removed in time as the twentieth century is from Yurokon'.[3] This is also the chart of the destruction of the world of the colonized.

The second stage will be determined largely by the status of conquest of the colonized. To quote Wilson Harris once again: 'The force of ritual bounty lies in the status of conquest within which the victorious side apparently succeeds in pressing the face or faces of the vanquished into the dust of uniform conviction so that the reality or play of contrasts is eclipsed within an order of self-deception.'[4] In such a state of 'self-deception-in-self-definition' the vanquished

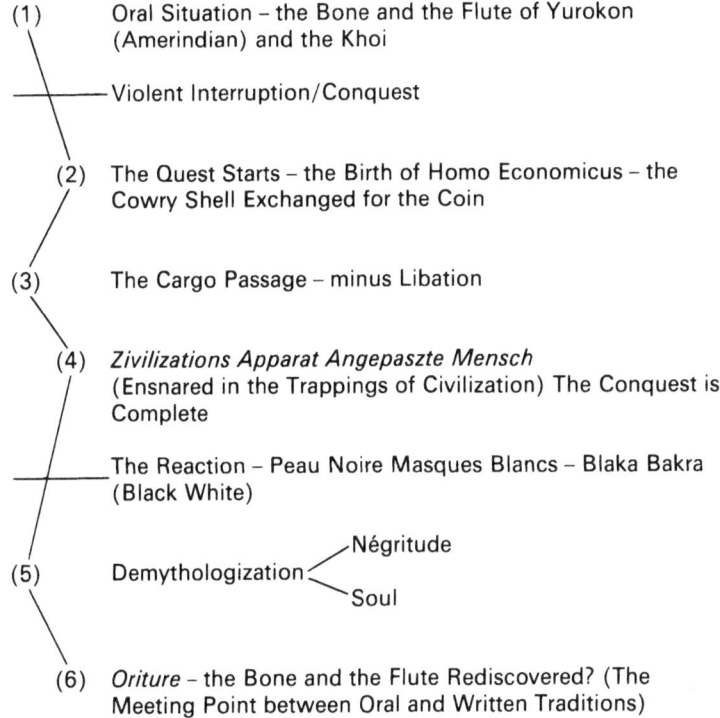

Figure 1. *From the Oral to Oriture*

abandons or forgets his own situation and starts aspiring to the ritual bounty of the vanquisher. This forces him into becoming a Homo Economicus, that is, he abandons his cowry shell for the coin. He is now like the cargo cultists (but this time with no libation), with no prospect of ever returning to contribute to a harmony in his community. The journey takes place without any ancestral blessing.

When the return becomes impossible, however, he becomes a slave of, and completely ensnared in, the trappings of civilization. This stage I have labelled *Zivilizations Apparat Angepaszte Mensch*, a term used by the German educationist Freier. Ironically, in this state of exile the vanquished recognizes his own 'self-deception-in-self-definition'. This stage, however, is often responsible for a duality. Thus, the revolt is halted by a desire for 'roots' and an unwillingness

And Bid Him Sing

to abandon the 'ritual bounty'. This led variously in the 1930s to an anomic situation among the French-speaking Antilleans and West Africans, studying in Paris, culminating ideologically and culturally in négritude. Soul-brotherism in America some decades later appears to have its roots in similar conditions.

Finally, in the typology presented here, cargo is only possible if there is a recognition that the African finds himself in a state of *oriture* (a term used by the Kenyan writer Micere) which I have defined as a recognition of his cosmological world order, as found in the oral tradition, and of the road travelled from the oral world as a consequence of the invasions. This term covers the syncretistic meeting point between the oral and the written.

The early invaders who came to South Africa had definite ideas about the original inhabitants of that country, the Khoi and the San. They called the Khoi 'Hottentots',[5] a term of derision, and the San, mockingly, Bushmen.[5] Travelogue after travelogue called these people 'brown apes', people who smelled a 'fathom in the wind', creatures (from the Dutch *schepselen*) with disgusting eating habits. In one publication concerning the Cornelis de Houtman voyage in 1597, one reads that the Dutch sailor considered himself superior to these 'Hottentots' whom he could split apart with one kick of his boots.[6]

The language of the Khoi was labelled 'clucking like turkeys'; they were compared to people in Switzerland with apparently similar speech impediments as a result of the hardness of the snow, that is, they had a goitred manner of speaking. One example will suffice. In the very important *Verhael* (1597), an anonymous writer aboard the ship made the following observation of the Khoi language: 'They also spoke very strangely with gestures like children at home play with their mouths, clucking like male turkeys (*als clockende als calcoensche hanen*).[7]

At the risk of being facetious I would like to demonstrate what could conceivably have happened at this first traumatic and linguistic confrontation between Khoi and invader at the Cape during the sixteenth and early seventeenth centuries. Imagine two robust, ruddy-faced, big-boned Dutchmen confronted by the Khoi who were fleet-footed, small in stature and of a colouration ranging from 'brown to peach'. The first reaction of these Dutchmen could have been: '*Godverdomme, moet je dat zoodje bruine aapjes zien.*' ('God dammit, just look at those sods of little brown apes.')

Ilizwi LikaJakobi Kodwa Isandla Sika-Esau

Mercifully, we have no written record of the Khoi reaction to the first Dutch spoken at the Cape. The fate of the Khoi is, of course, well known. They were either felled by epidemics or, as Shula Marks observed, miscegenated out of existence.[8]

This linguistic arrogance was to repeat itself in 1857 when an American missionary, the Reverend J.L. Döhne who, according to his own testimony, had spent twenty years among the Nguni, wrote in his *Zulu-Kafir Dictionary*:

> Some have expected to find much poetry among the Zulu-Kafirs, but there is in fact none. Poetical language is extremely rare and we meet with only a few pieces of prose. The Zulu nation is more fond of *ukuhlabelela*, i.e. singing, and engages more in 'ukuvuma amagama ezinkosi', i.e. singing the praises of the chiefs, than any other Kafir-tribe. But their capabilities in this respect are very limited. The highest song of praise for their King is composed entirely of a few hyperbolic expressions (see uku-kuleka) ... But nothing like poetry or song exists, no metre, no rhyme, nothing that interests or soothes the feelings or arrests the passions, no admiration of the heavenly bodies, or taste for the beauties of creation. We miss the cultivated mind which delights in seizing on these subjects and embodying them in suitable language.[9]

This holy and learned missionary Döhne, was a dupe of his own Eurocentric approach. In his inability to find metre, rhyme, Shakespearean sonnet schemes or Petrarchan sonnets, he boldly concluded that the Nguni had no poetic traditions. And in the process he failed to come to grips with, let alone understand, that wonderful phenomenon known as *praise poetry* in Nguni.

The important point is that African languages were not considered 'cultured', 'civilized' or a suitable or noble means of communication. Again, A. C. Jordan reminds us that language cannot be seen outside the social context in which it occurs. Language is not just a question of phoneme, word or idea, combined in certain contexts to communicate ideas.

> These sounds are combined in systems and evolved and conventionalised and recognised by common usage at any given period in the history of the human race within a given

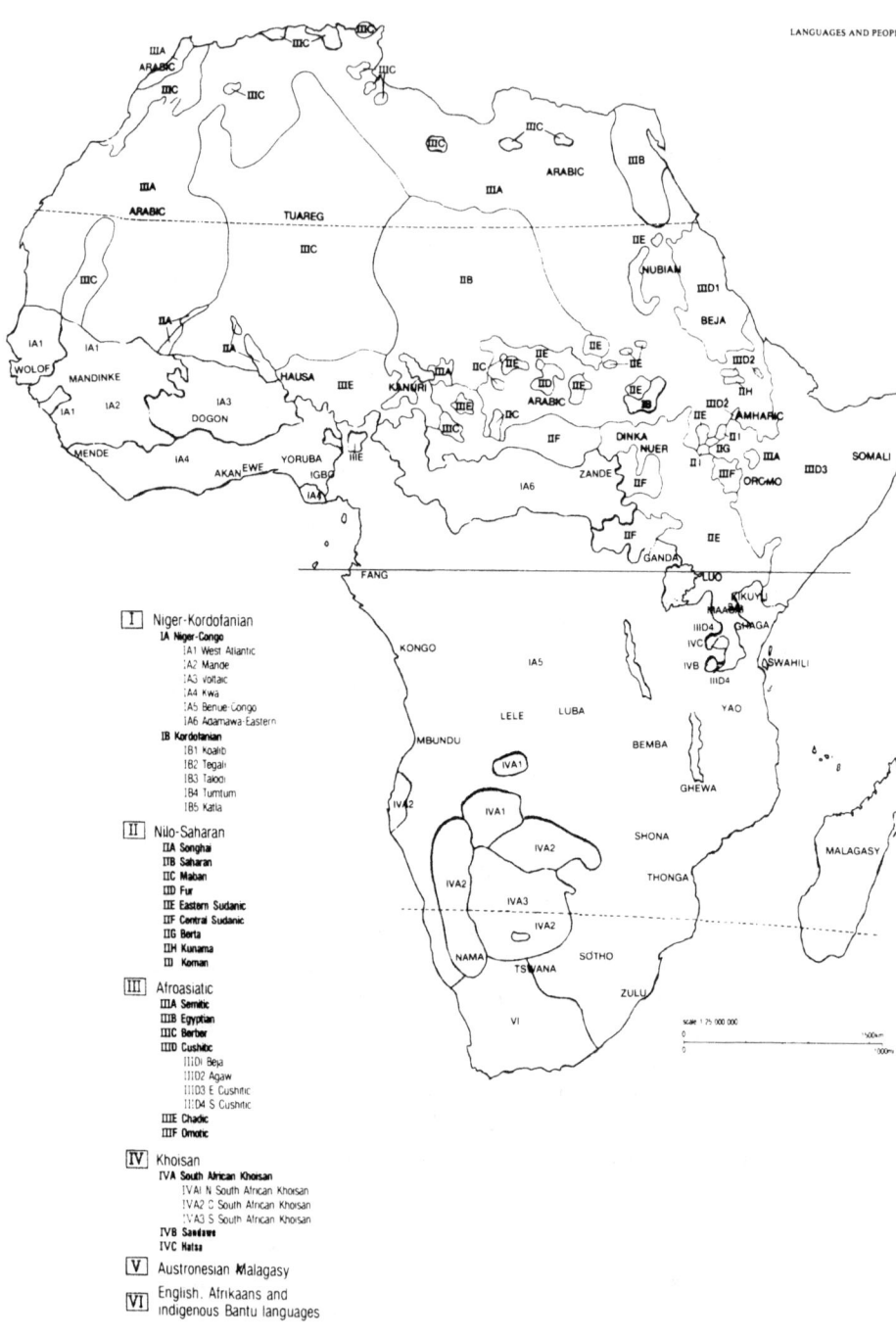

Map 1. *A Cross-Section of Language Distribution in Africa*

community that they are mutually intelligible to all normal members of such a community.[10]

Map 1 gives an indication of the spread of language families in Africa (after Greenberg). Extant Khoi languages are Nama and Korana.
A table of languages spoken inside South Africa (including the number of speakers of the language in question) gives a clearer insight into the situation. The following table is taken from Dennis Makhudu's thesis,[11] in which the languages spoken in South Africa are clearly indicated.

Languages Spoken in South Africa*

Type of Language	Language	No. of Speakers
A. Official languages: (Germanic)	1. Afrikaans	3,421,000
	2. English	1,423,000
	Total:	4,844,000†
B. Immigrant languages: (European)	1. French	9,000
	2. German	49,000
	3. Greek	20,000
	4. Dutch	18,000
	5. Italian	19,000
	6. Portuguese	42,000
	Total:	157,000
C. Indigenous languages: (Bantu)		
a. Nguni languages:	1. Zulu	4,026,000
	2. Xhosa	3,929,000
	3. Swazi	499,000
	4. Ndebele (S & N)	410,000‡
b. Sotho languages:	1. Tswana	1,719,000
	2. Sepedi (NS)	1,604,000
	3. Sesotho (SS)	1,453,000

And Bid Him Sing

c. Tsonga (Nguni-related)		737,000
d. Venda (Sotho-related)		358,000
e. Foreign (e.g. Kalanga)		318,000
	Total:	15,053,000
D. Dravidian/Indian languages:	1. Tamil	154,000
	2. Hindi	117,000
	3. Gujerati, Urdu, Telegu	116,000
	Total:	387,000

* Based on the 'latest official figures to the nearest 1,000'.
† This figure also includes the 'coloureds', a fraction of whom use English as a first language. Bilingual speakers are 1,022,000.
‡ S = South, N = North.

Unfortunately, there is no mention in Makhudu's table of the Khoisan languages in South Africa. For material on these languages we are largely dependent on the works of linguists (mostly from abroad) and anthropologists. The outstanding name in this respect is the German scholar, Carl Meinhof, who became known in this field through his book, *Die Sprache der Hamiten* (Berlin, 1912) and *Lehrbuch der Nama Sprachen* (1909) which contains texts, a grammar and a bibliography. For the languages of the San the name of Dorothea Bleek is of importance. It was Bleek who distinguished three language groups, namely, the Southern, the Northern and the Central. Her 'Distribution of Bushmen Languages in South Africa' appeared in the *Festschrift* for the linguist Carl Meinhof in 1927. Bleek's *A Bushman Dictionary* was published in the United States in 1956. One of the best dictionaries by Kroenlein, *Wortschatz der Khoi-Khoin*, first published in 1889, was republished in 1969 in South Africa and in 1971 in Farnborough, England.

Schapera observes in his work, *The Khoisan Peoples of South Africa*:

> The Bushmen, at one time spread over almost the whole of South Africa, are today confined principally to the Central and Northern Kalahari and adjacent districts... They all speak

languages of a uniform and easily recognizable type, phonetically, especially for the great prevalence of 'click' consonants.[12]

Of the Khoi-Khoin he writes:

> The Hottentots formerly occupied most of the Western half of the region, but are now found chiefly in the Southern parts of South-West Africa. They are closely allied to the Bushmen race, and their languages are of a somewhat similar type, although in both respects certain differences are also observable.

The Khoisan people have been pushed into areas in what is now Botswana, Namibia and western and central portions of South Africa, principally the Cape of Good Hope. The San, who were formerly also to be found in Zimbabwe, have now disappeared from these parts. This disappearance is not accidental but finds its origin in historical and political developments. The Khoisan presence in South Africa dispels the lie that the country was a 'terra-nullius' – an empty space – when the first invaders arrived.

The fate of the Khoisan people of South Africa serves as a paradigm for the fate of other black people, pushed into windswept, desolate areas, far from the big cities, or in so-called tribal areas, euphemistically known as Homelands. The mass removal of the original inhabitants paved the way for the acceptance, some 200 years later, of South Africa as a 'terra-nullius' when the Dutch arrived. As a result of this process whites could once more justify their occupation of the country.

Map 2, culled from Schapera, gives an indication of the distribution of the Khoisan peoples of South Africa before the whites established geographic, economic and political control over that part of the world.[13]

The following examples, culled from Meinhof and Schapera,[14] are given as an illustration of some features of Khoisan languages; wherever possible the examples are taken from Nama, one of the extant Khoisan languages. Schapera notes (p. 422) that '. . . extensive use of suffixes is one of the most characteristic features in the grammatical mechanisms of the Khoisan languages and the number of different suffixes as well as the variety of uses to which they are put

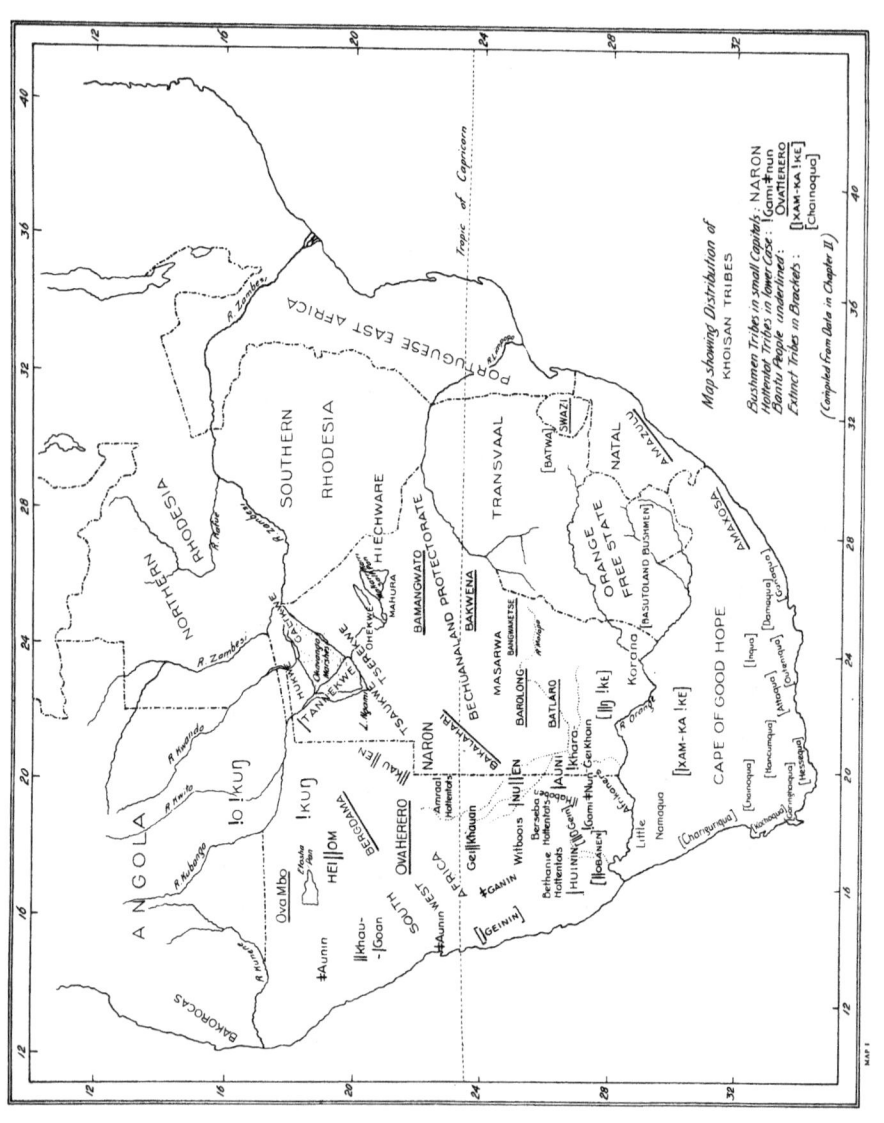

Map 2. Distribution of Khoisan

Ilizwi LikaJakobi Kodwa Isandla Sika-Esau

is extremely great'. In Nama, for example, sexual gender is generally dependent on the form of the suffix.

Suffixes in Nama

	Masc.(Sing.)	Fem.(Sing.)	Common(Sing.)
	-b	-s	-i
Substantive: Khoi	Khoib (Man)	Khois (Woman)	Khoii (Person)

The plurals in Nama are again dependent on the sexual gender:

	-gu	-ti	-n
Substantive: Khoi	Khoigu (Men)	Khoiti (Women)	Khoin (People)

The following are the plural suffixes for the languages Auen, !Khu and Hie:

	Plural suffix	Substantive (Sing.)	Plural
Auen	si	!Num (Stone)	!Numsi (Stones)
!Khu	-Siŋ- ŋ	Gaox(Chief)	Gaoxiŋ(Chiefs)
Hie	-re or ra	Kxam (Lion)	Kxamre (Lions)

The exception is Xam, the language of the 'Cape Bushmen' in which the plural is formed by means of reduplicating the singular:

Substantive: Kou (Stone, Sing.) = Koukən (Stones, Pl.)
Go/Go (Whirlwind, Sing.) = Gogən/Gogən (Whirlwinds, Pl.)

In all Khoisan languages three classes of persons are recognized. These are:

1. The person speaking;
2. The person spoken to;
3. The thing or person spoken of.

We learn further that Nama distinguishes between persons present and persons not present or persons about whom one is speaking, i.e., in the third person. Schapera notes:

> The notion of time in all Khoisan languages is to a very large extent expressed mainly by means of special auxiliary particles, which generally precede the verbal root, except in Naron and Nama where an inverted form is found.[15]

And Bid Him Sing

The important auxiliary particles for Nama are:

Auxiliary Particles in Nama

Present: Ta
Example: You see = *Sats ta mũ*
Note that *ta* = *ra* after a vowel, e.g. I see = *Tita ra mũ*.

Recent Past is expressed by *go*
Example: I have seen = *Tita go mũ*

Perfect = *Gje, Gjegje*
Example: I saw = *Tita gje mũ* or *Mũ ta gje*

Pluperfect The rule is that you place *hã ĩ* after the Perfect form of the verb.
Example: I had seen = *Tita gje mũ hã ĩ*

Future = *Ni*
Example: I shall see = *Tita ni mũ* or *Mũ ta ni*

Future Perfect is formed by placing *hã ĩ* after the future tense.
Example: I shall have seen = *Tita ni mũ hã ĩ*

Continuous Action
Here suffixes are used which are not attached to the verbal stem but to the auxiliary particles.

Imperfect = *Ro*
Example: I used to see = *Tita goro mũ*

Pluperfect and *Perfect* = *Re*
Example: I had the habit of seeing = *Tita gjere mũ hã ĩ*

    Many words in Khoisan languages are only distinguishable according to their tone. According to Schapera (p. 422) there are 'five significant tone levels . . . high level, mid level, low level, falling and rising'.
    In Carl Meinhof's *Die Sprache der Hamiten* one reads:

> Im Hottentotische spielt der musikalische Ton eine grosse Rolle. Ich glaube nicht zu irren, wenn ich das darauf zurückführe, dass eine grosse Menge Sprachgut aus den

Buschmannsprache in den Hottentottische eingedrungen ist, uns die Tonhöhenunterschiede hauptsächlich daher kommen.[16]

'In the Hottentot language musicality plays an important role. I do not believe I am mistaken when I trace this back to the fact that a great many lexical items from Bushmen languages have penetrated that of the Hottentots and that the difference in tone is chiefly derived from this.' (trans.)

In this rather too cursory look at one or two features of Khoisan languages it would be an oversight not to refer to the much-discussed clicks which also surface in Bantu languages in Southern Africa as non-Bantu phonemes drawn from Khoisan languages. These clicks occupy four different positions, namely:[17]

Position:	Symbol:
Dental	/
Alveolar	≠
Palato-Alveolar	!
Lateral	//

The implosive consonants are a characteristic feature of South African languages.

Westerman and Ward define implosive consonants as 'sounds of a plosive nature i.e. made by a stop and a release, in which the air is sucked inwards instead of being expelled'.[18] The following diagrams, also in Westerman and Ward (p.99) illustrate the formation of some of the most commonest clicks in Bantu languages, namely, the Dental, the Palato-Alveolar and the Lateral.

The clicks are a convenient point to make the transition to Bantu languages, for not only were they incorporated into these languages but they also serve as a living symbol of the meeting point between Bantu-language-speaker and Khoisan-speaker in South Africa.

The first Bantu language publication of which we have a record is Cardoso's translation into Kongo of Jorge's *Doctrina Christaa*,[19] printed in 1624 in Lisbon. The second book in a Bantu language was Pacconio and de Conto's *Gentio de Angola* (1643), a catechism in Mbundu or Kimbundu. Between 1650 and 1660 there were numerous works and references to works in Bantu languages. One of the early

And Bid Him Sing

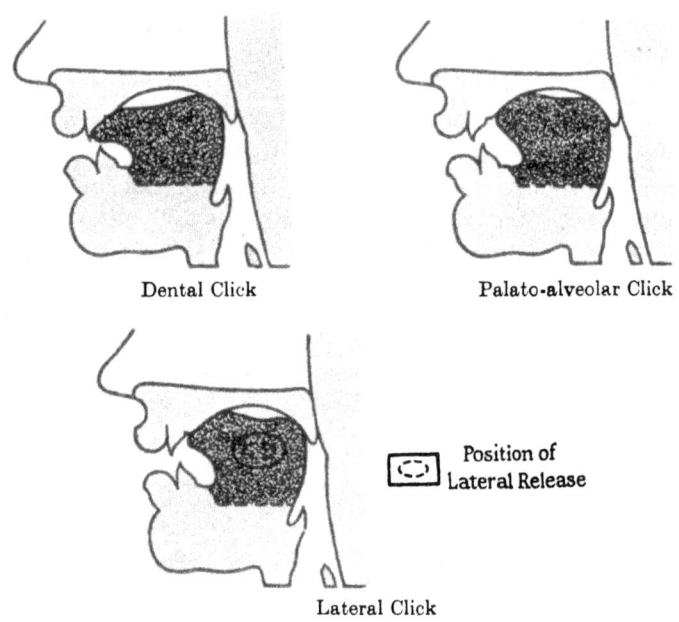

Dental Click

Palato-alveolar Click

Position of Lateral Release

Lateral Click

pioneers was Giacinto Brusciotto who published two books in 1650, namely, his *Quadrilingual Dictionary* and his *Christian Doctrine*. He established his reputation with the publication of the first Bantu language study, the first grammar, in 1659, entitled: *Regulae quadem pro difficilius Congensium idiomatis faciliori captu ad grammaticae nomen redactae*, translated in 1882 by H. Grattan-Guinnes as *Grammar of the Congo Language as Spoken Two Hundred Years ago Translated from the Latin of Brusciotto*.

For South Africa, the Swede Sparrmann's *Vocabulary of 'Caffre' in his Voyage to the Cape of Good Hope Towards the Antarctic Polar Circle and Round the World in 1785*, was the first of its kind for a South African Bantu language; in this particular case, Xhosa. Let me clear up one or two misconceptions concerning the word Bantu, as used in South Africa in a twentieth-century political context. The word is nothing but a class two noun, being the plural form of the singular *umntu*, meaning a person. *Bantu* is therefore the word for *people*. As one scholar facetiously pointed out, to the Xhosa and the Zulu, even the Afrikaners and the English are *Bantu*, that is, people. The word has acquired a deliberate racial connotation (often with the

Ilizwi LikaJakobi Kodwa Isandla Sika-Esau

implication of inferiority) and is applied only to black people within the socio-political context of apartheid. As I point out in *Mind Your Colour* (1981) the Afrikaans word *Bantoevolk* (lit. meaning People-Nation) is nothing else but tautological nonsense.[20]

Map 3 gives an illustration of the language distribution of the Nguni- and Sotho-speakers in South Africa as found in Schapera's book, *The Bantu-Speaking Tribes of South Africa* (1946). Note that Bechuanaland, Basutoland and Southern Rhodesia were all still under colonial rule. They are now independent and known respectively as Botswana, Lesotho and Zimbabwe.

I shall use as my example Xhosa, the language I am most familiar with grammatically and otherwise. The Cape Nguni Xhosa are to be found in the entire Cape Province. The Nguni speak nine mutually intelligible dialects. Xhosa constitutes the literary dialect of the Cape Nguni. The language was first committed to paper in 1823 at Gwali, previously Lovedale. Missionaries, in particular, were responsible for the spread of the language. The most important were the Presbyterians, the Anglicans and the Wesleyans. The first Xhosa-speaking preachers were from the Cape Province. Primus inter pares was Tiyo Soga (1821–79), a product of Lovedale who had also studied in Scotland. He was the first Xhosa speaker to be ordained as a minister of the church in 1856. Soga translated Bunyan's *Pilgrim's Progress* and was the author of *Lizalis' Idinga Lakho Tixo We Nyaniso* (*Fulfil Thy Promise God of Truth*). Soga also cooperated with Kropf, Bryce Ross and Rubusana to produce a translation of the New Testament, regarded as a work of outstanding literary quality, namely: *Incwadi Yezibalo ezingcwele ize ze-Testamente Endala neze-Testamente Entsha* (1931). A classic work was produced by the Xhosa writer, S. E. Krune Mqhayi, called: *Ityala Lama-Wele* (1914); he was also responsible for an excellent anthology of poetry: *ImiHobe nemiBongo* (1927).

Important Zulu writers include the poet Benedict Wallet Vilakazi. Thomas Mofolo towers over other Sotho writers. The latter is especially remembered for his book *Moeti oa Bochabela* (1907) and for the novel *Chaka* (1925), withheld from the general public because the missionary press at Morija did not consider the theme and the treatment of the subject matter as being consonant with their ideas of good, clean Christian writing. Solomon Plaatje was responsible for the translation of Shakespeare's *Julius Caesar* into Tswana, that is, *Dintshontsho tsa bo Juliuse Kesara* (1937).

Map 3. *Bantu-speaking Groups in South Africa circa 1946*

Ilizwi LikaJakobi Kodwa Isandla Sika-Esau

One of the charges against African languages was that they were not economical and could not express succinctly that which the Westerner wishes to say. A. C. Jordan clears up some of these misconceptions in his excellent series on language, referred to earlier. He shows how the internal structure of Xhosa is of such a nature that a single word can express what, in a Western language, requires several words. He uses as an example the Xhosa word for sleep, *lala*.[21]

Lala (Sleep)
Ulele (He is asleep)
Elele (He being asleep)
Ezakulala (He being about to sleep)
Walaliswa (He was put to sleep)
Elalisizwe (He having been put to sleep)
Ezakulaliswa (He being about to put to sleep)
Ma kalaliswe (He had better be put to sleep)

'But all that this reveals', he comments, 'is that Xhosa in this one respect is more economical than English.' He continues with this very telling observation: 'It was a failure to grasp this principle that led some philologists to believe that 'in the languages of savage peoples the vocabulary averages about three hundred words'.[22] Other charges, according to A. C. Jordan, were that 'in the Bantu-languages adjectives are very few and various devices have to be employed in order to make up for this deficiency'.[23]

Jordan points out the great incidence of bilinguality in the areas of Herschel, Matatiele, Aliwal North and Mt Fletcher where Xhosa and Sotho speakers conversed freely with one another despite the fact that these two languages are not mutually intelligible. A similar incidence of bilinguality was to be found between Zulu and Sotho speakers in the area of Bethlehem, Harrismith, Hindley and Reitz.

As in the case of Khoisan languages, certain features of Xhosa will also be identified here. The noun generally consists of a prefix and a stem. For example, the word for person in Xhosa = *Umntu*. In the 3rd person an article precedes the prefix:

1. Article – U
2. Prefix – M
3. Stem – Ntu

And Bid Him Sing

Nouns in Xhosa are divided into various classes according to their prefix and the concords related to the prefix. Examples:

Singular
(U) *mntu* (person)
(I) *sintu* (human style)
(U) *buntu* (human nature)
(U) *luntu* (mankind)

Plural
(A) *bantu* (people)

All these words belong to five different classes for, although they all share a common stem, *ntu*, they have different prefixes. Proper names in Xhosa do not have a prefix. Thus one simply writes Nomsa, Themba. In a sentence, any word related to any of the nouns stands in relation to that noun by means of concords, related to the prefix. Thus, the following sentence is expressed in Xhosa as follows:
All people want freedom = *Bonke abantu bafuna inkululeko*.
The whole of mankind wants freedom = *Lonke uluntu lufuna inkululeko*.

It follows that each noun has its own set of concords, since concords are related to the prefixes. Xhosa distinguishes sixteen noun classes. Class sixteen is, however, no longer in use and that which remains functions as an adverb, for example, *phantsi* (ground-side), phezulu (sky-side) and phesheya (further-side). Classes 12 and 13 do not exist in Xhosa. A tabulation of the noun classes in Xhosa would reveal the following pattern:

Noun Classes in Xhosa

	Article	Prefix	Stem	Meaning
Class 1 (singular)	u	m	ntu	person
Class 2 (plural)	a	ba	ntu	people
1a (singular)	u	–	Nomsa	proper name
2a (plural)	oo	–	Nomsa	proper name
Class 3 (singular)	u	m	thi	tree
Class 4 (plural)	i	mi	thi	trees
Class 5 (singular): This prefix *li* is found before. Monosyllabic stems only	i	li	tye	stone

84

before disyllabic and polysyllabic it is omitted	i (ihase)	li	haʃe	horse	
Class 6 (plural)	a	ma	tye	stones	
	a	ma	haʃe	horses	
Class 7 (singular): before stem starting with consonant	i	si	fundo	lesson	
before stem starting with vowel	i		sonka	bread	
Class 8 (plural): before stems starting in consonant	i	zi	fundo	lessons	
before stems starting in vowel	i		zandla	hands	
Class 9 (singular)					
(i) n-before t	i		nto	thing	
d	i		ndawo	place	
z	i		nzulu	depth	
j	i		nja	dog	
k	i		nkomo	cattle	
g	i		ngubo	blanket	
c	i		ncwadi	book	
x	i		nxhanxhosi	secretary bird	
g	i		nqawa	pipe	
(i) m-before p	i		mpumlo	nose	
b	i		mbila	pot	
f	i		mfazwe	war	
v	i		mvu	fat-tailed sheep	
(i) ny-before vowels	i		nyama	meat	
(i) before n & m	i		namba	python	
n & m	i		mini	day-time	
Class 10 (plural): before monosyllabic stems in t, d, x, j,	i	zi	nja	dogs	
k, g, c, z, q	i	zi	nto	things	
before disyllabic and polysyllabic stems in t, d, z	ii	–	ntombi	girls	
	ii	–	ngcango	doors	
before monosyllabic stems in p, b, f, v	i	zi	mpi	armies	
before disyllabic and polysyllabic stems ending in p, b, f, v	i	zi	mfe	sugar canes	
	ii	–	mpuku	mice	
	ii	–	mbiza	pots	

And Bid Him Sing

Class 11 becomes *uluthi* = stick before monosyllabic stems. Before consonants starting in 'a' or 'e' it becomes

and

$$ulu + azi \searrow\swarrow = w = ulwazi$$

$$ulu + oyiko \searrow\swarrow = o = uloyiko$$

Class 14   u   -   busuku   night
Class 15   u   -   kutya   food

These infinitives or verbal nouns all belong to class fifteen.

In these pages I have given the noun-class system as it is found in Xhosa. For comparative purposes the noun-class system of Zulu and Southern Sotho, taken from Meinhof and used by Doke in his article in Schapera's book, *The Bantu-Speaking Tribes of South Africa* (1946), is reprinted here.[24]

	Zulu	*Southern Sotho*
Class 1.	umu-umuntu (person)	mō-mōthō
2.	aba-abantu (people)	ba-bathō
3.	umu-umuzi (village)	mō-mōtse
4.	imi-imizi (villages)	me-metse
5.	ili-, i-izinyo (tooth)	le-leinò
6.	ama-amazinyo (teeth)	ma menò
7.	isi-isifuba (chest)	se sefuba
8.	izi-izifuba (chests)	li-lifuba
9.	im-, in- into (thing)	n-nthò
10.	izim-izin-iznto (things)	lin-, li-linthò
11.	ulu-u-uthango (fence)	....
14.	ubu-ubuhlungu (pain)	bō-bōhlōkö
15.	uku-ukudla (food)	hō-hoja

In the long form one substitutes *-ile* for the final vowel of the present stem. Example:

Hamba = Hambile
Sebenza (work) = Sebenzile.

In the short form one substitutes -*e* for the final vowel of the present stem. Example:

Hamba = Hambe
Sebenza = Sebenze.

The following exceptions are those ending in *ala* with high-low intonation and *ana*.
'Al,a as in 'lal, a (sleep) form the perfect stem by changing – ' al,a into 'el,e. The perfect form of l'al,a (sleep) = l'el,e. So also 'an,a into 'en,e e.g. lib'al,a (forget) becomes li,b'el,e.
Verbs with a different intonation pattern ending in *ana* and *ala* follow the general rule. Example:

v,al'a (close) becomes v,alile
q'al,a (begin) becomes q,alile.

The Recent Past is formed from the Perfect of the verb stem. The -*i* of the suffix -*ile* has a high-falling intonation. Example: ndiphumi,le
The negative is formed by substituting -*anga* for the final -*i* as in the following example:

Engatheti = Engathethanga
(he not speaking – he not having spoken).

The Remote Past has a similar formation to primary modality, except that -*yo* is suffixed to the verb stem. Example:

ndaathetha (I spoke . . . long ago).
Remote Past = *Nd*,aathethayo, with a low intonation of the subject concord (I have spoken . . . long ago).

Strong adjectives in Xhosa consist of an adjectival stem and a class prefix which is placed before the stem. In this case, the class prefixes are identical to the noun-class prefixes. Since there are sixteen noun classes in Xhosa and since the class prefixes of the strong adjectives are identical to the noun-class prefixes, it follows naturally that the class prefixes of strong adjectives will vary according to the noun class to which the adjective is related.

Strong demonstratives have three positional types in Xhosa, the first position indicating something nearer the speaker, the second something nearer the hearer than the speaker and the third, remote from both speaker and hearer. The last feature in this rather cursory look at some of the features of the Xhosa language is known as

ideophones. They have been defined by A. C. Jordan as half-adjectival and half-adverbial with onomatopoeic sounds.²⁵
Example:

Uboya bekathi *Bumfumfum* (the hair of the cat is soft-silky).
Isela Lathi *Qumpu, Qumpu, Qumpu* (the frog splashes in the water).
Xhegwazana phek' iphapha! Xhegwazana phek' iphapha!, resembling the sound of a steam-driven train through the veld and the mountains.

As the trains rush through the African landscape we finally arrive at a point where the presence of Afrikaans as a language in South Africa *cannot* be ignored. There are several important aspects in discussing the Afrikaans language situation inside South Africa. No matter from what particular angle one looks at Afrikaans, the political issue always rears its head. For the Afrikaner, Afrikaans is historically and emotionally tied up with Afrikaner nationalism and the search for identity. The first Afrikaans language movement of 1875²⁶ had its origin just before the first war between the English and the Boers (1881) and the second Anglo-Boer War (1899–1901).

Understandably, the aim of the Genootskap vir Regte Afrikaners (The Society for Proper Afrikaners) in 1875 was to stand for 'our language, nation and our country'. Black people did not feature as human beings in their early poetry and culture. They were functional only as decoration. The Afrikaner was only preoccupied with one thing: to gain control over South Africa, culturally, politically and economically. The basis for this was laid in their early language struggles.

It is no accident that one of the leading figures in the second language movement was Dr Malan, the first Afrikaner National Party Prime Minister in 1948. This language movement was first started in 1905 and achieved its reward in 1925 when Afrikaans was officially recognized.

Afrikaans as a potent weapon in the Afrikaner struggle for identity is a factor which cannot be ignored in Afrikaner nationalism. Another significant factor is the exploitation of Afrikaans by the Afrikaner to enforce the *ethnos* concept in which South Africa is regarded as a country consisting of many nations and different ethnic cultures which do not form a single state but a multi-national state. This ideological approach is used to justify Bantustans²⁷ and the Group Areas Acts in South Africa, whereby blacks become noncitizens in the country. The policy of Christian National Education[28] paved the way for Bantu Education,[29] whereby the Afrikaner was assured of a regular and cheap source of labour. Naturally, the foisting of Afrikaans on blacks was important in this respect. One analyst of the situation observed: 'Moedertaal-onderwys" is masqueraded as "mother-tongue" instruction, whereas in fact it is no more than the political enforcement of Afrikaans as medium in schools.'[30]

The enforcement of Afrikaans as a medium of instruction in black schools was a direct cause of the revolt of the youngsters in Soweto and elsewhere in 1976. It culminated in the blunt *Asingeni* (We shall not enter) by black pupils which, in turn, was answered by the regime with brutal repression.

But, there is yet another facet to Afrikaans, White Afrikaners look upon their language as a pure Germanic language. Blood-mixing of the various European groups at the Cape, e.g. Dutch, German and French, was used as a linguistic determinant. Thus, Afrikaans in the eyes of Afrikaner linguists could only be a 'Diets' language with Romance influences. It is, therefore, not so surprising that the linguist, Marius Valkhoff, one of the propounders of the theory that Afrikaans is a creole language, should accuse Afrikaner linguists of synchronistic purism, the tendency to 'transfer their ideal of purity of the white race to their mother-tongue and its history.'[31]

The debate concerning the creole nature of Afrikaans is still very much alive. The latest thesis of the South African, Dennis Makhudu, deals with Flytaal (Flaaitaal), formerly referred to as Tsotsi-Taal by blacks. Significantly, it is called: Is Afrikaans a Creole Language? (1984).

I observed in my work, *Mind Your Colour* (1981): 'Historically it is an indisputable fact that the Khoi, the slaves and later the so-called 'Cape-Coloured' have all contributed to the rise of Afrikaans as a language'.[32] The earliest attempts to explain the origin of Afrikaans came from Dr Th. Hahn in 1882 at a lecture in Cape Town, in which he clearly stated that Afrikaans was 'psychologically an essentially Hottentot idiom'.[33]

Research in the archives reveals many examples of Afrikaans spoken by the Khoi (referred to in books as 'Hottentots-Afrikaans'). In 1672, for example, two colonists were threatened by a Khoi with the following words: 'Duytsman een woort calm, ons U kelum.' (If white man one word speaks us you kill.) In 1710 the following

sentence was reported verbally: 'Ons denkum ons altijd Baas, maar ja Zienom Duitsman meer Baas.' (We think we are always Boss, but we have seen white man more Boss.)[34]
'The verbal suffix *-m, -um, -om*, which is no longer found in the actual language is, according to the Leiden linguist, J. Voorhoeve, a general characteristic of pidgin found, for example, in Cameroun pidgin English and Melanesian pidgin English. It also formally resembles the prominal object in Dutch.'[35]

Similarly, the Romance origin of the Afrikaans double negative is now rejected by some linguists and its origin sought in Khoisan languages. The incidence of spoken Malayan-Portuguese at the Cape during the eighteenth century (in 1820 the Wesleyans were still preaching in this language to the slaves) and the demographic picture of Cape Town at that time throw new light on the language situation. From *Opgaaf* (Annual Tax Rolls) lists we know that Cape Town was a male-dominated society. The list is as follows:[36] 4,871 male adults made up of 1,243 Burghers, 75 Free Black, 83 Knechten (i.e. soldiers and sailors released by the DEIC to work for Burghers) and 3,470 slaves. The *opgaaf* lists 1,721 adult women made up of 774 Burghers' widows and 91 Free Black women of whom 23 were married, 3 widowed and 856 slaves. This figure does not include the company slaves (approx. 650) and the Khoisan who found themselves within the orbit of the company. The slaves at the Cape came from various shores of the Indian Ocean, namely, India, Sri Lanka, Mozambique, sometimes even the Philippines and Thailand. According to the figures, in 1831 the free population was more than double that of 1806, the number being 13,359. In the South-Western Cape there was also a definite interplay between Khoi and whites. These demographic figures serve to dispel the lie of purism which surrounds the question of the Afrikaans language.

Two other aspects concerning Afrikaans need to be mentioned here: one, the emergence of Fanakalo and the use of Flytaal (Flaaitaal). Of Fanakalo A. C. Jordan wrote in his series of articles:

> *Fanakalo* (or Kitchen Kaffir) is confined to the Rand Mines and Durban kitchens, despised and hated by those who have to use it, never used in the 'married quarters', where the mine clerks live a relatively normal life with their families...
>
> Fanakalo basically employs Nguni words but ignoring both morphological and syntactic structure of Nguni, it transplants

isolated Nguni words into an English syntactic word order. E.g. Yini wena funa? for Ufuna ni? (What do you want?), Iphi wena hamba? for Uyaphi? (Where are you going?) . . . In the 'twenties', an Anglican minister 'translated' the Lords prayer into *Fanakalo* to use among the mineworkers. His church was deserted.[37]

To my mind, the MA thesis by Dennis Makhudu (1984) is the first full-scale study by an African from South Africa to come to grips linguistically with creolization processes within the socio-political context of South Africa. His is one of several critical studies by black South Africans.

Of Flytaal (spelt Flaaitaal by Schuring) Makhudu says:

Another variety of Afrikaans is known to have existed for some time among the putative Bantu-speaking groups. . . there are stable varieties of Afrikaans among the Blacks to a greater extent than has been previously supposed. In actuality, South African urban societies thrive on the constant interaction among different language groups. The most vibrant contact comes about between the Indo-European and Bantu languages . . . The dominance of Afrikaans as an official language has resulted in its use in the domains of school, labor market and government circles, such as post-offices and railway stations. It is not surprising, therefore, that in Black residential areas and urban townships a new form of communication has arisen. In order to survive in the urban cauldron, Bantu-speaking Blacks have created a communication system that combines Afrikaans, several Bantu languages and some English.[38]

Makhudu refers to the stigma clinging to Tsotsi-Taal, often looked upon as 'an esoteric jargon' of Afrikaans interlaced with Bantu and English words, and spoken by young men of a criminal bent . . . but that is not the whole story. Black South Africans of all social classes use it frequently among themselves to identify themselves as city-dwellers or 'the city-wise'. The stigma that attaches to Tsotsi-Taal has recently disappeared and speakers nowadays prefer to call it Flytaal or FT.

The writer and poet, Sipho Sepamla, demonstrated this in no

And Bid Him Sing

uncertain terms when he read his poem, 'Come Duze Baby',[39] i.e., 'Come Closer Baby', written in Flytaal, at the English-language festival held at Grahamstown in 1974. And, he added rather mockingly, in front of his largely English-speaking audience, that if there were people present who did not understand the language then they should reflect seriously on the extent of their South Africanness. The basilar of the poem which follows is Afrikaans. G. K. Schuring comments as follows:

> The poem consists of 167 orthographic words. Of these 114 are comparable with Afrikaans and 40 with English. The 40 in English also include some in slang. For the rest, it contains 13 words from South African languages spoken by Blacks, namely, ten from Zulu, two from Southern Sotho, and one from Tsonga . . .[40]

Come Duze Baby[41]

COME *DUZE* BABY	COME CLOSER BABY
Hela baby!	Hi! baby!
Zwakala daarso	Listen here
Of hoe sê ek?	Or what am I saying?
Jy moet my *notch*	Notice me
Kyk my mooi sweetie	Look pretty sweetie
Ek is nie een van hulle	I'm not one of them
Jy ken mos	You know me mos
Die Hillbrow type.	The Hillbrow type.
Hela Sisi!	Hi! Sister!
Look sharp	Be clever
Otherwise sal jy val	Otherwise you'll fall
Met my '*M*'	With my 'M' (mother)
Jy sal val soos 'n sak kool.	Like a bag of potatoes.
Ek wil jou *weedie*	I want to talk to you
Of praat jy net met situations	Or do you only talk to well-situated ones
Die manne met 'n *ntanjana*	The men wearing ties

Ilizwi LikaJakobi Kodwa Isandla Sika-Esau

Die Stetson oukies	The ones with stetson hats
Die Mpala-mpala outies	The okes driving Mpala-Chevvies
Wat jou *rwa*	who turn your head with promises
Met *Manyeledi*	of the wild games park at Manyeledi
And *Mgababa*	the holiday resort at Mgababa
Of hoe sê ek?	Or what am I saying?
Baby jy's 'n washout	Baby you're a washout
Hulle vang jou	They catch you
Sluit jou toe	lock you up
For Immorality	For immorality
'Strue met my '*P*'	'Strue as my '*P*' (Father)
Jy's 'n has-been	You're a has-been.
Kyk, ek *mca* jou baby	Look, I love you
Ek is serious	I'm serious
My hart maak *shandies*	My heart is bouncing wildly
Jy ken mos.	You know mos
Die downtown beat	The downtown beat
Van Jimmy Smith se *mojo*	Of Jimmy Smith's magic
Ek praat die real ding	I'm talking about the real thing
Moenie dink	Don't think
Ek *wala-wala* net stof	I'm just kicking up dust
Ek wil jou *cover*	I want to hold you
Ek wil jou *smekana*	I want to give you protection
Jy ken mos	You know mos
Die movie-star ding.	The movie-star thing.
Jy's my number one *mbuzana*	You're my number one sweetie-pie
Die *neneweet*	The good Lord knows
Jy's my eie ding	You're my one and only thing
Met my ma!	'Strue as my mother lives
Baby come *duze*!	Baby come closer
Come duze baby!	Come closer baby!

I have made no attempt to recreate the local colour of the poem. All the elements necessary for pidginization are there. The language of the dominant group – in this case Afrikaans – acts as the base. This type of language draws heavily – at least lexically – on various African languages, e.g. Nguni (Zulu). To what extent it will act as a means of communication between various language-speaking communities who cannot communicate with one another in their respective languages is, as yet, hard to tell. It is certainly not the new brand of South African English as anyone unfamiliar with pidginization might believe. Flytaal may, possibly, indicate the way in which Afrikaans can survive in a post-apartheid South Africa. As such, it might already carry within it the seeds of a future language form which was once only associated with apartheid. G. K. Schuring comments: 'Flaaitaal (or tsotsi language) is the slang spoken by urban Blacks ... (it) was used as early as 1935 and probably earlier.'[42]

In this respect the language of the people of the Cape is also an important facet of the Afrikaans language within the African context.[43] There are no indications that any of the Dravidian/Indian languages in South Africa have undergone similar changes to those of, for example, Surinam, where Sarnami is now regarded as a language with creolizations; its origin was either among the depots before shipment to Surinam or in Surinam itself.

The language question in South Africa cannot be discussed as an isolated phenomenon. The pressure of the socio-historical and political climate is visible everywhere. The South African regime has exploited the existence of various language communities in the country to justify their *ethnos* theories of divide and rule. The language situation has been politicized to such an extent that honest research is sometimes well-nigh impossible. Everything is geared to the fallacious notion that South Africa is a white man's country and not a part of Africa. When it is seen as a part of Africa then it usually becomes a special part, set aside from the rest of Africa.

It is not without significance that Caliban is made to say:

> 'You taught me language, and my profit on't
> Is, I know how to curse.'[44]

Perhaps the *cri de coeur* of the Khoi in 1710 is just as relevant today as when he called out: 'Ons denkum ons altijd baas, maar ja zienom

Ilizwi LikaJakobi Kodwa Isandla Sika-Esau

duitsman meer baas.' (We think we are always Boss, but we have seen white man more Boss.)[45]

In a discussion of the language question of South Africa, as indeed in the discussions of all forms of oppression in that country, it is essential to remember that a people desiring to emancipate itself must first know the bonds of its enslavement. I have attempted here to come to grips with some of those bonds.

The tendency of the dispossessed to avoid serious debate about the language question inside South Africa is largely the result of the 'self-deception-in-self-definition', referred to earlier. A.C. Jordan's plea in 1958 is still valid to this day. He stated at that time:

> Then we shall hear no more of *herrenvolk* and mental slaves who admire and profess to appreciate Austrian folk dances, but condemn Zulu folk dances as 'tribal antics', and no more of those progressives who readily accept the myth of the *Quest of the Golden Fleece* but sneer at the Africa myth of the *Quest of the Nabulele* because to retell it is to 'revive tribal mythology'.[46]

For in the streets of the South African urban ghettoes the youngsters are re-echoing the words of one of the original inhabitants of South Africa, a Khoi, who, in 1672 uttered these words: 'Duytsman een woort calm, ons U kelum.' ('If white man one word speaks, us you kill.)[47] And, ironically, the use of *ons* instead of the Dutch *wij* can, even as early as 1672, not be attributed to the Afrikaner but, rather, to the Khoi.

Notes

1. *Inggumbo Yeminyanya*, published by Jonathan Cape, London, 1954, was written by A. C. Jordan, eminent Nguni scholar. V. E. Rylate, i.e., very late, was the pseudonym of Hosea Jaffe, a prominent opposer of the apartheid regime who was closely associated with the Unity Movement in the 1950s.
2. See also V. A. February, *From the Arsenal*, Afrika Studiecentrum, Leiden, 1983, pp. 232–77.
3. 'The Native Phenomenon', paper delivered at conference on Commonwealth Literature, Aarhus, 1971.
4. ibid, p. 4.

5. The terms 'Hottentot' and 'Bushmen' are regarded as derogatory terms by the dispossessed in South Africa. The preference is for the terms Khoi and San respectively.
6. See G. Hooijer, *De eerste schipvaart der Nederlanders naar Oost-Indië onder Cornelis de Houtman 1595-1597 door Willem Lodewycksz*, De Bussy, Amsterdam, 1921, p. 11.
7. G. P. Rouffaer & W. J. Ijzerman (eds.), *De eerste schipvaart der Nederlanders naar Oost-Indië onder Cornelis de Houtman 1595-1597*, Martinus Nijhoff's-Gravenhage, 1925, p. 7.
8. 'Khoisan Resistance to the Dutch in the Seventeenth and Eighteenth Centuries', *Journal of African History*, vol. 13, no. 1, 1972, pp. 55-80, Cambridge University Press.
9. J. L. Döhne, *Zulu-Kafir Dictionary*, Gregg Press, Farnborough, England 1967 (originally published 1857).
10. See February, op. cit., p. 255. See also A. C. Jordan, 'The Language Question', *The Educational Journal*, vol. XXIX, no. 2, September 1957.
11. 'Is Afrikaans a Creole Language?' Carbondale, Illinois, 1984. The thesis is on Flytaal (Flaaitaal), the language used in an urban setting by Africans. It was formerly referred to as Tsotsitaal (with a derogatory connotation). See also G. K. Schuring, 'Die basilek van flaaitaal', *Tydskrif* vol. 21, no. 2, 1981, pp. 122-30.
12. George Routledge & Sons, London, 1930, p. 3.
13. ibid.
14. Meinhof, *Die Sprache der Hamiten*, L. Friederichson, Hamburg, 1912; Schapera, 1930, op. cit., pp. 419-38.
15. Schapera, 1930, op. cit., p. 432.
16. Meinhof, op. cit., p. 16.
17. Schapera, 1930, op. cit., p. 421.
18. D. Westermann & I. C. Ward, *Practical Phonetics for Students of African Languages*, Oxford University Press, London, 1964, p. 92.
19. C. M. Doke, 'Early Bantu Literature', *Bantu Studies*, vol. 9, no. 2, Johannesburg, June 1935.
20. See V. A. February, 1981, p. 3.
21. See A. C. Jordan in V. A. February, *From the Arsenal*, 1983, p. 259. Also A. C. Jordan 'The Language Question' (i), *The Educational Journal*, vol. XXIX, no. 2, September 1957.
22. ibid.
23. ibid., p. 260.
24. Schapera, 1946, op. cit., p. 320.
25. Culled from lecture notes of A. C. Jordan while I was his student during 1959-1960 at the University of Cape Town.
26. See V. A. February, *White Minorities, Black Majorities*, Afrika Studiecentrum, Leiden, 1976/1; see especially the article on the Afrikaans language, pp. 11-23. See also P. J. Nienaber, *Mylpale in die geskiedenis van die Afrikaanse taal en letterkunde*, Afrikaanse Pers-Boekhandel, Johannesburg, 1951.
27. In South African political ideology Bantustans are those areas set

aside, since the 1913 Land Act, for Africans of various language groups. These areas, according to the whites, coincide with the traditional areas of settlement of the Africans in South Africa. No account is taken of the wars of dispossession in which the African lost much of his land. Bantustans are also referred to as Homelands. According to the government, Africans can only realize their political aspirations in the Bantustans. Inside South Africa he can only be a visitor. The large majority of urban blacks make a mockery of this claim. The Bantustan areas are generally impoverished and totally dependent on South Africa.
28. This policy was devised to provide a Christian basis for the ideology of apartheid. For a fuller account see V. A. February, *Mind Your Colour*, Kegan Paul Int., London, 1981; see especially note 6 of chapter 6, 'A Voice in the Wilderness', p. 208.
29. A special system of education, designed for blacks by whites, to ensure that they have a regular labour reservoir and a docile black man. See *Bantu Education. Oppression or Opportunity*, published by the pro-government group SABRA (South African Bureau of Racial Affairs), Stellenbosch, 1955. For an African voice read I. B. Tabata, *Education for Barbarism*, n.d.
30. For 'Moedertaal-onderwijs' see February, op. cit., 1983, p. 277; also *The Educational Journal*, vol. XXVIII, no. 3, Sept. 1956.
31. *Portuguese and Creole with Special Reference to South Africa*, Witwatersrand University Press, Johannesburg, 1966; see also February, op. cit., 1983, p. 22.
32. February, op. cit. 1981, p. 20.
33. For Th. Hahn see February, op. cit., 1981, p. 21; see also D. B. Bosman, *Oor die ontstaan van Afrikaans*, Swets & Zeitlinger, Amsterdam, 1928, p. 16.
34. February, op. cit. 1981, p. 21.
35. Ibid.
36. Robert Ross, 'Oppression, Sexuality and Slavery at the Cape of Good Hope', *Reflections Historique*, vol. 6, no. 2, 1979, pp. 421–33; see also Ross, 'Cape Town 1750–1850: Synthesis in Dialectic of Continents', in Ross & G. Telkamp (eds.), *Colonial Cities*, Dordrecht/Boston/Lancaster/Nijhoff, Waterloo University, Canada, 1985.
37. See February, op. cit., 1983, pp. 262–3; see also A. C. Jordan, 'The Language Question', *The Educational Journal*, vol. XXIX, no. 3, October 1957.
38. Makhudu, op. cit., p. 31–2.
39. See G. K. Schuring, 'Die basilek van flaaitaal', *Tydskrif vir Geesteswetenskappe*, vol. 21, no. 2, 1981, pp. 123–4.
40. ibid., p. 124.
41. Duze = from Zulu eduze = closer.
    Hela = South Sotho interjection = Hallo, Hi!
    Zwakala = Zulu 'be heard'; in this context, Listen here!
    Notch = slang for notice.
    M = mother; P = Pa.

Weedie = to talk to.
Ntanjana = from Zulu intanjana = string
Mpala-mpala = Sotho reference to the Chevrolet-Impala model.
Rwa = from English 'rob' or Xhosa 'rwaya'.
Manyeledi (Manyeleti) = a Tsonga word = a games park for blacks near Acornhoek.
Mgababa = holiday resort for blacks near Durban.
Mca = I love you.
Shandy = from English shandy (beer).
Mojo = magic.
Wala-wala = to kick up lots of dust, to kick up a racket.
Cover and smekana = both with the meaning of wanting to protect.
Mbuzana = sweetheart.
Neneweet = from Zulu inene = gentleman, Sir; in Xhosa inene means the truth; in this context, The Lord knows.
Come duze baby = Come closer baby (sweetheart) and also a plea to stop resisting = give in, surrender to the lover's charms.
42. G. K. Schuring, op. cit., p. 122.
43. February, op. cit., 1981, pp. 89–100.
44. William Shakespeare, *The Tempest*, Act. 1, Scene 2, lines 65–6.
45. February, op. cit. 1981, p. 21.
46. See V. A. February, op. cit. 1983, p. 276; see also Jordan, *Towards an African Literature*, University of California Press, Los Angeles, 1974.
47. February, op. cit., 1981, p. 21.

Bibliography

Bastiaanse (1956): 'Moedertaal-onderwijs: Afrikanerizing Instrument'. In: *The Educational Journal*, Vol. XXVIII, 3 (Sept.), Cape Town. See also: V. A. February, *From the Arsenal*, (Leiden, Afrika Studiecentrum 1983), pp. 277–82.
Döhne, J. L. (1967): *Zulu-Kafir Dictionary* (Farnborough, Hants, England, Gregg. Press), originally published in 1857.
Doke, C. (1935): *Early Bantu Literature* in *Bantu Studies*, 9, 2, Johannesburg.
Doke, C.: Language, in: I. Schapera, *The Bantu-speaking Tribes of South Africa* (London, G. Routledge & Sons).
February, V. A. (1976): *White Minorities, Black Majorities* (Leiden, Afrika Studiecentrum).
February, V. A. (1981): *Mind Your Colour* (London, Kegan Paul Int.).
February, V. A. (1983): *From the Arsenal* (Leiden, Afrika Studiecentrum).
Harris, Wilson (1971): 'The Native Phenomenon' (Aarhus).
Hooijer, (1921): *De Eerste Schipvaart der Nederlanders naar Oost-Indië onder Cornelis de Houtman 1595–1597 door Willem Lodewycksz*. In opdracht van het Koloniaal Institut... (Amsterdam, De Bussy).

Jordan, A. C. (1957): 'The Language Question'. In: *The Educational Journal* (Cape Town, 29, 3: 6–8; 29, 5, 10–12. See especially V. A. February, *From the Arsenal*, Leiden, 1983.

Marks, Shula (1972): 'Khoisan Resistance to the Dutch in the Seventeenth and the Eighteenth Centuries'. In: *Journal of African History*, 13, 1: 55–80.

Makhudu, D. (1984): *Is Afrikaans a Creole Language?* (Southern Illinois University at Carbondale), M.A.-thesis.

Meinhof, C. (1912): *Die Sprache der Hamiten* (Hamburg, L. Friederichson).

Nienaber, P. J. (1951): *Mylpale* in die Geskiedenis van die Afrikaanse Taal en Letterkunde (Johannesburg, Afrikaanse Pers-Boekhandel).

Rouffaer, G. P. & Ijzerman, J. W. (1925): *De eerste schipvaart der Nederlanders naar Oost-Indië onder Cornelis de Houtman 1595–1597* ('s-Gravenhage).

Ross, Robert (1979): 'Oppression, Sexuality and Slavery at the Cape of Good Hope' in: *Reflections Historique*, 6.2. See also: 'Synthesis in Dialectic of Continents'. In: R. Ross & G. Telkamp (eds.) *Colonial Cities* Dordrecht/Boston/Lancaster, Nijhoff, Waterloo University, Canada, 1985.

Schapera, I. (1930): *The Khoisan People of South Africa*, (London, George Routledge & Sons).

Schapera, I. (1946): *The Bantu-Speaking Tribes of South Africa* (London, George Routledge & Sons).

Shakespeare, W. (1954): See: *The Tempest* (ed.) F. Kermode, London.

Valkhoff, Marius (1966): *Studies in Portuguese and Creole with special reference to South Africa* (Johannesburg, Witwatersrand University Press).

Westermann, D. & Ward, Ida C. (1964): *Practical Phonetics for Students of African Languages*, (London, Oxford University Press).

7

Asingeni – We Shall not Enter[1]

The Afrikaans Language and Soweto 1976

English! English! Only English!
that one hears or sees;
in our schools and in our churches
our mother-tongue is murdered there.[2]

These opening lines are taken from a poem by C. P. Hoogenhout, one of the stalwarts of the early phase of the Afrikaans language. Although poetically weak, this poem is an example of the way in which the Afrikaners reacted when their language or culture was in danger. These lines were written when Afrikaans was still in its infancy. The struggle for the recognition of Afrikaans was part and parcel of the Afrikaner struggle for recognition as a people. Even to this day, some Afrikaners still raise the English bogey from time to time.

The revolts at Soweto against Afrikaans as a medium of instruction, resulting in numerous deaths, reminded one of the Afrikaner opposition to English, almost a century earlier. Yet, in 1976, the Afrikaner had no qualms about foisting his brand of language imperialism onto the African.

Language in a colonial situation has always been a most powerful instrument, responsible for pulverizing the 'native' into uniformity and conformity. The reaction of the African population in South Africa against Afrikaans assumes even greater significance when one surveys the attitudes of colonized people in Africa, the West Indies and Asia. In the French territories, in particular, the French language proved to be a very important instrument of colonialism, the effects of which are still visible in Africa and the West Indian islands. The French imposed their cultural pattern on the African and Antillean child through the school system, the books prescribed and the expatriates and civil servants who were present in the colonies to bolster up the colonial scheme.

Frantz Fanon, in his *Black Skin, White Masks*, rightly starts with a discussion of the status of language for the colonized. A mastery of the language of the colonial overlord was essential if one wanted to make any advance in society. He observes: 'The negro of the Antilles will be proportionately whiter, that is, he will become closer to being a real human being in direct relation to his mastery of the French language.'[3] In adopting the language of the colonizer, the colonized sometimes imbibed prejudices and attitudes of the colonial overlord towards indigenous culture.

Once more Fanon gives evidence of his deep understanding of the colonial trauma when he writes:

> Every colonized people – in other words, every people in whose soul an inferiority complex has been created by the death and burial of its local cultural originality – finds itself face to face with the language of the civilising nation; that is, with the culture of the mother country. The colonized is elevated above his jungle status in proportion to his adoption of the mother country's cultural standards.[4]

The policy of assimilation induced in West Africans and Antilleans a reverence for the mother-country, France. Paris was the ultimate dream. In the thirties, however, those students studying in the metropolis soon discovered that they were not treated as full human beings. They simply could not shed their 'negroness'. This led to a reaction which resulted, in French-speaking areas, in a rediscovery of Africa, African culture and roots. The movement, known as négritude, was both cultural and ideological. Peculiarly black attributes were imputed to black men in one poetic effusion after another. Négritude, as an epidermic, psychological and ideological reaction, was a phenomenon confined to French territories.

In English-speaking colonies no attempt was made to Anglicize the 'native' The effect of English habits and customs was, however, no less forceful.

The eminent novelist, critic and short-story writer, Chinua Achebe, makes the following terse observations:

> Yet the fact remains that Nigeria was created by the British for their own ends. Let us give the devil his due: colonialism in Africa disrupted many things, but it did create political units where there were small scattered ones before.[5]

Achebe's appreciation for the English language stems from a similar type of analysis:

> Those of us who have inherited the English language may not be in a position to appreciate the value of the inheritance. Or we may go on resenting it because it came as part of a package deal which included many other items of doubtful value and the positive atrocity of racial arrogance and prejudice which may yet set the world on fire. But let us not, in rejecting the evil, throw out the good with it.[6]

The activities and publications of several African authors have helped greatly in the process of demythologization. Achebe is astute enough to recognize that the Queen's English must, of necessity, undergo a change in the hands of, for example, a Nigerian or South African author. Wisely he states:

> The African writer should aim to use English in a way that brings out his message without altering the language to the extent that its value as a medium of international exchange will be lost. He should aim at fashioning out an English which is at once universal and able to carry his particular experience.[7]

In the case of both French and English colonies the language, used as a colonial instrument, serves as a medium of international exchange. Ironically, when the black man did object to language in a colonial situation, it was invariably against the way in which the black man was made to use the white man's language so that it only confirmed that he was dumb and incapable of learning anything. He was made to say 'I nono' instead of I don't know. This was the case in, for example, Surinam, the former Dutch West Indies, and is possibly still so in the Dutch Antilles. Creole in Surinam (now known as Sranan Tongo, i.e., the Surinamese tongue) and Papiamento (the Antillean creole language) were scorned by the local population and discouraged as a medium of instruction in schools. In the French Antilles creole was despised;

> Creole is for black people
> Creole is for the people
> Creole is for silly Negroes who cannot
> Read or write . . .[8]

But even creole came to be discovered during the process of demythologization and nationalism. Reactions against colonialism and the white man and his culture (in particular) turned creole into a symbol of respectability as is evident from the remarks of Koenders on Surinamese creole.

> That is not what they call negro-English or Negro tongue. Negro-English is that broken English which a negro speaks: 'mi no no' instead of 'I don't know'. The 'Negro tongue' is the language of all negroes . . . A people that has neglected its language or lost it, or heaps insults on it for the sake of another language, whichever it may be, is more stupid than our forefathers.[9]

The conditions described in former English and French colonies differ significantly from those obtaining inside South Africa. First of all, there is an indigenous white population which controls the country, politically and economically, by a system of oppression. Assimilation, in so far as it is allowed, can only take place within the institutionalized structures of the country, that is, within the framework of apartheid. Lord Lugard's system of Indirect Rule seems to linger on in the form of Bantustans. The African worker subsists peripherally near the white urban areas, with no political rights.

Being in white areas as labourers, Africans must perforce deal with the two languages of the whites, namely, English and Afrikaans. English is, of course, a means of international exchange. Afrikaans is the language of the Afrikaner, the power-holders who implement the system of apartheid. The language itself has a spate of terms by which the black man is abused. Thus, Africans are referred to as Kaffirs and 'coloureds' as Hotnots (Hottentots). Afrikaans, for the majority of the oppressed, is the language of the oppressor. There is reason to assume that, for many blacks, Afrikaans is synonymous with Afrikaner = white man = oppressor.

Ostensibly, then, the attempts of the white authorities to ram Afrikaans down the throats of black youngsters in Soweto seem of recent date. In reality, the role of Afrikaans as an instrument of oppression is traceable to the first attempts of the Afrikaners to gain recognition for their language in 1875. At that time a group of ardent people started the Genootskap vir regte Afrikaners (Society for Proper Afrikaners). The first language movement laid the basis for a peculiar brand of Afrikaner nationalism. One of the chief aims of the movement was 'to stand for our language, our nation and our country'. Here one stumbles upon the first germs of Christian National Education[10] in embryonic form.

The main concern was nationalistic. Afrikaans and Afrikaner was already synonymous with 'white' in the early phase. Although most of the protagonists would have endorsed the maxim of the Flemish language pioneer, Jan Frans Willems, that 'de taal is gansch het volk' ('the language is the entire people'),[11] they were not prepared to include the 'coloureds' who spoke Afrikaans in their concept of the nation or *volk*.[12] The earliest literary efforts concentrated on factors such as pride, religion and Afrikaner history. Many of the first writings were didactic in tone, anti-English and nationalistic. The Afrikaner was, himself, in the process of changing from a Dutchman into an Afrikaner, from a member of a group to a member of a tribe, from a tribe into a nation with political aspirations. The first poetic products were a reflection of these aspirations.

> Where Table Mountain starts till deep into Transvaal
> There lives a people unified – one language known to all:
> A People formerly despised, a language suppressed.
> But now well-known and honoured in East, West, South and North.[13]

Afrikaans became charmingly naïve in a poem by Leon Cachet: 'A poor Boer lass despised by many but still of noble blood.' He ends his poem rather prophetically that, should he wave the magic wand:

> ... Mother-tongue,
> The whole land follows in my wake,
> And I am shortly
> Queen of South Africa![14]

Black South Africans as cultural and rational human beings were unthinkable in early Afrikaans poetry. They were either savages at, the most, 'noble savages', or were present to supply the comic note. The Afrikaner was still so occupied with gaining control politically and culturally over the English that black South Africa simply did not exist.

The second language movement (1903) was a continuation of the struggle; Afrikaans was finally recognized in schools in 1925. One of the stalwarts of the movement was Dr Malan, who became the first Nationalist Prime Minister in 1948. The Afrikanerization of South Africa is a long and continuous process and had its origin in the language movement started in 1875.

It was Dr Malan who envisaged that separation be practised between all races in South Africa. For the first time there was talk of separation between the whites and the 'coloureds' in the Cape. While, traditionally, South African schools have always practised segregation, excluding the early schools under the Dutch East India Company, black and white students at least sat for the same exams. The national government of Malan and his followers was to change fundamentally that situation. Language, as we have already noted, can serve as an important instrument of enslavement and colonialism. Afrikaners recognized this and started the institution of ethnic fragmentation by appointing several commissions. Most important of these were the De Villiers Commission (1948), the Eiselen Commission (1949–51) and the De Vos Malan Commission (1953–5).

The De Villiers Report consisted of 300 pages of which only twenty-eight were devoted to the education of blacks. The report advocated compulsory (free) education for white children and proposed the following. White children should attend a nursery school between the ages of three to five, they should be at primary schools between six and twelve, at junior high between twelve and fifteen and at senior level from fifteen onwards. Educationally, therefore, they would be well equipped to play the role of overlord, since no provision was made for such compulsory education among blacks. The De Villiers Report paved the way for the superiority of the white child. The black child ('coloured' and African) was to be prepared for his subservient role as a labourer in the economic and socio-political system. This is even more evident from the syllabuses envisaged for 'coloured' and African children.

The Eiselen Commission prepared the way for the re-tribalization of the African, whereas the De Vos Malan Commission had to reshape the 'coloureds' into a special tribe. Totally in accordance with the country's needs, the syllabuses concentrated on the following aspects: religious instruction (always an excellent opiate), literacy in a Bantu language (necessary for the re-tribalization process), a knowledge of, and literacy in, one or both of the official languages (essential for fulfilling a proper role in the labour process) and, naturally, a knowledge of technical skills in agriculture and trade.

In Bloemfontein, in 1948, the Afrikaner devised a system of education called Christelike Nasionale Onderwys (CNO, i.e., Christnia National Education, CNE), described by opponents as being neither Christian nor National, let alone a system of education. This system envisaged that every white child should be a Christian. CNO was to prevent the African from succumbing to heathen ideologies. One of the pillars of this system was 'Moedertaalonderrig', that is, mother-tongue instruction. With this type of education, the black man would be adequately equipped for his role in the apartheid society of South Africa.

For this reason, it was necessary to devise a special system of education for Africans under the supervision of a special Native Affairs Department (NAD). Commenting on the intentions of the Afrikaner government, with respect to the education of the African, the Teachers League of South Africa wrote in the *Educational Journal* in 1955:

> The separation of white and African education by the transfer of the latter to the state department was carefully conceived to enslave not only the African child, the worker of tomorrow, but also the African teacher, as potentially the most important instrument in this dastardly operation. The main aim of 'Bantu' education, as devised by the Herrenvolk experts on the theory and practice of slave-driving, is not only to produce an inferior type of teacher of the miserable 'ja-baas'-variety. The long-term perspective of 'Bantu' education envisages therefore the Eiselenising of the African teacher through the system of

teacher training; to condition him also to accept inferiority without questioning, so that he in turn shall indoctrinate the mind of the child within this inferiority and its by-products and condition his behaviour accordingly; that he shall condition the minds of the African children for a new kind of 'aparte' society in which Africans will not desire in the words of the inimitable Dr. Verwoerd, to 'graze in the green pastures of European society'.[15]

Under the type of 'Bantu' education devised, African teachers were subject to conditions under which they could be dismissed if they were hostile to the state, identified themselves with political parties or engaged in political activities, dangerous for the maintenance of the status quo. Eiselen had a type of education in mind for the African which would make the African teacher a willing prey of the Native Affairs Department in the early fifties. A perusal of the 'Bantuized Higher Primary Course' of the early fifties reveals the following. One reads, on page 169, that 'in regard to the instruction of the child in the primary school, it is important to collect a store of facts rather than to reason about them.'

The 'Bantu' child must be made to realize that 'he is a member of a particular community and that he is tied by various ties to particular groups of people as they are represented by *his* home, *his* church, *his* village, *his* tribe. The African child must thus be fully cognizant of his *andersoortigheid* (his differentness).[16]

The programme also made provision for the study of 'Bantu culture'.

2. The study of a Bantu tribe and preferably the tribe of the majority of the pupils.
3. The coming of the Bantu to South Africa – the Great Trek of the Bantu from Central Africa – the main streams of Bantu immigration [to prove that the African arrived on the scene later than the white man] and to show 'how a Bantu child is bound to the people of his home through birth, izibongo, totem, language'.

This programme is liberally spiced with practical subjects such as treeplanting, metalwork, woodwork, gardening, in short, manual labour.

There can, of course, be no valid objection to an emphasis on the mother tongue *per se*. Within the South African setting, however, mother-tongue instruction through a Bantu language, for example, means only one thing: an attempt to re-tribalize the urban African. Its implementation is political and not inspired by linguistic motives. The attempts to foist Afrikaans on non-speakers of the language can, and must, be seen against the overall policy of apartheid. One should bear in mind that there are several languages spoken in South Africa. A random selection would reveal the following: Xhosa, Zulu, Southern Sotho, Northern Sotho, Venda, English and Afrikaans. As languages, as means of communication, none of these languages is superior to the others. Afrikaans is as ethnically confined to a specific group as is, for example, Zulu, Venda or Xhosa. The only language in the group which stands out is English, serving as an instrument of international communication. There is, therefore, no pressing reason why the African should learn another language which is confined to one particular ethnic group. The only real reason would be political.

The African is, after all, indispensable in the labour process and, as such, it would be useful if he could make himself understood in the language of the overlord or at least understand the commands given in the language.

Ever since a special type of 'Bantu education' was designed for the Africans, that is, between the early fifties and 1974, 'mother tongue' instruction was propagated for the African child. Africans themselves deeply resented this trend. Auerbach, a noted educationist, commented in the *Star* (19 June 1976):

> The government would have liked to extend the mother-tongue principle to Standard 10 if it were possible. As long as it was impossible, the rule was that half of the subjects was in English and half in Afrikaans in the high school – with concessions where this was impracticable.

Lanham, from the University of Witwatersrand, writing on the language ruling of the Bantu Education Department, observed:

> Research findings are not yet conclusive about the merits of the mother-tongue as opposed to a world language as a medium, for teaching subjects from the higher primary stage upwards, but there is no support in the literature for the simultaneous

introduction of two foreign languages for African pupils in the first years of the lower primary school and, in particular, the sudden change to the use of both media of instruction in the secondary school.[17]

In 1973, the Bantu Education Department ruled that Africans in schools should choose their medium of instruction in consultation with the department where mother-tongue instruction was not the rule. In 1974 the Southern Transvaal region of the Bantu Education Department issued a circular to the effect that English and Afrikaans should be taught on a 50-50 basis in junior secondary schools. The problems posed by this ruling were enormous. There were many teachers in African schools who were simply not proficient in the Afrikaans language. Were they now to be dismissed? One school principal spelt out the dilemma quite clearly when he commented:

> I have a new teacher who has completed her training in Natal. She got almost full marks for social studies in her final year, but I cannot use her because she does not understand Afrikaans, let alone know how to teach it.[18]

The enforcement of the language rule was a cause of concern to many a black teacher who did not fail to grasp the political implications. Thus Lawrence Vusmusi observed: 'White children can choose their medium of instruction, which is either English or Afrikaans. They are not forced to study through an African language.'[19] Another African, Mr Sithembiso, reminded the authorities of the resentment among blacks against Afrikaans: 'Are the authorities aware that Afrikaans is a hated language among blacks?'[20]

Black children responded by refusing to enter the classrooms. They used the slogan '*Asingeni*,' that is, 'We shall not enter.' Despite the objections by black pupils and educators, government spokesmen denied that they were ramming Afrikaans down the throats of black pupils. Cronje, chairman of the National Party Bantu Education group claimed that 'In fact the 50-50-rule is applied most leniently.'[21] This viewpoint was strongly endorsed by the then Deputy Minister of Bantu Education, Dr Treurnicht, who averred that

> The policy of 50% Afrikaans and 50% English in the secondary

schools is being applied in such a lenient manner that in practice the instruction in matric is virtually 100% in English as against nil in Afrikaans. I think one could almost say: 95 percent English and 5 percent Afrikaans . . . this is the case in spite of the fact that the official policy is 50-50 . . .[22]

Cronje reiterated the principles of CNO when he categorically stated: 'Our point of view over the years, and this we have done for ourselves, is that mother-tongue instruction is the foundation-stone of personality.'[23]

This, then, is what the Afrikaners are foisting upon the African child: that he choose, in addition to his mother tongue, i.e., a Bantu language which already curtails his entry into the wider world, Afrikaans, the language of the rulers. The purely linguistic aspect is but a part of the problem. Obviously, the reason for this Afrikaner approach must be sought in the takeover of organized industry and labour. The Anglo-Boer war had left in its wake a great many poor whites who were forced to settle in urban areas. To complicate matters these poor whites were then confronted with the already emerging pattern of cheap black labour. They were now expected to compete with the urban blacks. One of the major aims of the Afrikaner was to change from a *bekvelder*[24] into a homo economicus. *Afrikaans thus had to become the language of industry and commerce.*

V. E. Rylate, in a vicious examination of Afrikaans, commented in the Teachers League of South Africa's *Educational Journal*:

> Afrikaans became the 'werktaal' of the platteland, reflecting all its particular viciousness, vulgarity, coarseness, barbarism and backwardness. The townward migration of the Afrikaners between the two wars spread Afrikaans into the peri-urban and even into the urban areas. Since they constituted the main bulk of the white labour aristocracy . . . Afrikaans tended to become a 'werktaal' also in the cities, thereby reinforcing the Afrikaans spoken by non-European workers who had migrated from the country to the town and acting as human wall between the non-Europeans and English.[25]

The policy to win over the blacks has gone on unabated. In the case of the 'coloureds', English was introduced at a later stage when Afrikaans was the first language. Moreover, when English was noted as the first language the authorities were over-zealous in introducing Afrikaans at a very early stage. This whole question of *moedertaal-onderwys* was laid bare with uncanny insight by J. Bastiaanse, in an article in the *Educational Journal* of the Teachers League of South Africa, as far back as 1956. Bastiaanse was proved right a full twenty years later in the black townships of Soweto, Langa and Bonteheuvel.

The author observed at that time: 'Moedertaal-onderwys is masqueraded as 'mother-tongue' instruction, whereas in fact it is no more than the political enforcement of Afrikaans as medium in schools.'[26] Bastiaanse gives a very clear analysis of mother-tongue instruction as it operated via CNO. At the same time he made it quite clear that he was not attacking the language as a medium of communication, but rather the use to which it was put by Afrikaners:

> Thus, when attacking this policy of language of the C.N.O. . . . we are not attacking Afrikaans as a language. For there can hardly be valid objection to the use of any language as a social instrument as a means of communication between man and man . . . What is being attacked, is the use of Afrikaans as a political weapon, not only for the supremacy of one section of the Herrenvolk over the other section, but, worse still, for its use as an agency of domination over the millions of non-Whites in this country.[27]

The author stressed that a preference for English did not imply the superiority of one language over the other. It only gives recognition to the following fact:

> . . . the plea is for the use and knowledge of that language which can fit us for present-day world society. It is a choice between, to say the least, cultural and intellectual isolation, even starvation, and genuine full development as a human being.[28]

Rightly does Bastiaanse observe: 'The fight, therefore, is not only to 'Afrikanerize' the other white section but, more important, to 'Afrikanerize' the non-white millions and so gain their sympathy and retard, isolate and divide them.'[29]

The reaction of black students in Soweto and elsewhere in South Africa towards this process of Afrikanerization was also an indica-

Asingeni – We Shall not Enter

tion of the growth in political consciousness among the oppressed generation of the seventies. Even among the 'coloureds', who were generally speaking in closer touch with Afrikaans, there was a change in attitude.

In his study of the 'coloureds' of Johannesburg, the late Dr Edelstein found that 16 per cent preferred English as the medium of instruction against 2 per cent which opted for Afrikaans. His study also revealed that 74 per cent of the 'coloureds' in Johannesburg preferred to read English newspapers as opposed to 2 per cent which read Afrikaans newspapers; 44 per cent divulged as their reason for doing so that it was easier for them to read English than Afrikaans. While in the Cape the picture would no doubt reveal different figures, one would still come across similar attitudes among the 'coloureds'.[30]

Prior to the eruptions at Soweto Dr Edelstein had warned that: 'Hostile attitudes which can lead or even threaten to lead to social violence have the greatest significance and importance for they may develop into war, revolutions and social upheavals . . .'[31] Ironically, Edelstein, who worked for the 'Bantu' authorities in Soweto, was one of the first whites to be killed in Soweto. Concerning African attitudes towards the medium of instruction Edelstein found that 85 per cent of pupils preferred to be taught in English. The following table is a clear indication of African attitudes towards language preferences inside South Africa.

Language in Which Bantu Pupils would Prefer Their Child to be Educated[32]

Language	Frequency	%
Afrikaans	4	2·0
English	177	88·5
Vernacular	19	9·5
Total	200	100·00

The South African government was given ample warning that their language policy would lead to disaster. The authorities were, however, oblivious to all these protestations.

And Bid Him Sing

Early in June 1967, at six schools with a total of 1,500 pupils, an entire school board resigned on learning that history and mathematics would henceforth be taught in Afrikaans; this held no sway with the Afrikaner who was determined to enforce the Afrikaans language policy in black areas. The extent to which the government was out of touch with, or oblivious to, African objections, became even clearer from the statement of the Deputy Minister of Bantu Education, Dr Treurnicht, who openly asserted:

> In the white areas of South Africa, where the government supplies the subsidies and pays the teachers, it is surely right to determine the distribution of language . . . Our attitude still remains that a knowledge of both Afrikaans and English will be of advantage to the pupil in future.[33]

The central, or key, word here is *advantage*. Possibly, one should interpret the Minister's statement against the background of that uttered by J. de Klerk when he was still Minister of Labour: 'What the Afrikaner must always bear in mind is that he must maintain his position in our multi-racial country'.[34]

The African, it is obvious, would only benefit from Afrikaans in that he would be able to harmonize with the labour process. A knowledge of Afrikaans would stand him in good stead as a labourer in the mines, the factories, and in his daily communication with the Afrikaner.

Although the pro-government daily, *Die Burger*, still tried to blame agitators for inciting young people against Afrikaans, it was realistic enough to admit that the basic issue at stake was the African in urban areas – not just the language question. Following the events at Soweto, *Die Burger* carried this leading article:

> The direct use of violence . . . is the opposition to the use of Afrikaans in the schools of Soweto. It should be borne in mind that the objection is not against learning Afrikaans or against Afrikaans as a subject at school, but against the fact that half of the subjects would be taught in Afrikaans and the other half in English.
> There are of course many good and important reasons for this, yet it is a matter which will be viewed with, at least, mixed feelings by the Afrikaans-speaking people in the light of their

own desire not to have their children receive instruction in another language, and also, because they consider it educationally unsound ... To what extent the children themselves came to this conclusion and to what extent it was prompted to them, or even forced upon them by others, who regard Afrikaans as the language of the oppressor, will be hard to find out ... After all said and done, there is the whole question of the black man in the city, which has once again been high-lighted by the eruptions.[35]

Fanie Oliver, the Afrikaner poet, in parodying the lines of the poet and dramatist Adam Small, may have unconsciously pointed out the appropriate epitaph for the whites if they continue on this path of keeping blacks in perpetual submission:

> White man, why worry,
> Your mauser's slung o'er your shoulder,
> The noose gets tighter and tighter,
> But your mauser's o'er your shoulder,
> White man why worry?[36]

Notes

1. Revised version of 'The Afrikaans Language-Afrikanerizing Instrument', '*White Minorities, Black Majorities*' (ed. V. A. February), Afrika Studiecentrum, Leiden, 1976, pp.11–23.
2. The poem is by C. P. Hoogenhout; see D. J. Opperman, *Groot Verseboek*, Nasionale Boekhandel, Bloemfontein, 1964, p. 8. The text in Afrikaans is as follows:

    > Engels! Engels! Alles Engels!
    > Engels! Engels! Alles Engels! Engels wat jij sien en hoor;
    > In ons skole, in ons kerke word ons moedertaal vermoor.

3. Grove Inc. Press, New York, 1967.
4. ibid., p. 18.
5. *Morning Yet on Creation Day*, Heinemann Educational Books, London, 1975; see especially 'The African Writer and the English Language' p. 57.
6. ibid, p. 58.
7. ibid, p. 61.

And Bid Him Sing

8. See G. R. Coulthard, *Race and Colour in Caribbean Literature*, Oxford University Press, London, 1962, p. 44; see especially the poem by Frank Fouché, chapter 11, 'Rejection of European Culture'.
9. J. Voorhoeve & U. Lichtveld (eds.), *Creole Drum*, Yale University Press, New Haven 1975, pp. 138–9.
10. Christian National Education (CNE) and, in Afrikaans, Christelike Nasionale Onderwys (CNO), constitutes one of the cornerstones of Afrikaner nationalism. See V. A. February, *Mind Your Colour*, Kegan Paul Int., London, 1981, pp. 30, 173, 208, note 5.
11. Jan Frans Willems (1793–1846), one of the leading figures in the Flemish language and cultural movement.
12. The word *volk* has, in Afrikaner mythology, an almost magic tinge. Volk is reserved for the Afrikaner people in this context. Many people see, in this, parallels with the ideology of the Nazis.
13. See D. J. Opperman, op. cit., pp. 7–8. Poem by C. P. Hoogenhout, entitled 'Ons toekomsige Volkslied', of which this is an excerpt. The original text is:

> Waar Tafelberg begint tot vêr in die Transvaal
> Woon één verenigd volk, één algemene taal;
> 'n Volk voorheen miskend, 'n taal voorheen gesmoord.
> Maar nou beroemd, geëerd, in oos, wes, suid en
>   noord.

14. See D. J. Opperman, op. cit., pp. 14–15. Poem by J. Lion Cachet, entitled 'Die Afrikaanse Taal' of which this is an excerpt. The original text is:

> . . . Moedertaal,
> Dan volg die land my na,
> En ek is netnou koningin
> Van heel Suid-Afrika!

15. The Teachers League of South Africa was a 'coloured' teachers' organization, founded in 1913. The main initiators were Dr Abdurahman and Harold Cressy. See the *Educational Journal*, Cape Town, 1955.
16. See V. A. February (ed.), *White Minorities, Black Majorities*, Afrika Studiecentrum, Leiden, 1976, p. 17; see especially 'The Afrikaans Language', pp. 11–23.
17. ibid., pp. 17–18.
18. See the *Star*, 19 June 1976; also quoted in V. A. February, op. cit., p. 18.
19. ibid., p. 18.
20. ibid.
21. ibid.
22. ibid.
23. ibid.
24. *Bekvelder*: someone from the rural areas.
25. 'A Short History of the Language Question in South Africa',

Educational Journal, 28 May 1956; see also V. A. February, *From the Arsenal*, Afrika Studiecentrum, Leiden, 1983, p. 239.
26. 'Moedertaal-Onderwys: (1) Afrikanerizing Instrument', *Educational Journal*, 28 March 1956; see also V. A. February, *From the Arsenal*, p. 277.
27. ibid., p. 278.
28. ibid.
29. ibid., p. 279.
30. See M. L. Edelstein, *What Do the Coloureds Think?*, Labour & Community Consultants, Johannesburg, 1974, p. 78 (tables 24 & 25).
31. *What Do Young Africans Think?*, South African Institute of Race Relations, Johannesburg, 1972, p. 12.
32. ibid. p. 114. The word 'Bantu' is rejected by blacks. It means 'people'. Bantu pupils would therefore mean 'people pupils'; *Bantoevolk* – 'people nation', a tautological monstrosity created by architects of apartheid.
33. See Andries Treurnicht in *Die Burger*, 17 June 1976; also quoted in V. A. February (ed.), *White Minorities, Black Majorities*, Afrika Studiecentrum, Leiden, 1976 p. 21.
34. ibid.
35. *Die Burger*, 18 June 1976; see also V. A. February, op. cit., p. 21.
36. The original poem by Adam Small reads as follows:

> Bruinman hoekom kommer
> jy't jou kitaar oor jou skouer
> die strop trek nouer en nouer
> maar jy't jou kitaar oor die skouer
> bruinman hoekom kommer?

The literal translation is:

> Brownman why worry?
> Your guitar's slung o'er your shoulder
> The noose gets tighter and tighter
> But your guitar's slung o'er your shoulder
> Brownman why worry.

Bibliography

1. Achebe, Chinua (1975): *Morning Yet on Creation Day*, London, Heinemann Educational Books
2. Bastiaanse, J. (1956): 'Moedertaal-Onderwys' In: *The Educational Journal*, Cape Town, 28, 3, Sept., 1956; see also: V. A. February, *From the Arsenal*, Leiden, 1983, pp. 277–81.
3. Coulthard, G. R. (1962): *Race and Colour in Caribbean Literature*, London, Oxford University Press.

4. Edelstein, M. (1972): *What do Young Africans Think?* Johannesburg, South African Institute of Race Relations
5. Edelstein, M. (1974): *What do the Coloureds Think?* Johannesburg, Labour & Community Consultants
6. Fanon, F. (1967): *Black Skin White Masks* (translated by Charles Markmann), New York, Grove Inc. Press. originally as: *Peau Noire Masques Blancs*, Paris, 1952
7. February, V. A. (1976): *White Minorities Black Majorities*, Leiden, African Studies Centre
8. February, V. A. (1981): *Mind Your Colour*, London, Kegan Paul Int.
9. February, V. A. (1983): *From the Arsenal*, Leiden, African Studies Centre
10. Jaffe, H. (1956/57): 'A Short History of the Language Question in South Africa' In: *The Educational Journal*, Cape Town, 28, 4, Oct. '56 (1); 28, 5, Nov.–Dec., '56 (11); 28, 6, Jan–Feb. '56 (111); 29, 7, March, '57 (1V). see also: V. A. February, *From the Arsenal*, Leiden, 1983, pp. 232–277.
11. Jordan, A. C. (1957/58): 'The Language Question' In: *The Educational Journal*, Cape Town, 29, 2, Sept. '57 (1); 29, 3, Oct. '57 (11); 29, 4, Nov.–Dec. '57 (111); 29, 5, Jan.–Feb. '58 (1V). see also: V. A. February, *From the Arsenal*, Leiden, 1983, pp. 232–277.
12. Opperman, D. J. (1964): *Groot Verse Boek*, Bloemfontein/Johannesburg, Nasionale Boekhandel
13. Voorhoeve, J. & U. Lichtveld (eds.) (1975): *Creole Drum*, with English translations by Vernie A. February, New Haven, Yale University Press.

8

Trefossa – Posthumous Homage to a Creole Poet[1]

Surinamese creole literature is not widely known or easily accessible to scholars of African, Afro-Caribbean and Afro-American literature. This is partly due to Surinam's history as a Dutch colony, where Dutch customs prevailed and the Dutch language was spoken. No doubt these factors proved inhibiting to some scholars. Apart from the book by Herskovits on Surinamese culture and Richard Price's scholarly works on the Maroons, very little is known about Surinam in the Americas.

Inevitably, and understandably, information on Surinam found its way to other parts of the world via the Netherlands where several scholars were responsible for the dissemination of knowledge on Surinam. Prominent amongst these was the late J. Voorhoeve of Leiden University who did much to acquaint the Dutch and, later on, the English world with Surinamese literature and Sranan Tongo, i.e., the Surinamese tongue.

Articles by the linguist Hellinga from Amsterdam caught the eye. Surinamese contributors to the greater awareness of the Surinamese world included the linguist Hein Eersel, Ursy Lichtveld and the novelist and short-story writer and essayist, Albert Helman.

The major form of creativity in Surinam is, as in so many pre-literate societies, poetry. J. Voorhoeve and U. Lichtveld sought to introduce the Dutch reader to Surinamese texts in their *Suriname:*

And Bid Him Sing

Spiegel der Vaderlandsche Kooplieden. Een Historisch Leesboek (1958). The first comprehensive and critical anthology of Surinamese creole literature from slavery until the present day, *Creole Drum* (1975), came about as a result of the joint efforts of Voorhoeve, Lichtveld and February. *Creole Drum* gives an historical insight into the rise of creole as a language of culture.

The language itself was variously referred to in rather derisive terms as the negro's tongue, taki-taki, nengre English and, of late, Surinamese creole, Sranan (Surinamese) or Sranan Tongo (the Surinamese tongue). Serving initially as a contact language between master and slave and also between slaves with different backgrounds, the language, in a space of 250 years, developed into a lingua franca between Creole and Javanese, Hindustani and Chinese, as well as some of the Amerindians.

We learn that the earliest text in creole was published in 1718[2] and that, after the emancipation of the slaves in 1863, it remained the language of the lower-class creole. Attitudes towards creole as a language followed similar patterns in other colonies. The language was despised and children were discouraged from using it. The badge of shame which clung to French creole in the Antilles is also noticeable in Surinam. These attitudes were, of course, a reflection of the egocentric approach of the colonial overlord who looked upon *his language* and *his culture* as the *highest form of civilization*.

It was left to Papa Koenders (1886–1957) who, in his *Foetoe-boi*,[3] heralded a cultural and nationalistic revival in the forties. In his publication he staunchly and vigorously defended his language, his customs and his culture. Like George Padmore and Marcus Aurelius Garvey he, too, urged his countrymen to shed their inferiority complexes and show a pride in the black achievement. Papa Koenders, with his pithy motto, *Yu kan kibri granmama ma yu no kan tapu kosokoso*, i.e., You can hide your mother but you cannot prevent her from coughing, can be looked upon as one of the earliest cultural and nationalist leaders in Surinam. He deserves to be ranked alongside those other black writers in the 1930s and forties who sought, in word and deed, to instill black pride and a sense of history into the oppressed.

If Koenders was the spearhead of this revival then Trefossa, the poet and teacher, was the philosophical focal point. In his poems he disproved the lie that creole was only fit for the lower classes and unsuited to such higher pursuits as poetry. Born in 1916 as Frans

Trefossa – Posthumous Homage to a Creole Poet

Henri de Ziel, Trefossa, as he came to be known, was trained as a teacher, then worked as a male nurse and, finally, received training in Holland as a librarian.

The early fifties in Holland were, as is so clear from *Creole Drum*, interesting from the Surinamese point of view. The many Surinamese students in Holland – the promised land – and, in particular, in Amsterdam – the cultural metropolis – soon had incontrovertible proof that they were not so welcome. Like the West African and Antillean students in France in the thirties, they too discovered that a knowledge of the Dutch language and culture was not sufficient to qualify for the European epithet of civilized. Thus they, too, experienced the deflation of their dream. And, as with the black students in Paris, the Surinamese also came together and started their own organization, Wie Eegie Sanie (Our Own Things), recalling the efforts of students in France in the thirties with their Légitime Défense and l'Etudiant Noir.

Wie Eegie Sanie was a cultural, nationalistic movement, bent on the implementation of those very ideas so ably and vociferously propounded by Papa Koenders during the forties. While, in the words of Voorhoeve,[4] Trefossa played no active role in the organization, he certainly gave a boost to it through his poems. When creole was looked upon as a language of scorn and low cultural status, Trefossa conclusively dispelled the notion that one cannot write poetry in it by producing that beautiful poem 'Bro'. Seen against the historical and cultural setting, this was probably one of the most significant and revolutionary creative acts in Surinam.

The Surinamese would no longer suffer the illusion that creole is mere child's prattle or a slave hangover. Its reputation as a means of poetic expression was beyond dispute. And the man responsible for this cultural volte-face was Trefossa. He is practically unknown outside the geographic confines of Surinam and, sadly, remembered by only a few in Holland. His death in 1975 in Holland hardly attracted any attention among scholars of African, Afro-Caribbean and Afro-American literature.

One of the people largely responsible for the propagation of Surinamese creole literature and language in Holland, the late Prof. J. Voorhoeve, was intimately acquainted with Trefossa for many years. In 1957 Voorhoeve was responsible for a publication, called *Trotji*, in which he analysed some of Trefossa's poems, in particular 'Kopenhagen'.

And Bid Him Sing

Voorhoeve analyses the poem 'Kopenhagen' in detail and provides useful information about the Surinamese language situation in general. In 1975, with the appearance of *Creole Drum* in English, the first comprehensive anthology for a creole language and literature which covered texts from slavery until the present day, Trefossa was, naturally, assigned a proper place in the literature of Surinam. Subsequently, in 1977, the Bureau Volkslectuur in Paramaribo published a posthumous homage to Trefossa in which scholars and friends recalled the writer and the man. It was an interesting publication which, regrettably, is only accessible to readers of Dutch. The book was simply called *Trefossa*.

I would like to examine here the way in which Trefossa is revealed through this posthumous publication. It was, after all, Trefossa who indicated the vast linguistic possibilities locked within Sranan Tongo in the mid-forties. He, together with Papa Koenders, helped to dispel the 'nigger-tongue' aura which formerly surrounded the Surinamese creole language.

The posthumous homage is far more extensive than the two pages dedicated to Trefossa in *Creole Drum*. There is an introduction by the creologist J. Voorhoeve, followed by a discussion by Ronnie Klimsop, a personal friend of the poet. Towards the end, there are one or two analytical passages by Voorhoeve and the Surinamese author, Albert Helman; it is a very knowledgeable cast indeed.

Trefossa was remarkable in more than one respect. For instance, he kept a diary in a society which was largely pre-literate. This in itself might have suggested that more of the man would be revealed in *Trefossa*. Klimsop, who acknowledges an emotional and intellectual debt to the poet, does the student of Surinamese creole literature a disservice by either censoring or withholding information. One suspects that this is done to protect living descendants or out of sheer embarrassment. In Trefossa's diary of 19 January 1936 one reads: 'For especially these days, I was besieged by a strong urge to go and work in order to earn money, because I can no longer bear the poverty mother finds herself in.'[5]

One would have liked to know more about Trefossa's personal relationship with his mother, his family circumstances and the effect of this on him as a poet. Instead, the reader is presented with the biographical 'laundry list', in which one finds out how much Trefossa earned as a student nurse, a teacher, a head master. This may very well be interesting to the educated in an independent Surinam, by way of comparing salaries, but adds nothing to our understanding of Trefossa, the man and poet.

One learns further that the poet underwent a rather strict Christian education. According to Klimsop, the series of Christmas poems towards the end of Trefossa's life are directly traceable to these early Christian influences. The poet had a great admiration for his grandfather. He comes across as a withdrawn child, fond of books in a society which did not cater for such luxuries if one was black. He is a sensitive youngster and teacher who is deeply involved in his work. At times, an almost ethereal quality and lyricism is evident in his diary. He himself writes: 'I would like to be a good, well-written and beautiful book in the community which could be of use to people.'[6]

The well-known poem, 'Bro' ('Repose'), is contained in his notes of 3 January 1933. That Trefossa was an excellent personality within the Surinamese context is further illustrated by one of his ex-teachers, Mr Lauriers: 'I got to know Henny de Ziel in 1932 . . . Henny was one of my pupils (6th class). I was struck by his polish and friendliness. . . He loved making speeches . . . He was a very sensitive young man who cared a lot for honest friendship.'[7]

Trefossa worked variously as a male nurse, a librarian and a teacher. He returned to Holland for good, forced to do so by ill health and, according to Klimsop, by the moral decay and decadence in Surinam. While in Holland he was encouraged by J. Voorhoeve to work on the diaries of the bush negro prophet, Johannes King, and prepare it for publication.

Trefossa's remarks on the Surinamese language and literature are very illuminating when seen in the proper historical context. In a personal conversation with Klimsop, he maintained:

> We transplant our personal uncertainties about the Dutch language onto our pupils without realizing it. The painful thing is that we do not know or do not wish to know, that we are uncertain in our attitude towards the Dutch language. We handle the language differently from the thorough-bred Dutchman, and that, to my mind, is the most natural thing in the world. But we must be prepared to draw the consequences from all this.[8]

The poet gives a detailed and interesting account of language and culture within the sociological framework of Surinam. It is an eloquent plea for the use of their own (creole) language, although Trefossa was the last person to deny the value of Dutch as a language. In a sense, his plea was also a political one, for the question of language in a colonial or post-colonial situation is fundamental to a country trying to carve out its own cultural identity. Of Sranan Tongo he wrote:

> It is deeply immoral to neglect or kill a cultural phenomenon (a language) born out of the interchange and historical circumstances of the entire society. Under no circumstances, whatsoever, should one do so, even if it meant that one would add a few problems to our existence.[9]

Trefossa's poems can, in my opinion, generally be divided into:

1. poems of reflection, e.g. the earlier 'Bro';
2. poems of national and historic interest, e.g. 'Joli Coeur' and 'Refensi';
3. political poems, e.g. 'Nanga wan ai';
4. poems of exile, e.g. 'Kopenhagen' and 'Mi go – M'e kon';
5. poems concerning the act of creativity, e.g. 'Wan troe poewema' and 'Santa'; and, lastly, what I would like to call
6. his Christological poems, e.g. 'Hoemor in èksèlsis', 'Pin-pin Jesus' and 'Josef ori-tjar Maria'.

To Trefossa, a 'true poem was a struggle unto death'.[10] Rightly does Voorhoeve comment in his foreword that the act of creativity was literally a process of re-creation. His struggle to write in creole was also a blow against the Dutch colonial policy. This theme of a deadly struggle is reiterated in 'Santa':

> No one
> shall know my sadness
> if this unwritten scrap
> shall wait in vain
> because I did not delve deep enough
> to dip my pen
> in the black
> of my deep blood.[11]

The creative act was, in the case of Trefossa, both historical and political. He recalls the South African poet, James Matthews, for whom the creative act was even more of a political act:

> It is said
> that poets write of beauty
> of form, of flowers, of love
> but the words I write
> are of pain and rage.[12]

The Afro-American poet and dramatist, Le Roi Jones speaks of 'poems that kill'.[13]

Of the poems of exile, as I call them, the two most cited are 'Mi go M'e kon' and 'Kopenhagen'. Voorhoeve gave an extensive analysis of the latter poem in a publication, *Trotji* (1957). The central theme in 'Kopenhagen' is a mermaid and, in particular, the statue of the mermaid in the harbour of Copenhagen. The subtle way in which the poet uses the mermaid to highlight a peculiarly Surinamese cultural situation is one of the striking features of this poem. Trefossa starts off the image of the mermaid in a Western milieu and then proceeds to establish a Surinamese context. He knows the mermaid from Surinamese folklore and is surprised to find it also in Europe. After the initial shock, the poet informs his readers that the Surinamese mermaid has a golden comb on her head. The difference between the Surinamese and the Western mermaid is now crystal clear. The authentic mermaid is, after all, still in Surinam. Thus, a well-known European landmark afforded the poet a chance of delving into his own Surinamese cultural background. At the same time his loneliness and longing for home surfaces in the poem.

The second poem, 'Mi go, M'e kon', deals even more explicitly with the trauma of exile. Trefossa describes a Creole who is a product of cultural ambivalence, divided between his colonial Dutchness, on the one hand, and his Surinameseness on the other. This duality is amusingly reflected in the symbolic exploitation of the different types of food eaten by the Surinamese and the Dutch.

> Sister Mina potatoes are so nice
> But you boyo has no peer.[14]

In 'Nanga wan ai' Trefossa fulminates against the hypocrites who deceive people but enrich themselves:

And Bid Him Sing

> With one eye they look
> as if they are doing good work.
> With the other eye
> they carry on their underhanded business....[15]

He can write lyrically, as in 'Yu ay':

> Thy hair frames thy face
> so festively,
> like when the dry season is about to dawn.[16]

But he can also be threatening, as in 'Wan enkri gado-momenti':

> Woe unto me
> when I don't succeed
> to penetrate
> time's hide.[17]

Towards the end of his life Trefossa wrote a sequence of poems in which Christ and Mary feature prominently. Voorhoeve, in his foreword to the posthumous anthology of Trefossa, maintains that, in these poems, the poet had at last found the right form (presumably inner harmony and the right combination of words, symbols and imagery). Helman, the Surinamese writer, gives a very penetrating analysis of at least one of these poems, namely 'Hoemor in Eksèlsis'.[18] He shows how Trefossa resorts to the typical sonnet form of the Western European tradition. At the same time, he points out how specifically Surinamese the poem is in parts. Trefossa wrote a humorous poem. Yet, his humour is neither bitingly sarcastic nor vehemently anti-clerical, as in the case of the French Antillean négritude poets of the 1930s. It is the laughter of someone who is free from ideological restraints and arises out of what Helman calls 'freedom and self-liberation'.

Trefossa was a great poet and will one day hopefully be known to other teachers of African, Afro-Caribbean and Afro-American literature. I can find no more fitting tribute to him than the following lines from his poem 'Gronmama':

> I am not myself
> as long as my roots

Trefossa – Posthumous Homage to a Creole Poet

don't penetrate, don't shoot,
earth mother of mine
into your heart.[19]

Notes

1. First published in E. D. Jones (ed.), *African Literature Today*, no. 12, Heinemann, London, 1982, pp. 204–11.Trefossa was the pseudonym of the Creole poet Frans Henri de Ziel (1916–75).
2. See J. Voorhoeve & U. Lichtveld (eds.), *Creole Drum* (trans. V. A. February) Yale, New Haven, 1975, preface.
3. ibid., pp. 135–63.
4. *Trefossa*, Bureau Volkslectuur, Paramaribo, 1977, p. 26.
5. ibid. Original quote reads: 'Want juist dezer dagen kwam geweldige drang in me op om te werken en geld te verdienen, omdat ik niet langer kan aanzien de armoede en ellende, waarin moeder verkeert'.
6. ibid., p. 21. Original quote reads: 'Ik wil in de samenleving kunnen zijn als een goed en mooi geschreven boek, waaraan de mensen iets hebben.'
7. ibid., pp. 23–24. Original quote reads: 'Ik heb Henny de Ziel leren kennen in 1932 . . . Henny behoorde toen tot één van mijn leerlingen (6e klas). Hij viel op door zijn beschaafdheid en vriendelijkheid . . . Hij hield veel van speechen . . . Hij was een uiterst gevoelige jongeman die onnoemelijk veel gaf om "goede" vriendschap.'
8. ibid., pp. 33–4. Original quote reads:

   Onze onzekerheid m.b.t. het Nederlands brengen wij op onze leerlingen over zonder het zelf te beseffen. Het pijnlijke is dat velen van ons niet weten of niet willen weten, dat we in onze houding t.o.v. het Nederlands onzeker zijn. Wij hanteren die taal anders dan de geboren Nederlander en dat is volgens mij de meest natuurlijke zaak van de wereld, maar wij moeten bereid gevonden worden om konsekwenties hieraan te verbinden.

9. ibid., p. 37. Original quote reads:

   Het is diep immoreel om een cultuurverschijnsel (een taal) geboren uit wisselwerking en geschiedenis van de gehele gemeenschap, te verwaarlozen of te doden. Om geen enkele reden zou men dat mogen doen, dus ook niet omdat het aan onze problemen nog enkele zou toevoegen.

10. ibid., p. 45; Voorhoeve & Lichtveld, op. cit., pp. 198–9.

11. ibid., p. 46. Original poem reads:
    > No wan sma
    > sa sabi mi sari,
    > te na krin papira disi
    > sa wakti f'soso
    > foe di m' no doekroen fara nofo
    > fo foeroe mi pen
    > nanga na braka
    > foe mi dipi broedoe.

12. James Matthews & Gladys Thomas, *Cry Rage*, Raven Press, Johannesburg, 1972, p. 1.
13. See 'Blackart' in Stephen Henderson, *Understanding the New Black Poetry*, William Morrow & Co, New York, 1973.
14. See Voorhoeve & Lichtveld, op. cit., p. 105. Original poem reads:
    > -s'sa Mina, ptata bun,
    > -ma boyo fu yu kir-kiri.

15. Voorhoeve, op. cit., p. 80. Original poem reads:
    > Nanga wàn ai d'e loekoe
    > lek d'e doe den wroko boemoe,
    > nanga a trawan d'e nogosi
    > wan kron-kron nogosi
    > foe lai den botri.

16. Voorhoeve & Lichtveld, op. cit., pp. 207-8. Original poem reads:
    > Edewiwiri lontu yu fesi
    > so prisiri,
    > lek te dreyten e kon.

17. Voorhoeve & Lichtveld, op. cit., pp. 202-3. Original poem reads:
    > Elu fu mi!
    > ef mi no doro
    > fu boro
    > buba fu ten.

18. Voorhoeve, op. cit., p. 155.
19. Voorhoeve & Lichtveld, op. cit., p. 50. Original poem reads:
    > Mi a no mi
    > Solanga mi loetoe
    > n'e saka, n'e soetoe
    > mi gronmama, te na joe ati.

Bibliography

1. Matthews, J. & Thomas, G. (1972): *Cry Rage*, Johannesburg, Ravan Press.
2. Voorhoeve, J. (ed.) (1957): *Trotji, puëma fu Trefossa*, Amsterdam, Noord-Hollandse Uitgevers Maatschappij.
3. Voorhoeve, J. & Lichtveld, U. (1975): *Creole Drum*, English translations by V. A. February, New Haven, Yale.
4. Voorhoeve, J. (ed.) (1977): *Trefossa*, Paramaribo, Bureau Volkslectuur.
5. Henderson, Stephen (1973): *Understanding the New Black Poetry*, New York, William Morrow and Co.

9

Boesi Sa Tek' Mi Baka – Let the Bush Receive Me Once Again[1]

Edgar Cairo – Surinamese Writer

Edgar Cairo is one of the most prolific writers in the Netherlands. An excellent performer and reader of his own poetry, a story-teller of considerable finesse, he has succeeded, in only a few years, in becoming almost a household name in the Netherlands. Born in Surinam, the former Dutch Guyana in 1948, he showed promise even while at home. Cairo comes from the Para District, an important fact insofar as he grew up in close proximity to the old creole (slave) culture. He is therefore fully conversant with the *banya* and the *laku* (song/dance and drama), as well as the *anansi tori* (spider tales brought over from Africa and adapted to the new environment in Latin America). He also knows the *srafuten tori* (tales from slavery), *winti* (Afro – Caribbean slave religion) and the concept of *kra* (soul), as it still functions in lower creole culture in and around Paramaribo. In a sense, then, Cairo combines within himself all the characteristics of the African oral artist (his heritage), and reminds one during performances very strongly of the *imbongi* (the praise poet). Invariably he is accompanied on the drums by a fellow Creole who, like him, is as steeped in creole culture. He has written twenty-five books. The following selection of his publications will give an indication of the man's productivity:

1969 *Temekoe* (*Kopzorg* or *Headache*), a novel in Sranan Tongo (creole).
1970 *Kra* (*Soul* or *Spirit*), 'poewesie' i.e., poetry in the Surinamese creole language, Sranan Tongo.
1975 *Obja Sa Tan a Brewa!* (*There Will Never be an End to the Brewing of Magic*) – poetry with analysis.
1976 *Brokositon* (*Rubble*), an historical play of song and dance.
1976 *Famir'man – Sani oftewel Kollektieve Schuld* (*Collective Guilt*), a novel.
1977 *Adoebe-Lobi* (*Alles tegen Alles* or *All against All*).
1978 *Djari* (*Erven*, or *Life in the Backyards*), a novel.
1979 *Koewatra Djodjo* (In de Geest van Mijn Kultuur or *In the Spirit of My Culture*), a novel.
1979 *Kopzorg* (author's translation of *Temekoe* into Dutch and therefore accessible for the first time to the non-creole speaker in a European language), a novel.
1980 *Mi Boto Doro* (*Droomboot Havenloos* or *Dreamboat Rudderless*).
1980 *Ik ga Dood om Jullie Hoofd* (*I'd Die for You*), a collection of articles in Surinamese-Dutch as columnist of the well-known Dutch daily, *De Volkskrant*.
1980 *Jeje/Disi*.
1982 *Dat Vuur der Grote Drama's*.

In addition, Cairo is also responsible for one or two plays in which, for example, he exploits the *anansi* motif within the Latin American-creole context: *Ba Anansi WOI! WOI! WOI!* (1977). In addition, *Elzaro! Elzaro!* (1978), the *Doodsboodschapsvogel* (according to tradition the *jorkafowroe* – a night swallow, harbinger of death), *Foe Jowe Disi/om het oer* (1978) and work for Dutch radio in which he answers questions about Surinamese culture, language and literature and his own role as a writer and poet, give an inkling of the life this very creative Surinamese Creole artist leads. Cairo's views on language are very illuminating. He himself studied language and literature at the University of Amsterdam, of which he is a graduate.

His weekly column in *De Volkskrant* was written in Surinamese-Dutch, that is, an almost phonetic transcription (in his view) of the

Boesi Sa Tek' Mi Baka

Dutch spoken by his countrymen. In this respect, he is an iconoclast, a young Surinamese who treads in the footsteps of that Creole nationalist, Papa Koenders[2] and the doyen of Surinamese poets, Trefossa.[3]

During 1971 and 1983 I worked with the Creologist, J. Voorhoeve and the linguist, U. Lichtveld, on the first full-length creole anthology in English (published in 1975 by Yale University Press). While in Surinam, to introduce African and Caribbean literature, I was asked to look up Cairo when I returned to Holland. Cairo, of course, has the distinction of being the only novelist to date who has ever written a full-length novel in a creole language. *Creole Drum* includes an extract of this novel, *Temekoe*, in English translation.

The novel, *Temekoe*, is remarkable, full of pain, pathos and lyrically sad at times, a cri-de-coeur to understand his father. It is autobiographical. This, in itself, is an achievement for autobiographies are few and far between in creole-Surinamese culture and literature. Creoles simply don't care to wash their dirty linen in public. The Anglo-Saxon scholar may be familiar with the poetry of the Jamaican, Joan Bennett, or have heard of the Sierra Leonean, Thomas Dekker. In the Dutch Antilles some of the major novelists preferred to write in Dutch. Even the Antillean, Frank Martinus Arion, despite his black nationalism and feelings for Africa, has still written his three major novels in standard Dutch. Cairo's *Temekoe* has a psychological theme. The reader is confronted with the relationship which exists (or does not exist) between the young impressionable Edgar Cairo and his father. Cairo himself is confronted with 'negro traumas', to use his own words. In a article in a Dutch magazine (*De Tijd*, 1979), he formulates his problem in the following manner: 'You must be aware of your own culture when you land up in a strange world. It is like meeting a tiger in the forest: then you must back-pedal without falling into something.'[4]

Hugo Pos, one of the few people in Holland intimately involved with Surinamese literature and culture maintains: 'I do not know whether we fully realise how creative an artist, poet and dramatist Edgar Cairo really is. His lyrical verse-dramas based as they are on the oral-Creole culture, are completely unique in form, melody and theme.'[5]

Cairo is not loth to air his opinions on Surinamese culture and language in Dutch magazines, newspapers and periodicals. He swipes at the *bakra* (white man) and the *blakaman* (black man, mostly

Surinamese) with condescension and a conciliatory smile. Yet, at the same time, he ostensibly demeans himself, thereby playing out his *anansi* role the animal which survives the ravages of slavery because of his cunning, the lowly, the despised who outwits his superior. In an interview in the weekly *Pipel* he, himself, stated in no uncertain terms: 'I have set it as my goal to undo various colonial traumas.'[6]

For Cairo, language is not only 'a means of communication but an instrument of regulating the emotions'. He makes no secret about his love for, and devotion to, his mother tongue, Sranan Tongo. In the interview in *Pipel* he says:

> Sranan Tongo has been reviled and ridiculed to such an extent that no one wants to identify him/her self with it psychologically. One is confronted with the reality that everyone rejects Sranan Tongo.
> Then I started writing in Dutch but in a completely different manner. But as a child I was busy with Sranan Tongo. I still have a scar on my forehead from one of the teachers who 'hari mi wan baks' because I had spoken Sranan Tongo at school. That scar has remained and I think that the entire language question is tied up with colonialism and its consequences.[7]

Cairo is especially concerned about the fact that the Surinamese themselves have forgotten their language. They must now struggle with a foreign language, Dutch, which they speak and write badly – or differently. Not unnaturally, Edgar Cairo refers to himself as a 'word workman' (a literal translation of the Dutch term used by him, '*woord werkman*; see *Het Parool*).[8]

He realizes that many of his countrymen are products of 'self-deception-in-self-definition'. They are *blakabakras* – outwardly black but inwardly white. Conscious of the fact that these are colonial traumas he, therefore, hammers at his own countrymen and Dutchmen. The Surinamese, in his eyes, 'have grown up with a bakra-mouth – that is, a Dutch mouth – and, in reality, with a bakra-head also' (see *Het Parool*, 26 October 1979). If this led to forms of schizophrenia in many of his countrymen, then Edgar Cairo seems to have escaped the ravages of colonialism. In the same interview in *Het Parool* (1979) he stated: 'My family was indeed very negroid. They never told me not to be a nigger. From inside, I have had no opposition. On the contrary, I have always identified myself with my blackness. Not to get bogged down in it; but to choose clearly for my background.'⁹

This statement characterizes Cairo and his seemingly lonely fight as a Surinamese Creole in Holland against total assimilation and, eventually, total annihilation. A Dutch reporter once remarked in a newspaper that, in his fight for Sranan Tongo, Cairo could very well have culled his motto from the writings of the celebrated Dutch (Flemish) poet, Guido Gezelle, who once wrote: 'Where there is no language, there is no nation. Where there is no nation there is no land' (see *Trouw*, April 1980).¹⁰

Edgar Cairo realizes that language has often been used by the conqueror to colonize and enslave. English was the language of the colonizer in India and Africa, Dutch in Indonesia, Portuguese in Africa and Latin America. The examples are numerous and the effects equally traumatic. One could paraphrase Frantz Fanon and state that the Surinamese black man was civilized in proportion to his mastery of the Dutch language. Yet, the blacks in Surinam either spoke Dutch incorrectly or differently – or else whites and others were amazed that they spoke it so well at all. Cairo recalls a light-skinned woman – the narcissism of small differences is very much alive in Surinam – who said to him: 'My God, you speak Dutch well – for a negro' (see *De Tijd*, 6 July 1979).¹¹ The writer's virtuosity lies in his knowledge of his mother tongue, Sranan Tongo. He even writes 'deep Sranan' – understanding the sentence structure, word order, melody and thought processes of the Surinamese Dutch so well that he single-handedly created a new Surinamese-Dutch orthography and style. At the same time, he can express his thoughts beautifully in standard Dutch.

For Edgar Cairo, 'One of the faults of the Dutch and the Surinamese is that they think of a writer as good only when he writes about his own country. But for me, a writer is only good when he can enlarge and extend the small framework of his youth to embrace the universal'. Echoes of Frantz Fanon, Henny de Ziel (Trefossa) and Papa Koenders, as well as those of other black writers, are found in most of the statements of this very prolific Surinamese writer.

Cairo studied the Dutch language at university level, wrote in Sranan Tongo and campaigned relentlessly for the recognition of Sranan as the national language. In fact, he is very much preoccupied with this question of language. He, too, was brought up with the standard prejudices against his mother tongue. He realized that the

Creole's prime concern was to erase his 'negroness' in the land of the white man in Holland. Dobru (pseudonym of the late Robin Ravales which, in Sranan Tongo, means double R), poet, nationalist and, at one time, deputy Minister of Culture (1980), recalls in his autobiography, *Wan Monki Fri*, that his mother once hit him in the mouth for daring to speak Sranan Tongo.

Cairo naturally realizes that writing in Sranan Tongo imposes certain limitations upon him as a creative artist. Moreover, it means sacrificing international recognition. The Surinamese themselves have hitherto refrained from introducing Sranan Tongo as the main language of instruction. Cairo once referred to language as a 'means of separation and to shit on others'. Apart from *Temekoe* and some of his poetry, his novels are therefore written in Surinamese Dutch. This choice, in turn, also posed problems. His brand of Surinamese Dutch has been labelled by him, in comic-ironic vein, as Cairoaans and, in a sense, it is not so far off the mark. His humorous articles in the Dutch Daily, *De Volkskrant*, now published in book form under the title, *Ik ga Dood om Jullie Hoofd* (*I'd Die for You*), caused many a Surinamese and Dutchman to write to the newspaper. Many felt that he was ridiculing the Surinamese Creoles. The attitude expressed by 'coloureds' in South Africa towards the language used by the South African poet, Small, is similar to that of some Surinamese towards Cairo's literary products (see V. February, *Mind Your Colour*, Kegan Paul Int., London, 1981, p. 95).

The charge that he ridiculed his own people must have hurt Cairo who does so much for Surinamese culture and literature. In any case, he was sensitive to this charge.

The author himself justifies his prolonged stay in Holland in the following, rather unconvincing, manner:

> It is my artistic nature which keeps me here. I am afraid that I won't be able to do this if I return to Surinam. Then I'll be destroyed as an artist, not because of Surinam, but because conditions over there are so miserable. Writing is my profession . . . my life. I'd rather die than down my pen.[12]

Cairo's weapon is the pen. In Holland he lambasts the Dutch for having turned the Surinamese into pseudo-Dutchmen. On the stage, he amuses his half-literate, semi-proletarian countrymen in Holland who sublimate nostalgically when they hear him perform. For the man is an excellent performer, someone who understands the creole culture of the lower classes intimately. It is no accident that Edgar Cairo exploits the *laku* and the *banya* the way he does. Nor is it surprising that he constantly refers to *winti* (Afro-Caribbean slave religion) and the *kra* (soul). Charles Wooding, another Creole with an intimate knowledge of lower-class creole culture, has written clearly on the subject of *winti* in his thesis. *Creole Drum* (1975) stresses the importance of these phenomena in chapter two. Cairo realizes that they constitute the sinews of creole life. The importance of song in Surinamese society is stressed in *Creole Drum*: 'In Creole society songs can be tender or humorous, but they can also be used as deadly weapons ... Surinam is possibly one of the few places in the world where concerts have been repeatedly forbidden by law.'[13]

Cairo understands the essence of the 'dramatized banya and the laku' and reaches his Creole audience in a very direct manner. To the outsider, his plays may then be cumbersome at times, too full of digression and non-functional parts, as with his play, *Ba Anansi WOI! WOI! WOI!* The Creole audiences react differently and enjoy every minute of it. Recognition of aspects of their own culture elicits guffaws from the Creole.

In *Temekoe*,[14] the main character is not the son but the father. The reader is confronted with an ordinary labourer, ensnared in ordinary humdrum activities and his attempts to survive his poverty-stricken conditions. Cairo's novella does not concentrate solely on illuminating his creole existence, neither is it purely a product of social protest, in the vein of many a black writer. It is not a book about the process of growing up, initiation into adulthood, such as one finds with the Caribbean writers (see George Lamming, *In the Castle of My Skin* (1953); Michael Anthony, *The Year in San Fernando* (1976); Geoffrey Drayton, *Christopher* (1959); Samuel Selvon, *A Brighter Sun* (1952)). While it does not have the biting satire of a Naipaul, it is never truly devoid of laughter and humour. In this respect, the comi-tragic operatic portrayals of the lower class Creoles, the verbal diarrhoea characterizing the fights of the women on the back-lots of Paramaribo, come to mind. The novella has been called a 'psychological jewel' by a critic of Surinamese life.

Temekoe is not merely an attempt at social realism by a black writer, but a frenetic search by a son to understand his father – a withdrawn and complex human being. The father is the product of the *Para* world of spirits: *winti*, *wisiman* (bewitcher), *kra* (soul) and *tori's* (tales/stories). This psychological dimension saves the book from being merely 'an everyman of poverty work of art', so commonly found in the fiction of black writers. The language of his poetry and prose is sometimes reminiscent of one big, convoluted lyrical effusion of word and image. Cairo is capable of a social realism which recalls the best descriptive parts of the South African novelist, Alex La Guma (see *A Walk in the Night* (1962)). Some of the graphic descriptive parts in *Temekoe* recall the rot and decay of the Ghanaian novelist, Ayi Kwei Armah, in *The Beautyful Ones are Not Yet Born* (1968). But, Cairo stops short of the faeces world of Armah and others.

Yet, as a powerful undercurrent in *Temekoe*, there are always indications and signs of the phantasmagorical, supra-natural world of the blacks in Surinam created by, and existing in, the slave experience. The world of the *obeah* (*obja*), the *wisiman* (bewitcher), the supernatural explanations for certain occurrences, surface strongly in what, to the Western reader, may seem digressions. But, these *tori's* (tales) are decidedly functional in their socio-historical context. Cairo is the *tori-man* (story-teller) par excellence – true descendant that he is of the traditional oral artist, transported via the middle passage to Surinam.

Cairo's poetry and prose has an ideophonic quality in which the sounds and the gestures, the movements and the tabloid way of life of the non-urban black, ensconced as he/she is between *obja*, *winti*, *wisiman* and *bonoeman*, as also the semi-proletarian existence on the back-lots of Paramaribo, bare the pulsating heart of Surinam blacks with excitement and candour.

The novelist invokes everything, exploits devices such as pathetic fallacy when it so suits him, enthralls and bewitches. The Dutch critic of Surinamese literature and culture, Hugo Pos, in his inability to account for Cairo's rich and ebullient Sranan Tongo, even sees parallels with Flemish writers who are similarly praised for their rich brand of Dutch. 'Perhaps Cairo was a Fleming in a former life. That would possibly account for his juicy, rich, sometimes ebullient and extravagant, violent Cairoian language usage.'[15] Pos concludes his review: 'It was as if I had listened to a long-playing record. Cairo has bewitched me, used black magic on me.' Throughout the novel, one is forcibly reminded of that other Surinamese world existing beyond the ravages of colonialism.

Jan Voorhoeve, noted scholar of Surinamese creole culture,

observes of *Temekoe*: 'In the hands of this writer the enigma of the proud father and the lonely worker's son, slowly becomes crystal clear, more searing than any unpalatable indictment. The book ends with an insane declaration of love for his father.'[16] This extract from the *Temekoe's* ending was culled from the translation in *Creole Drum*:

> There were so many places to work in town, but there is only one where a man had worked for thirty years. Not three days. That is something to rejoice about, to praise God that He had granted you this for such a long time. That man was my father. But just dare to speak about it. 'People have nothing to do with it. I did not go and work to get publicity', Nelis answered them. He disliked being cock of the walk. 'Father, you're going to hold a big feast, aren't you'? When he heard someone saying that, he called out, 'Oh, don't shout like that' – he himself was shouting – 'Why don't you broadcast it or spread it among the gossips? There won't be any feast here. What for? You're successful today, you're successful tomorrow, the day after tomorrow you're on the street'. With this he put an end to it. Yes, yes, truly father, how I came to know you . . .
>
> See how strong he is, how weak he is, how human he is. The man who could stand for three-quarters of an hour in front of the radio with an alarm clock in his hand only to find out the right time before he goes out; the man who arrived at his work so early, allowed himself no time for pausing because when the siren goes off and the gates open up to suck in the workers, then he would have run, run, run through all the doors, all the rooms, conceal his head, his back, his body, run up all the stairs, take all the elevators, take an ambulance, a police car, put on the siren, yell, yell, pour out his heart to the whole world.[16]

It was a happy coincidence for Edgar Cairo that the Dutch Organization Novib (an organization for aid and development to Latin American and African countries) decided to start a special series of third-world authors in Dutch. The author had had many rejection slips in his box from Dutch publishers who simply did not have the courage and the foresight to publish his extraordinary novels. Novib had on its board critics who were well disposed towards Cairo; *Famir'man-sani oftewel Kollektieve Schuld (Collective*

Guilt) was his first novel to be published by a Dutch publisher. The novel had a fair reception in the Dutch press. Cairo himself stimulated interest by performing passages to Dutch and Surinamese audiences. His countrymen simply loved it and hastened to buy the novel. Not all critics were enamoured of it, however. Voorhoeve, in particular, found fault with certain aspects but he conceded that, apart from Cairo, there is no one writing in Surinam who approaches the language of the Surinam proletariat so closely. Cairo is particularly strong in his graphic descriptions, his dialogue.

Cairo confronts us with a Surinamese creole 'famiri'. For the purposes of the reader he even produces a family chart. We are introduced to them one by one. Cairo is no Galsworthy and operates firmly within the framework of his creole background. The Dutch reader is inundated with *winti*, that Surinamese Afro-American religion, in typical Cairoian style.

The other Surinamese Creole, possessed as Cairo with creole society, is Charles Wooding. He has written a thesis on *winti* (see *Winti: Een Afro-amerikaanse godsdienst*, Boom, Meppel, 1972). In his introduction, Wooding writes:

> During the period of slavery various members of tribes were brought from West Africa to Surinam for the benefit of the white masters. By far the majority consisted of Fante-Akan, Ewe-Fon and West Bantu; a relatively small section of these slaves consisted of Mandingo, Ibo and Yoruba. The majority thus came from kingdoms which in terms of religion showed great similarities.
>
> The descendants of these slaves were assimilated into the population group now known as Creoles in Surinam, and from these original religions, a new one arose, namely, 'Winti', which reveals a pattern of worship and great similarities with the original.

Richard Price, the American scholar, says of Wooding's thesis:

> The heart of the book is the extremely rich system of belief and ritual itself. It quickly becomes clear that *Winti* in its internal complexity and in the role it plays in people's daily lives, is as fully elaborated as any that is known in Afro-America. And one sees that in a strange way it has 'Institutionalized' its own

developmental history that it holds up a mirror for its adherents of their own tortuous past . . . *Winti's* uniqueness and much of its more general significance then, would lie in the degree to which it has remained isolated from the gradual westernization that has prevailed elsewhere.[17]

In *Famir'man-sani* Cairo gives literary form to Wooding's excellent theoretical exposé of *winti* – a phenomenon so essential for an understanding of Surinamese creoledom. The novel is, however, tedious at times, perhaps even difficult for those who have not been initiated into the Cairo oeuvre or the creole world. Again, one would do well to read Wooding's chapter 8 on the *Winti-pré* (1972, p. 293).

The theme of *Famir'man-sani* is the debt of an ordinary Surinamese family to the Gods and the ancestors. The novelist also refers to the collective freedom of the slaves; the slaves were freed in Surinam in 1863. The first part of the novel is concerned with the collection of money for a collective ceremonial feast, the so-called *winti-pré* (game of the Gods). This task is entrusted to Auntie Lien who now has to pay visits to all the family and collect the money. Cairo uses this to present the reader with a kaleidoscopic picture of lower class Surinamese life. Marjana the mother of the clan, is almost blind. Some of the grandchildren are half-castes from the city of Amsterdam. Marjana has a sister Dana whose son's behaviour is far from impeccable. The younger generation debate topics of a political nature, in particular, the issue of independence. All these people have different reactions to this request for money. The bigoted sister-in-law is married to a white-collar worker who refuses to get involved in such matters. They are a motley collection.

Cairo crowds his novel with information, reveals to us his Surinamese creole society in all its bigotry, prejudices, its sadness and laughter. Through his presentation of the *kra* (soul), *bonoeman* (Witch doctor) and the *Winti-Pré*, Cairo destroys the colonial picture of the Surinamese Creole as a product, sadly and only, of plantation slavery and Dutch colonialism. Rudy's return to Surinam with his *bakra* (white/Dutch) wife and his *moksi-moksi* (half-caste) daughter is used by the author to reveal the schizophrenia prevalent among Surinamese Creoles as a result of Dutch colonialism. The book has its moments of laughter. But the essential and prime movement is centred round the ceremony.

Voorhoeve comments on the ceremony that the writer is obviously very familiar with it, with the songs, the stories, the characteristics. Then he challenges Cairo in the following manner:

> There are gross mistakes in the ceremonies described, the gods, the words are in the wrong order, invoked sometimes through wrong people, the prayers are literary litanies, actions are wrongly interpreted. I do not plead for ethnological accuracy. I accept completely historical untruth, when it is functional in the story.[18]

But his most vehement attack he reserves for the eventual dénouement of the novel. He fulminates against Marjana and her trance as well as the punishments meted out:

> This is all absolute nonsense in a state where witchcraft laws have not been applied since 1920, and recently and rightly so, abolished, worse still, a writer must not introduce his reader to a family only to dispose of them in a fake trial... Is it a bad novel? Certainly. But what a fascinating failure. I have seldom come across such a realistic portrayal of a Surinamese family.[18]

Cairo was not the person to take this lying down. In a letter circulated to some close associates (among others, myself) he launched a vehement attack on Voorhoeve. Scathingly, he referred to him in sarcastic terms as *Masra Jan*, evoking images of the relationship between the master and the slave. While expressing complete understanding for the role of the critic, he railed at Voorhoeve for arrogating unto himself the role of linguist, literary critic, sociologist, psychologist, psychiatrist, anthropologist and ethnologist. This is one of Cairo's weaknesses – his extreme sensitivity to criticism. His inability to incorporate constructive criticism is reflected in the weaknesses in his books. Voorhoeve had dared to suggest that Spanjoro, the rather soft-in-the-head character, was possibly the author himself. The author strongly refuted the charge that he fobbed off his reader with punishment as a result of witchcraft. He states emphatically: 'Death through the fault of Annalien, Johanna, Marianne. The woman died through the fault of the family and consequently we have a trial and punishment.'

He spells out his criticism boldly:

Boesi Sa Tek' Mi Baka

I see that THE ESSENCE OF THE BOOK AND IN PARTICULAR THE DÉNOUEMENT has escaped him completely. The fact that the old, blind woman dies is no fake! She MUST DIE AS A SYMBOL OF THE COLONIAL PERIOD. Her physical blindness runs parallel with her historical blindness. It is certainly no accident that almost the entire book is directed towards Freedom-Giving (Liberating) Contact with the Past. The *roots of the fathers* run via this woman, whose life (look at her birthdate, ca. end of slavery) and her death (shortly before independence) embraces a whole historical period.

The book deals with guilt at various levels: money guilt (debt), religious guilt, social guilt, political guilt, individual and collective guilt . . . psychological guilt and last but not least, judicial guilt. There is also (and in great measure) the question of historical guilt. . .

The book ends with a philosophical problem: we are confronted with our colonial past. Is it our fault when we do not know how to really come to grips with it? Are we not partly responsible for that past? Can we cast off that past unscathed (unpunished)? . . .[19]

The novel was the forerunner to several others which introduced the Dutch public to various aspects of Surinamese lower-class creole life.

Cairo is at his magnificent best when he bewitches and drags his reader into the world of secret language (*kromanti*), dance and ritual. The language and the idiom falls short of the trance. He hypnotizes when he performs, is an 'anaconda' on the Dutch literary scene. The *winti-pré* reaches a climax when old Ma Marjana herself is possessed and starts dancing. Listen to the pre-colonized, creole world of Edgar Cairo and Ma Marjana who dances herself orgiastically to death:

> Hunter who finds anew the true eagle, take me on your hunt through the ancestral world. Show me the prey which is mine. To whom shall I give it? My hands are so open, my face so loose . . . wild parrots screeching . . . or are these the voices in the kankantri. Wings trembling, this I feel, a kolibri opening up dimensions for me. Before the wind, an own breath-like rhythm.
>
> I know it not. I know not what shall become of them. Take

from me, old woman, the old chains. Mourn not because I am old, but because you are forsaken.
My veins are chilled. My bones creak under my hands. Wait, before you wash me in farewell, embrace me, passionately, passionately, now that I no longer travel to there where sleep is, but travel far away, to far off places.
Weep for me! Children, weep for my insane arrogance, which propels me from on high, far, far away, into flight of death...[20]

The book ends with the rather uncalled-for explication attacked earlier by the late Jan Voorhoeve in his review. It is not ethnological or historical correctness which is at fault. Rather, it is Cairo's annoying tendency to sacrifice functionality in his prose for digression and superfluousness. *Famir'man-sani* should have ended with the words of old Ma Marjana ... 'far, far away, into flight of death'. The rest should have been silence. This tendency to overdo or miscomprehend the art of the overkill, is one of Cairo's problems as a novelist. The main character in the novel, *Adoebe-Lobi*, which, according to a reviewer in the *Eindhovens Dagblad*, means 'epileptic love',[21] is Roy Carrolls, a high-school student sitting for his final examinations. Roy, one gathers, has just been on the verge of a nervous breakdown. He is fraught with inner conflicts and uncertain about his future in a country on the eve of independence. Wherever he turns, the future seems bleak to him and his friends, in particular, John and Marlon. The only way out seems to be Holland, Blanda, the land of the colonizer. John verbalizes the fears and inner conflicts when he says: 'This land is far too small'. Roy is idealistic and full of dreams. He visits the bureau for language research where he, himself, delves into Surinamese languages. Here he meets Mrs Marjette Wedde who, with her husband, would later on become some sort of benefactress to him during his difficult times. They give him a room where he can study in peace, far away from a constricting home environment. There is just a touch of the autobiographical in this relationship for the cognoscenti, although Cairo has tried to cover it very carefully.

Roy feels himself 'a stranger in his own country', a factor spelt out very crudely for him by his own brother who accuses him of having 'white manners'. His background is typical of the Cairo genre—congested, raucous, non-private and claustrophobic. The language used by Cairo is one of decay and threatening disorder – 'a brooding stinking warmth' enveloping everything. Roy is totally alienated from his brothers and sisters. His father resents him and fails to understand that such a big boy is still studying. After all, he would be much more useful if he contributed financially to the household. Roy's burning desire is to find himself in a physical and spiritual *frimangron* – free man's land. Edgar Cairo introduces the reader to a variety of personalities and facets of Surinamese life. Mr Geitepoot (lit. goat's foot) is a typical Dutchman and a language maniac pouring himself into Surinamese languages. The Yankees are guilty of cultural and literary piracy. Roy is a ship who is rudderless and anxiously, almost sickeningly, looking for a way out. Cairo gives us vignettes of the creole-Hindustani hostilities. As a golden thread through the novel there is the magic word (land), Blanda (Holland).

Like his friend John, Roy is seeking for clarity and a way out of his miserable environment. His friend John, in posturing his ideas, comes closest to a class, rather than an ethnic, approach in spelling out his Surinamese world view. Edgar Cairo's depiction of Surinam and Paramaribo, in particular, is reminiscent of one big *konfrijari* (fancy fair).

This problem of alienation is not new. George Lamming, the Barbadian has given excellent expression to it in his autobiographical novel, *In the Castle of My Skin* (1952). Samuel Selvon from Trinidad immortalized the exiles, in all their folly, sadness and serendipitious existence in London, in his marvellously comic-ironic book, *The Lonely Londoners* (1956). The Surinamese writers can learn from their illustrious West Indian counterparts.

In an unpublished paper at the MEDU Conference on South African Art and Liberation held in Botswana in 1981, the South African novelist, Nadine Gordimer, commented very astutely on this concept of alienation:

> I am not using the concept of alienation in the purely Marxist sense, as the consequence of man's relation to the means of production, although that is highly relevant in consideration of the industrialisation of millions of blacks under apartheid conditions – a subject in itself. There are many ways in which man becomes divided from others, distanced from himself. Alienation as such is a condition of rejecting and of being rejected. The black writer lives in a society that has rejected his culture for hundreds of years. He has now turned his alienation in the face of those who rejected him, and made his false

consciousness the inevitable point of departure towards his true self-hood, to be found or re-discovered by no eyes but his own.[22]

Gordimer could have written this last sentence exclusively for the Surinamese writer, Edgar Cairo.

Cairo is a champion par excellence of the lumpen proletariat, subsisting pitifully on the back-lots of Paramaribo. The bus trip by Roy and John to Marlon's place evokes parallels with the Ghanaian "mammy-wagons" and the Sierra Leone poda-poda's. Cairo's novels are scenes within scenes against the overall backdrop of the search for an identity in pre-independent Surinam. The novel was completed in 1974, just prior to independence.

Occasionally, Cairo finds it difficult to control his pen and dips it in venom which he, in turn, directs at people clearly recognizable within the Surinamese context. It is not so difficult for someone familiar with Surinamese society to recognize the Director of Education, Mr Peersel, as Cairo's horrible attempt at punning, Probeersel (lit. 'a try with the implication of failure'), an amiable, knowledgeable and respected creole academic. Cairo will have to learn that mudslinging is no substitute for irony, let alone the comic-ironic.

The Paramaribo of Edgar Cairo is a village existing by, and because of, the various ethnic groups imported (heavy-handedly or by trickery) from Asia and Africa. One wonders whether Edgar Cairo's gossip-mongering, claustrophobic world of Paramaribo is not one of nihilism only; he is perceptive but in a long-winded manner, leading to a certain tedium at times.

Roy Carrolls receives his certificate and departs for Holland – pathetically seen off by no one. 'Who waves good-bye for me? Who from amongst the crowds raises a hand for me? Friend? Girl friend? Acquaintance? An exit which is no last exit! For I shall return, I shall perhaps, perhaps, return.'[23] And the doubt is forever in the Surinamese mind – a cynicism born out of reality perhaps? Can one blame the Surinamese, in the throes of reconstruction, for interpreting this as defeatist literature?

Edgar Cairo's invocation of Aisa – the earth mother – in an attempt to explain the departure of the Surinamese, seems to confirm his roots and, at the same time, justify his own exile.

Aisa lon wan pikini de na go

Boesi Sa Tek' Mi Baka

Mama no mandi mi ba, gi mi w'an 'o!
(Thy Eye shall not shed a tear
for the child who departs
Mother be not in discord with me
be my support!)

Cairo himself writes, 'The Hindustani is caught concentrically within his own cultural pattern, the Creole in his utmost confusion.' *Mama Aisa* (Maisa) will be much in demand among the Surinamese in Holland.

Koewatra Djodjo (*In de Geest van Mijn Kultuur*) (1979), is Edgar Cairo's fourth novel: the middle passage in reverse. This trek to Holland, the mother country, started in earnest on the eve of independence (1975). The pundits had predicted a race war in Surinam – Demerara repeated – the Hindustani against the Creoles. Apart from a few buildings which went up in smoke, they were forced to swallow their prophecies. Surinam emerged an independent country, very much like a pupa from its chrysalis, ready for its new historic task.

As in other parts of the ex-colonial world, it soon became apparent that the new masters (*blakaman*) were no better than the old, colonial overlords (*bakra*). In fact, the mistakes made by other independent countries in Africa and Latin America, were even duplicated. The poor remained poor and the new rich black became richer. It was still largely a country of the cultured few.

In the motherland (the Netherlands), critics continued their critical tirades, thus helping to create a climate conducive to dissent and rebellion. At the same time, they created a mirage image of their own country. The conditions for the mass exodus of the Surinamese to the Netherlands were there: unequal distribution of the means of production, a weak infrastructure, an over-dependence on aid and development from the Netherlands, an over-emphasis on a monoculture (bauxite), and a tenuous political alliance between the various (ethnic) groups.

Koewatra Djodjo is set in the Netherlands and deals with those Creoles who made the 'middle passage' in reverse. The main characters are Max (apparently an assimilado), his wife Airis, and the newcomer, Buddy, one of those f.o.p's (fresh off the plane) come to Holland to find happiness. Unfortunately, the book is built round rather stock stereotyped situations. One has a sneaking suspicion that

And Bid Him Sing

Cairo's extreme attitude of 'socialized ambivalence', to use the term of the American anthropologist, Herskovits, precluded him from artistically portraying his Surinamese characters as people of flesh and blood. One is reminded of the charge by the South African critic and writer, Lewis Nkosi, when he indicts another South African novelist, Richard Rive, for producing characters of cardboard rather than flesh and blood. And cardboard characters, he continues, don't spill blood.

Generally, novels by Edgar Cairo are well received in the Dutch press. *Koewatra Djodjo* apparently irritated some Dutch critics who thought that it was not an easy book to read and had too many footnotes in it. The critic of the *Leeuwaarder Courant*, Ab Visser, failed to control himself when he railed: 'Cairo, who is tremendously ambitious (based on nationalistic feelings of inferiority?) defends himself in arrogant style against what he in turn calls the arrogant manner of his countrymen, who feel he must live in Surinam if he wants to do anything for the country.'[24] He continues: 'For what is left of his books when stripped of indigenous language usage and translated? Second rate novels, thirteen to a dozen.'

Visser, of course, only revealed his own ignorance of Surinamese literature, in general, and of Cairo the writer, in particular. His colleague, Barber van de Pol, laments the fact that 'In *Koewatra Djodjo* one does not come across one really nice Dutchman.'[25] These reviews tell us more about certain Dutch critics and their inability to understand Surinamese culture – after 300 years of involvement – than about the novelist, Edgar Cairo.

Cairo's novel falls far short of the writing of the Trinidadian, Samuel Selvon, who, in comic-ironic vein, gives form and content to the world of discrimination surrounding the West Indian exile in England, a world of poverty, alienation and an irrepressible zest for life. Nowhere does *Koewatra Djodjo* approach the richness of character, the humour – that one quality which makes for sanity under oppressive circumstances – of Samuel Selvon's *The Lonely Londoners*. Max will pass into oblivion while Selvon's Moses will continue to amuse and inform – a monument cast in words for the Islanders, those exiles, who, in the 1950s, left their 'Little England' for 'Big England'. Perhaps Cairo was so intent on writing a novel about a Surinamese exile for a Dutch public that he forgot to understate and worked firmly within the framework of the statement. For an essential difference between the Dutch and the English is that the former state and the latter understate. In this, too, Cairo and Selvon are true products of their respective colonial traumas. As opposed to Cairo's: 'Something has been done to me. I can't yell it out,' there is Selvon's unforgettable ending in *The Lonely Londoners*: 'It was a summer night; laughter fell softly: it was the sort of night that if you wasn't making love to a woman you feel you was the only person in the world like that.'[26]

Cairo's novel *Djari (Erven)* (back-plots) re-introduces the reader to the proletarian conditions of the poor in Paramaribo. These back-plots are tucked away behind the main house – evoking images of the slave-plantation situation in the South of the United States and servants' quarters in apartheid South Africa. According to cognoscenti, there are about 14,000 people subsisting in such miserable conditions in Paramaribo. In *Djari* the main character is Bo who lives on such a back-plot with his wife and four children. He had bought the plot from his father-in-law but was thinking of selling it in order to buy a piece of land which he could call his own. Bo still had a loan to pay off at the bank and owed his father-in-law some money.

The author makes it quite clear that a plot is not simply a plot, that there are certain emotional and spiritual ties between the owner and his piece of land. On the other hand, Bo's ambitions are directly responsible for his ensuing misfortunes. His leg troubles him and gets worse which, in turn, is interpreted as punishment. His neighbours on both sides pester him, not shying away from using magical practices. Bo's leg deteriorates to such an extent that he is confined to his house.

He has literally no leg to stand on. At the same time Bo is adamant and refuses to give in. This collage of lower-class creole life is filled with characters and scenes which remind us of a Hieronymus Bosch painting. We see them in their fights, their follies, their sadness and their laughter – a pot-pourri of races and classes.

One character, Schoorsteen, is, according to one Dutch critic, representative of Edgar Cairo's viewpoint. Thus Vogelaar writes in *De Groene Amsterdammer* 'And at the end even Bo who has now come to his senses, seems to resemble Schoorsteen...'[27] *Djari* was generally well received in the Dutch press. Cairo is so prolific as a writer that the critic and follower of his work hardly has time to digest one work when another appears on the bookshelves. Such is the versatility of the man that he can produce poetry, complete novels of 560 pages, write plays and perform on stage in a period of time which would take other mortals a lifetime. His play *Dagrati* deals with a slave revolt in Guyana in 1763; *Djop* details the relationship between Surinamese factory workers and their white foreman, as well as the ensuing tensions. *Ba Anansi WOI! WOI! WOI!* exploits the spider theme in a Surinam context in which Anansi lives by guile, satire and amusement. In 1981, in a circular, Cairo warned readers of his forthcoming magnum opus, *Jeje Disi (Karakter's Krachten)*.

Cairo's *Jeje Disi*, a monumental work of 560 pages, was hailed by himself and his publisher as his *magnum opus*. Some months later, Cairo gave his readers another surprise by announcing that he had just completed another masterpiece, this time called *Dat Vuur der Grote Drama's*, consisting of 474 pages.

Jeje Disi requires, as I have already indicated, a lesson in patience and endurance. At the same time it also gives an insight into Cairo's occupational *hebi's*, that is, areas of concern that he, as a black author, is set on decoding. For Cairo is obsessed with *blackness, negroness*, and leaves no stone unturned, no opportunity unused, to castigate his Dutch public, to ridicule them and to confront them with their colonial past and Surinamese countrymen.

In *Jeje Disi* Janki Verwoeven is a Dutchman who is working on his thesis. In Verwoeven one immediately recognizes the late Professor Jan Voorhoeve, Creole expert and linguist, who is severely subjected to Cairo's satirical pen. Janki, one learns, is sympathetic to Creole culture and this gives Cairo an opportunity to attack certain Dutchmen – liberal culture-vultures in his eyes. The author allows Janki to fall in love with a black woman whom he seduces (rapes?), as a result of which she becomes pregnant. At an occult dance festivity Evi's mother performs an abortion on her. The symbolism is crystal clear. Instead of procreation, there can only be abortion. Janki, the misguided liberal, is rejected by Creole culture and all his attempts at conciliation are abortive.

Gerben Mann, Janki's superviser, is, possibly, the Dutch linguist Hellinga. Ronalds De Moor van Venetië (an incredibly bad and cheap pun on his (Cairo's) victim's name), is easily recognizable as the mathematics teacher and one-time Minister of Education, Ronald Venetiaan. Eddy Brumals is, obviously, Eddy Bruma, lawyer, prominent politician and one of the prime figures in the nationalistic cultural movement, Wie Eegie Sanie, in Amsterdam in the fifties.

Cairo's interpretation of the activities of Wie Eegie Sanie is questionable, to say the least. He refers cursorily to négritude, scathingly dismisses the efforts of the first Surinamese nationalist writers who, after all, paved the way for other users of Sranan Tongo (including Cairo himself). It has become almost standard practice with Cairo to refer to that doyen of Surinamese poets, Trefossa, by ridiculing him for using the sonnet form and excluding *winti* from his poems. And, all too often, this unwarranted criticism of Trefossa goes unchallenged because the audience is in awe of Cairo or ignorant about their own culture. Cairo's satirical swipes sometimes border on pettiness, not compatible with his enormous talent. He is much more natural in his portrayal of the Creole boy, Mandwe, born of Nette, who gives solace to many but who finds herself in a helpless, penniless situation. Therefore, Mandwe is left in the care of his grandparents; his grandfather is a Catholic and his grandmother an adept of the slave religion, *winti*.

The late Jan Voorhoeve, one of the recipients of Cairo's venom in *Jeje Disi*, reviewed this voluminous novel in a leading Dutch socialist weekly, *Vrij Nederland* (1981). An earlier critic had hailed *Jeje Disi* as a key novel. Voorhoeve agreed that it was a key novel only insofar as certain dramatic personalities were clearly recognizable, even down to their names.

'... All these figures are true to type but not true to fact,' Voorhoeve commented succinctly in that review. He continues; 'If I ignore for a while the irritating verbal diarrhoea of the writer, then I must admit that I have seldom read such a convincing and honest description of the Surinamese people – at least of the Creole proletariat.'[28] In his last novel (for the time being at least) entitled, *Dat Vuur der Grote Drama's* (1982), the theme is part-historical, part-sociological, with recognizable areas of concern. The problem of 'socialized ambivalence', as spelt out by Herskovits, is clearly evident in the novel. The main character, Atti Tuurhart (Arthur in reverse), is such a product of socialized ambivalence – too long in Holland, too alienated, an uncle Tom basically. People like him are not *inboorlingen* (natives) but *aanboorlingen* (those who are grafted onto – an appendage) in Cairo's terminology. They are held responsible for economic malaise: the 'minorities' – the *allochthonen*, as opposed to the *autochthonen* – who, with the collapse of the European *wirtschaftswunder*, have become an embarrassing problem.

The reader is confronted with racism, *winti*, *kromanti*, a father who rejects his negroness and everything connected with it. The white girl Anna finds herself in an Othello-Desdemona relationship with Atti.

And Bid Him Sing

One is confronted by Berbice, the Maroons in Brazil, Haiti and Toussaint L'Ouverture and Boni. There are parallel histories – the white lover who dies in the slave uprising of Berbice – and the relationship of Anna and Atti in Holland.

Cairo is at his best when he does not behave as if everything he commits to paper is in reaction to colonialism or white culture. In the words of grandma Titi, 'You see how negro things follow negro's tail' – like a tapeworm whose body can be removed but whose head will soon grow another. This is the inevitable cycle within which the Surinamese black finds himself in the Netherlands. This is the extent of his alienation.

Cairo is also very prolific as a poet. He is one of those black writers who ignores accepted 'Western aesthetics' and creates his own. It is very difficult to draw a definite line between what, for him, constitutes poetry and what is prose. In this, too, he is a true descendant of his African oral past. Cairo's poetry is less known than his prose, although no less important in his entire oeuvre.

One of his early and interesting anthologies is called *Obja Sa Tan a Brewa* (There will Never be an End to the Brewing of Magic). Cairo leaves nothing to chance. In a note on *Obja*, he writes: 'Obja: magic object, derived from obeyer? To obey. The reality poses increasingly new problems for mankind. How shall he solve them? Shall he tackle the almost insoluble problems by invoking magical powers? This reality and the things flowing from them are his obja. He himself is, and remains, a medicine man, who magically transforms life into a completely modern style, reshapes reality . . .' Quite obviously, Cairo sees himself as a cultural, historico-literary *obja* man, magically transforming 'creole life' into a completely modern style, reshaping its reality.

Cairo cannot help posing as the teacher who acts as the conscience of his people. In his foreword and introduction he expounds his ideas on Surinamese literature, in no uncertain terms. And to crown it all, he has added some very thought-provoking theses. Despite all these efforts, however, one can only fully appreciate his poetry by listening to the man reciting, performing and singing. *His* is 'performance poetry' par excellence, which means that his poetry is difficult to commit to memory. Cairo is no Surinamese Shrinivasi, whose poetry is characterized by a beauty and simplicity of language which lingers on long after the poet has ceased his recital. The following simple, yet penetrating, lines of Shrinivasi come to mind:

Boesi Sa Tek' Mi Baka

> I am not there
> to disturb the equilibrium
> but to take that
> which is most beautiful
> in you
> and bring it to perfection.[29]

The poetry of that raconteur, nationalist and *imbongi* (praise poet), Dobru, leaves behind a similar impression. Of Dobru's celebrated poem, 'Wan Bon' ('One Tree'),[30] Edward Kamu Braithwaite wrote: 'Yet one of his finest poems accepted with tumultuous applause during the festival was 'Wan Bon' (One Tree) written in Surinamese.' Other beautiful examples can be culled from the works of the following Surinamese poets: Trefossa, Michael Slory and Johanna Schouten Elsenhout.

Cairo's poetry, instead, needs annotation, translation – even for the Surinamese – and an understanding of *his* Surinamese world. It is therefore not surprising that his anthology, *Obja Sa Tan a Brewa* needs a section called analysis 1. close reading; 2. conclusion and interpretation. All this does not help to make his poetry easily accessible to the ordinary (semi-literate) Surinamese public (let alone the Dutch reader!).

The author scathingly attacks literary critics who dare to say that they find it difficult to analyse his poems, for he operates from the simple maxim – if they're understandable to Cairo, then they are understandable to all and sundry.

Obja ... is a complicated lesson in Surinamese culture for the uninitiated, obscure for the literate and alive only when performed by the poet himself. Perhaps the following simple attempt at translation of a Cairo poem will do more justice to this anthology and to the poet than any detailed analysis of the poems.

Let This be Known unto Men

(*originally Kondre Sa Jere*)[31]

> You called me so insistently
> voice which did not linger

And Bid Him Sing

> Land hidden in my breath
> and from afar you sighed
> bringing my conscience to rebellion.
>
> Word upon word
> whirl-winded into a tropical storm
> in me
>
> How heavily you sighed
> How your whisper flew
> past the place
> to which I dragged myself
> – a moment's rest at least.
>
> My heart flies away
> but my blood
> is still battling.
> Indict me not
> Be not embittered
> Mother of mine.

'Mother' in this context is 'earth mother' – Aisa-Maisa for the Surinamese in exile.

Kra, meaning Soul, Spirit (in mundane terms, that which makes the Surinamese tick), a slim volume of poetry, was published in Surinam in 1970. Cairo's poem in which he spells out (or tries to) his search for identity under alienated circumstances is important for understanding the man as a whole:

> What am I
> Who am I
> What is happening to me
> Soon
> I shall be a god
> I shall be a devil
> even.
> Oh!
> Life passed me by
> death passed me by
> help me

Boesi Sa Tek' Mi Baka

>Oh! help me!
>I begin
>I end
>I become word.³²

The end of this poem is very important. Cairo himself has invented the word 'word workman'. The written word is important for him. Symbolically, one is reminded of St John's 'the word becomes flesh'; 'In the beginning was the word and the word (for the Surinamese Creole at least), 'was of Edgar Cairo.' This is his weapon, his *obja* in his struggle to restructure the history of his people, the Creoles. In his *Powema Di Rutu* (Amsterdam, 1982), his songs of Origin and Future, Cairo states: 'My poetry is a poem which finds its roots in black loins from within which I re-write the movements between people.'

In *Powema Di Rutu* we are confronted with a commentary on black culture, on colonialism, on revolution and on slavery. This is poetry with a message, interspersed with song and dance, myth and a humour which evokes both tears and laughter. It is a biting satire on historical events. Cairo, dressed up in tails on stage, acting out his role as a masra on a plantation, recalls Antonio Machado's depiction of Spain as 'dressed up in carnival mummery'. For 'the operative image of Cairo's Surinamese-Dutch world in *Powema Di Rutu* is 'carnival mummery'. It is poetry in drama form performed on stage.

Cairo is one of the most talented and prolific Surinamese authors in the Netherlands. His descriptive abilities are sometimes unparalleled. He exploits the novel as if black writing made the transition from the oral story to the written form with ease. He writes plays, pours out his heart in poetry, performs his literary products on stage, together with other Creoles, as if finally succumbing to some *winti* ritual on a slave plantation. In a sense he is an *anansi* incarnate – now castigating whites, now pouring scorn on his fellow blacks, educating, correcting, cajoling, playing the obsequious negro – but always with one aim in mind – to wipe out the 'negro traumas'.

He overplays his hand in the process, seems consumed by 'negro-white' *hebi's*. He produces novels which could do with a good editor who would prune it to manageable, readable proportions. In this respect his publisher serves him badly.

In 1983 Cairo made a trip to Africa, Nigeria in particular, which he then immortalized in an article in a Dutch weekly, *De Tijd*, as 'A negro in Negroland'. It was not a very flattering account for the

And Bid Him Sing

Nigerians. Cairo seemed to have fallen into the same trap as the illustrious author, Richard Wright, decades earlier. The latter was forced to conclude, after a trip to Ghana, that they were black and he was black but they did not understand one another. Hopefully, Cairo's orphic descent won't cause him to lose his Eurydice on the borderland of light and darkness. I can find no more fitting tribute for his writing than the following lament in Sranan Tongo which he, himself, once invoked in a newspaper article after the upheavals in Surinam:

> Boesi Sa Tek' mi Baka
> Boesi Sa Tek' mi Baka
> Boesi Sa Tek' mi Baka
> Boesi Sa Tek' mi Baka, ef'
> a kondre dis' no poer'
> en lelekoe! Boesi Sa Tek' mi Baka.[33]

Notes

1. First published in V. A. February & H. Wekker (eds), 'Essays in Memory of Jan Voorhoeve', *OSO*, vol. 3, no. 1, 1984, pp. 39–56. (This is a slightly revised version of the original.)
2. Papa Koenders – Julius Gustaaf Arnout Koenders, 1886–1957. Opposed the Dutch colonial policy, fought for the recognition of Sranan Tongo as a language. See his magazine *Foetoe-boi* (1946–56).
3. Trefossa (pseudonym of Frans Henri de Ziel), 1916–75. Pioneer Surinamese poet (see *Creole Drum*, 1975; see also V. A. February in *African Literature Today*, vol. 12, London, 1982, pp. 204–11.
4. 'Edgar Cairo en de Surinaamse Cultuur', interview with Corine Spoor, *De Tijd*, 6 July 1979, p. 21. Original quote reads: 'Je moet je bewust zijn van je eigen cultuur wanneer je in een vreemde wereld terecht komt. Het is net zo als wanneer je een tijger tegenkomt in het bos, dan moet je achteruit op je schreden kunnen terugkeren zonder dat je ergens in valt.'
5. 'De jonge literatuur van Suriname', Hugo Pos, *De Tijd*, 6 July 1979, p. 26.
6. 'Edgar Cairo – 'kolonial trauma's ongedaan maken', interview with Alfons Levens, *Pipel*, Paramaribo, 7 September 1979. Original quote reads: 'Wat ik tot taak heb gesteld is om allerlei koloniale trauma's ongedaan te maken.'
7. ibid. Original quote reads:

Boesi Sa Tek' Mi Baka

Sranan Tongo is zo belaagd en belast dat niemand zich psychisch ermee wil identificeren. Je komt voor het gegeven feit te staan dat iedereen Sranan Tongo afzweert. Toen ben ik Nederlands gaan schrijven, maar dan op een andere manier. Maar als kind heb ik me met Sranan Tongo bezig gehouden. Ik heb nog een litteken op mijn voorhoofd van een schoolmeester, *die hari mi wan baks*, omdat ik Sranan Tongo op school gesproken had. Dat litteken is gebleven en ik denk dat de hele taalkwestie te maken heeft met het kolonialisme en de gevolgen daarvan.

8. 'Ik ben 'n woord werkman', interview with Catherina van Houts, *Het Parool*, 26 October 1979.
9. Original quote reads: 'Mijn familie was inderdaad zeer negroïde. Ze hebben me nooit gezegd: je mag geen neger zijn. Van binnenuit heb ik nooit tegenwerking gehad. Ik heb me ook altijd met het zwart zijn geïdentificeerd. Niet om daarin te blijven plakken, maar om duidelijk stelling te kiezen voor m'n achtergrond'.
10. 'Taalgevecht van Edgar Cairo', Riet Diemer, *Trouw*, April 1980, p. 4. Original quote reads: 'Waar geen taal is, is geen volk. Waar geen volk is, is geen land'.
11. 'Edgar Cairo en de Surinaamse Cultuur', interview with Corine Spoor, *De Tijd*, 6 July 1979, p. 21. Original quote reads: 'Mijn God, wat spreek jij goed Nederlands . . . voor een neger'.
12. ibid. Original quote reads:

    Het is mijn artisticiteit die me hier houdt. Ik ben bang dat wanneer ik in Suriname ga zitten, ik dit niet meer kan. Dan ga ik artistiek kapot, niet omdat Suriname me kapot zou maken maar omdat omstandigheden daar zo beroerd zijn. Schrijven is mijn beroep . . . mijn leven. Ik ga nog liever dood dan dat ik mijn pen neerleg.

13. J. Voorhoeve and U. Lichtveld (eds.), Yale University Press, New Haven, 1975, p. 15.
14. Of this novel Cairo observed in *Het Parool* (26 October 1979): 'Temekoe heb ik geschreven toen ik achtien was. Het is een vreselijk eerlijk boek, helemaal autobiografisch . . . Die relatie met mijn vader is helemaal echt, ik als buiksluiter.'
    'I wrote *Temekoe* when I was eighteen years of age. It is a terribly honest book, completely autobiographical . . . The relationship with my father is very real, with me as the belly-closer (literally the last child).' (trans.)
15. 'Sappige taal' Hugo Pos, *Het Parool*, 26 October 1979. Original quote reads: 'Misschien is Cairo in een vorig leven een Vlaming geweest. Dat zou een verklaring zijn voor zijn rijk, sappig, soms overdadig en baldadig Cairoaans gebruik.'
16. See *Suriname Nummer*, Bzzlltth, The Hague, November 1976; see also: *Creole Drum* (1975), pp. 270–71.

And Bid Him Sing

17. See *American Anthropologist*, vol. 75, 1973, p. 1885.
18. See *Suriname nummer* van Bzzlltttn, The Hague, November 1976. Original quote reads:

    Er zitten grove fouten in de Beschreven ceremoniën, de goden worden in onjuiste volgorde opgeroepen via soms onjuiste liederen, de gebeden zijn literaire litaniën, handelingen zijn verkeerd geïnterpreteerd, etc. Ik pleit niet voor ethnologische juistheid. Ik accepteer ten volle historische onwaarheid, wanneer die maar functioneel is in het verhaal.

    [further]: Dit alles is niet alleen baarlijke nonsens in een staat waarin de afgoderijwetten sinds 1920 niet meer worden toegepast, en recentelijk zijn afgeschaft, erger is dat een schrijver lezers niet in kennis mag brengen met een familie om hen dan met een fake rechtbankverslag tevreden te stellen... Is het dus een slechte roman? Zeker. Maar wat een boeiende mislukking. Ik heb zelden zo'n levensecht portret van een Surinaamse familie gelezen.

19. 'Master Jan', said Cairo, 'does not know how to read well.' Original quote reads:

    Ik zie dat de essentie van het boek en vooral van de ontknoping zijn geheel aan hem voorbijgegaan. Want dat die oude, vrijwel blinde vrouw sterft is geen fake! Zij moet als symbool van een kolonialistische periode sterven. Haar fysieke blindheid loopt parallel met haar historische blindheid. Het is vooral niet voor niets dat vrijwel het hele boek is gericht op vrede-gevend (= bevrijdend) kontakt met het verleden. De *wortels van de vaderen* lopen via deze vrouw, wier leven (bekijk haar geboortejaar ± einde slavernij) en haar sterftejaar (vlak voór onafhankelijkheid) een gehele geschiedenisperiode omvat.

    Het boek behandelt schuld op verschillende nivo's: geldelijke schuld, religieuze schuld, maatschappelijke schuld, politieke schuld, individuele en kollektieve schuld, al of niet 'psychologisch', en niet te vergeten, de justitiële schuld. Er is ook (en in hoge mate) sprake van een historische schuld.

    Het boek eindigt met de filosofische vraagstelling: wij zijn belast met ons (koloniale) verleden. Is het onze schuld wanneer wij dat goed verwerken? Zijn wij zelf mede schuldig aan dat verleden? Kunnen wij ongeschonden (ongestraft) dat verleden van ons afwerpen, gewild of ongewild ermee breken?...

20. *Famir'man-Sani*, Wereldvenster, Baarn, 1975 pp. 184–5.
21. 'De vernieuwing in de Surinaamse literatuur', Archie Sumpter, *Eindhovens Dagblad*, 9 March 1978, p. 13.
22. 'Relevance and Commitment: Apprentices of Freedom'.
23. Original quote reads: 'Wie zwaait fo mij? Wie vanuit de menigte een opgestoken hand? Vriend? Vriendin? Kennis? Een uitgeleide die geen uitvaart is! Want ik kom terug, ik kom misschien, misschien, terug.'

24. 'Het apostolaat van Edgar Cairo', Ab Visser, *Leeuwaarder Courant*, 9 February 1980.
25. 'Een arrogante bakra' Barber van de Pol, *NRC* 1980.
26. Alan Wingate, London, 1956.
27. 'Het Stijve been van tegelzetter Bo', J. F. Vogelaar, *Groene Amsterdammer*, 28 March 1979, p. 23.
28. 'Jeje Disi: een sleutelroman ontsleuteld. De van Deysseliaanse toorn van Edgar Cairo', Jan Voorhoeve, *Vrij Nederland*, 25 September 1981.
29. Shrinivasi: (pseudonym of Martinus Harridat Lutchman), *Oog in Oog*, N. V. Drukkerij Eldorado, Paramaribo, 1974.
30. Robin Ravales wrote under the pseudonym, Dobru, meaning double R in Sranan Tongo; see *Flowers Must not Grow Today*, 'afi-kofi', Paramaribo, 1973, p. 7. Dobru's demise in 1983 was a great loss to the Surinamese literary and cultural world.
31. Original poem reads:

>Kondre sa jere...
>joe kar' mi sote
>sten di no wakti
>kondre di kibri
>in mi bro
>
>farawe joe seme
>èn koefta mi konsensi
>wortoe tap' wortoe
>in mi
>
>fa joe soktoe no ke
>fa joè froistri
>no fré psa na presi
>pe mi srepi
>mi srefi
>go sranga didon
>
>mi ati lowe
>ma mi broedoe et feti
>no kroetoe mi
>no mandi mi, mama.

32. Bureau Volkslektuur, Paramaribo, 1970, p. 7. Original poem reads:

>san a mi
>soema a mi
>san e ps'anga mi
>sitosito
>m'e trongado
>m'e tron didibri
>srefi
>ke
>m'e psa libi

And Bid Him Sing

> dede m'e pasa
> jep mi
> jep mioooii
> m'e bigin
> m'e kaba
> m'e tron wortoe

33. See *De Volkskrant*, 28 June 1980, p. 11. Translation reads:
> Let the Bush receive me once again
> Let the Bush receive me once again
> Let the Bush receive me once again
> Let the Bush receive me once again if this country is not freed from its evils and burdens. Let the Bush receive me once again.

Bibliography

n = novel; p = poetry; d = drama; s-t = Sranan Tongo; s-d = Surinamese-Dutch

Cairo, Edgar, (1969): *Temekoe* (s-t), Buro Volkslectuur, Paramaribo.
—— (1970): *Kra* (p. s-t), Buro Volkslectuur, Paramaribo.
—— (1975): *Obja Sa Tan a Brewa!* (p. s-t), E. Cairo, Amsterdam.
—— (1975): *Famir'man-sani oftewel Kollektieve Schuld* (n. s-d), Novib, Baarn, Wereldvenster, The Hague.
—— (1976): *Brokositon*, historical song and danceplay, E. Cairo, Amsterdam.
—— (1977): *Adoebe-Lobi* (n. s-d), In de Knipscheer, Amsterdam.
—— (1978): *Ba Anansi WOI! WOI! WOI!* (s.d.), Rotterdamse Kunststichting, Rotterdam.
—— (1978): *Foe Jowe Disi* (p. s-t), E. Cairo, Amsterdam.
—— (1978): *Neti Nanga Joe!* (d. s.-t), E. Cairo, Amsterdam.
—— (1978): *Djari* (n. s-d), In de Knipscheer, Amsterdam.
—— (1978): *Elzaro! Elzaro* (d), E. Cairo, Amsterdam.
—— (1978): *Masra* (a play for radio), E. Cairo, Amsterdam.
—— (1978): *Masra Kodokoe* (p. stories), E. Cairo, Amsterdam.
—— (1979): *Kopzorg* (Dutch trans. of *Temekoe*), In de Knipscheer, Amsterdam.
—— (1979): *Koewatra Djodjo* (n. s-d), In de Knipscheer, Amsterdam.
—— (1979): *Djop* (d), E. Cairo, Amsterdam.
—— (1980): *A Nowto Foe Mi Ai* (p), In de Knipscheer, Amsterdam.
—— (1980): *Dagrati, Dagrati* (d), E. Cairo, Amsterdam.

—— (1980): *Jeje Disi* (n. s-d), In de Knipscheer, Amsterdam.
—— (1980): *Ik ga Dood om Jullie Hoofd* (columns from the Dutch daily, *De Volkskrant*, In de Knipscheer, Amsterdam.
—— (1982): *Dat vuur der Grote Drama's* (n), In de Knipscheer, Amsterdam.
—— (1984): *Lelu! Lelu!* In de Knipscheer, Amsterdam.

10

From the Green Antilles

Frank Martinus Arion

Frank Martinus Arion was born in 1936 on the island of Curaçao where he attended high school until 1955. In 1957 he graduated from a Gymnasium in The Hague, the Netherlands. In that same year Martinus Arion served notice to the Dutch public and his fellow countrymen, in an anthology of his poems, *Stemmen uit Afrika* (*Voices from Africa*), that he would be a force to be reckoned with in the future. Between 1958–1965 he was enrolled as a student of Dutch literature at the University of Leiden which he left just before graduation. He returned to the Dutch Antilles and started a magazine, *Ruku*, in which Dutch cultural imperialism was a major target. In 1971 he returned to the Netherlands to complete his studies. Between 1971–5 he was attached to the teaching staff of Amsterdam University as a member of the Dutch department. His first novel, *Dubbelspel* was published in 1973, followed by *Afscheid van de Koningin* in 1975 and *Nobele Wilden* in 1979. These novels were all published by a reputable Dutch publisher, De Bezige Bij, in Amsterdam.

The Dutch Antilles is still, to this day, a part of the Netherlands, despite some form of self-government. The struggle for independence remains a difficult issue. Cola Debrot, the distinguished administrator and writer, commented:

And Bid Him Sing

The Netherlands Antilles are composed of two groups: the Leeward islands, lying near Venezuelan Coast, Aruba, Bonaire and Curaçao, and situated 580 miles to the north of them, the Windward islands, St Maarten, Saba and St Eustatius. The population originated from a mixture of Europeans and Africans, though on Aruba and Bonaire features of autochtons from the pre-Columbian period, the Arawaks, are in many cases clearly recognizable. On the Leeward islands the populations make use of Spanish and Papiamento... while on the Windward islands only English is spoken and written.[1]

The Leeward islands are generally referred to as the ABC group, i.e., Aruba, Bonaire and Curaçao, while the Windward islands are called the SSS group (St Maarten, St Eustatius and Saba).

In an unpublished paper the Antillean, Jorge Labadie Solano, commented on the use of Papiamento as follows: 'Papiamento is a creole language spoken by some 250,000 people, the majority of whom live on the Leeward islands of Aruba, Bonaire and Curaçao...'[2]

Cola Debrot commented on the literary situation as follows:

> We are faced with the complicated situation of having a folk literature that is expressed in two languages (Papiamento on the Leeward islands and English on the Windward islands), and a written literature that makes use of three languages, Spanish, Dutch and Papiamento.[3]

The survey which follows, brief though it may be, nevertheless gives an indication of the type of literature produced and the complicated situation referred to by Debrot.

Willem E. Kroon (1886–1949) wrote *Giambo Bieuw ta Bolbe na Wea* (*Old Love Does not Die*) in Papiamento. Nicolás Piña (1921–67) wrote in Dutch, Spanish and Papiamento, expressing a preference for the latter. He founded Papiamento periodicals on Curaçao and Aruba. A major writer in the Antilles was Cola Debrot (1902–83) whose first novel in 1935, *Mijn Zuster de Negerin* (*My Sister the Negress*), dealt with the search for roots and racial and ethnic relationships. In the Netherlands Tip Marugg (b. 1923) attracted attention with his novel, *Weekendpilgrimage* (1957) while Boelie van Leeuwen (b. 1922) enriched the Dutch literary scene with his novels,

From the Green Antilles

De Rots der Struikeling (*The Stumbling Rock* 1959), *Een Vreemde op Aarde* (*Stranger on Earth*, 1962) and *De Eerste Adam* (The First Adam, 1966). In these books the theme of death is prominent and existentialist overtones are visible.

This question of ethnic roots is also found in Guillermo Rosario's *E rais ku no ke muri* (*The Root Won't Die*, 1969). Of importance is also Edward de Jongh's *E dia di mas histórico* (1969–70), written in Papiamento and covering the riots of 1969. Diana Lebacs published her novel *Sherry* in 1971. Here too the question of race and socialized ambivalence is evident. René de Rooij, although of Surinamese origin, enriched Antillean drama with his *Juancho Picaflor* (1954), published in Papiamento. Jules de Palm attracted attention with his short stories.

Major figures in poetry were Pierre Lauffer (b. 1920) and Elis Juliana (b. 1927). Juliana is remembered for his typical depictions of the islanders. Cola Debrot considered Juliana 'a remarkable amalgamation of Spanish passion, Dutch intimacy and African humour or, could we say, of Spanish romanticism, Dutch realism and African popularization'.[4] He also observed that 'Pierre Lauffer's poetry owes its attractiveness to its exceptional sonority and variety of rhythm.'[5]

From the 1970s onward Frank Martinus Arion was to play a major role. All the critics in Holland agree that the Antillean poet, columnist and novelist is an excellent story-teller. Without exception they acknowledge that Curaçao has a very gifted novelist on its shores. And, ironically, despite the fact that he is from the colonies, they all embrace him as a Dutch writer. This is a fundamental departure from the general trend that a black writer, writing in the language of the colonial overlord, is welcomed because he is black and not because he is a writer. Frank Martinus Arion is, however, definitely regarded as a welcome addition to the Dutch literary scene.

Martinus Arion has thus succeeded in avoiding some of the pitfalls. Most reviewers of his work in the Netherlands do not fling the charge of exoticism in his face. He is not faulted for his usage of Dutch. Neither is he crucified for turning the Dutch language into something else, as happens in the case of the Surinamese writer, Edgar Cairo. And he has certainly not been mangled by Dutch critics, such as often happens when the former colonized write in the language of the colonizer.

His first novel, *Dubbelspel* was very well received. The title has the implication of a double game, double play, doubles (as in sport), with the suggestion of deception. It also means *changā*, that is, the domino has a number which can be placed at both ends of the game. For the novel is ostensibly about a game of dominoes played on the island of Curaçao by various players.

No one who has ever had the pleasure of meeting Frank Martinus Arion will even doubt that he is a very honest, sincere and committed writer, his umbilical cord stretching right into the very depths of Africa. It is, therefore, not so surprising to learn that, when Martinus Arion was awarded a prestigious Dutch literary prize (well-known recipients have included Simon Vestdijk and Gerard Reve) for *Dubbelspel*, he donated the money to two anti-apartheid organizations in the Netherlands.

His deep social concern with the fate of the African dispossessed in South Africa is expressed in a poem dedicated to the black miners killed at Carletonville in Johannesburg. The poem was called 'War against Gems'. I cite parts of it to show the extent to which Martinus Arion feels committed to the freedom cause in South Africa:

War against Gems[6]

Let's wage war against nobles and cigarettes
Let's wage war on nobles
Let's wage war on precious stones...
which work oppression on the country
which press human flesh underfoot

and under the ground
Let's wage war on their produce

Let's wage war on Olympic gold
And on wedding and engagement rings
Daughter of God wears no diamonds
out of South Africa
Daughter of God wears no gold

Remember before you write man –
Writing isn't indispensable

and writing with the wrong pen
just like writing with the wrong hand
can cost you your soul.

The main characters in *Dubbelspel* are Manchi Sanantonio, his wife, Solema, Juanchi Pau, Boeboe Fiel and his wife, Nora, and Chamon Nicholas who hails from Saba. The reader is confronted with deceptions at various levels. The male characters are involved in a game of dominoes. They are paired off, Manchi and Boeboe against Nicholas and Juanchi. But, there is also a double deception – one not so visible to the naked eye. Nicholas deceives his opponent, Boeboe, by sleeping with his wife Nora; and Juanchi deceives his opponent Manchi by sleeping with his wife Solema. We are witnesses to cuckoldry at various levels. A doubles game, double deception and *changā* – a double marked on the domino which can now be added to both sides. The entire novel is full of these double layers of double morality. The dominoes game provides the setting whereby Curaçao society will be unfolded to the reader.

The main characters are introduced one by one. We are treated to beautiful, humane, amusing and detailed descriptions of the various actors. Martinus Arion has an eye for detail. Manchi Sanantonio is a bailiff aspiring to be a judge and feverishly hoping to be admitted to the Lodge on the island. He has had a beautiful house built and desires a weekend retreat at West Point. To crown it all, he is the envy of all the men for being married to an educated (in Europe) coloured woman who plays the piano at home and the organ in church. These are quite impressive achievements for a black man on the island. Unfortunately, for Manchi, his wife loses her moral and intellectual ascendancy over him when she sleeps with a young lawyer. He can now only re-establish his position of power by forcing her to hand over to him a five-guilder note every week, as a sign that she is merely a cheap whore.

Manchi, the cuckolded husband, has another unique manner of sublimating his anger and feelings of revenge by telling his fellow domino players a dramatically faked story in which the actors in this drama are not Manchi and his wife, Solema, but a judge, his colleague and the judge's wife.

Of *Dubbelspel* the Dutch critic, J. F. Vogelaar, wrote in *Groene Amsterdammer*: 'The novel takes place one Sunday afternoon ... Each move is, as it were, a chain in the social conflict. It is seldom that one finds in Dutch literature a social novel written with such expertise and so much fantasy.'[7]

Martinus Arion describes his main characters with precision. In the first few pages of the novel he manages to give a very realistic portrayal of Manchi and Solema and, through them, of some of the social concerns in the novel. It is a caste society. The whites live in villages characteristically called Princess Village and Queens Village. Through Manchi we are afforded a peep into local politics (the Democratic Party and the People's National Party). The narcissism of small differences is also to be found here, that quality which I have described in my book, *Mind Your Colour*, as the peculiar ability of the dispossessed expertly to detect shades of dark and light not so visible to the outsider. Thus, Juanchi Pau is described as follows: 'And Juanchi Pau! He had some respect for the man, and moreover, he was also light of colour . . .'

Manchi is full of unfulfilled dreams and desires. His wife is 'a beautiful woman, who time and again caused the men of Wakota to describe her in lyrical terms . . .

'She has a slender waist and a flat stomach.

'. . . She had straight hair, Solema, which she however had cut short and deliberately turned into very many little curls to the annoyance of Manchi.'

Solema is certainly a departure from the stereotyped portrayal one generally finds of black women in most novels. She has a mind of her own and decidedly socialist ideas about developments on the island. Solema, the educated woman, and Juanchi Pau, the idealist, destined to become lovers, are the nearest to politically committed and ideologically orientated characters in the book.

Juanchi Pau is the loner who failed to complete his house after the death of his mother, who defecates in the bush and has a sparsely furnished house '. . . planks on the floor . . . a single bed of a fragile iron frame, a chair, a table and a two-flame kerosene stove and a drum in which he kept his drinking water which he fetched from a neighbouring well'.

Then there is Boeboe Fiel, the taxi-driver, who is about to become chairman of the taxi drivers' union. Boeboe Fiel, the black man, is as strong as an ox and secretly feared by Nicholas who is having an affair with his wife, Nora. Of Boeboe Fiel, Martinus Arion said in an interview in the *Haagse Post*:

I have come to love Boeboe Fiel. Objectively, he is a disgusting man, because he destroys himself. But I love him. Because, through him, I can show what I look upon as the positive side of misery. The way he handles the work. The ability to be philosophical about unimportant things. It's a flight, but it is creative, expressive.[8]

In that same interview Martinus Arion continued: 'And, yet, the discovery that he really finds life wonderful. The way the man drives across the island, completely relaxed, away from home, from misery, the skirt-chaser.'

Boeboe spends an evening with a whore, Micha, which turns into an orgy. He has already gambled away all his money which was intended for Nora who wants to buy shoes for their son at a top school on the island. It is almost as if Martinus Arion wanted to apologize for his seeming indulgence in erotic passages and the stereotyped portrayal of women when he said:

Here is an intrinsic cruelty which is terrible. The whore in the Campo, Micha, it is naturally an orgy in that house. But the woman can also be terribly natural and a woman. Then, you are up against the prejudice of the system. A normal woman is a nice whore. No. A whore is a woman who practises prostitution.[9]

Another attempt by the novelist to expose the double morality of his society?

Nora, Boeboe's wife, is larger than life. She slaves, pinches and is part of the long-suffering breed in deprived societies who, to quote the South African poet, Dennis Brutus, 'endures and endures'. She will not hesitate to sleep with a man (in this case, painfully for Boeboe, with Nicholas, one of his domino partners).

Dubbelspel is about life and death, love and hatred. But it is also about a colonial society, or the products of Dutch colonialism in the Antilles. In fact, the novel is structured in such a way that the Dutch critic of literature, Kees Fens, found fault with it for the following reasons. He thought that the novel was too contrived, too much under the direction of the author. Actions were too explicit and explanations far too many. Martinus Arion, in the view of Kees Fens, 'leaves little to chance'.[10] The critic continued: 'Against the risk that things have no meaning, he has taken an insurance, by giving a meaning to everything. Purposely and explicitly so.'

The novel is divided into three parts: the Sunday morning, the mid-afternoon and the evening, during which the dénouement will take place. Boeboe Fiel and Manchi Sanantonio, against all expectations, are trounced by Nicholas and Juanchi Pau. Boeboe is killed by Nicholas and, after the island-wide humiliation at the domino board, Manchi commits suicide when his wife leaves him for Juanchi.

The Antillean, Jos de Roo, has some interesting comments on the novel. Of Solema he observes that she is in favour of a society with a cooperative socialist basis because its origin is traceable to Africa. In her eyes this ideology is, 'of the existing ideologies, the one best suited to our people (who do like their personal freedom) but still do not think so individualistically . . . like the whites . . . After all, we find democracy and the cooperative organisational pattern in Africa and, formerly among the slaves . . . It is therefore also something of ourselves.'[11]

Jos de Roo also says of Solema and of Juanchi: 'The two characters who propagate political ideas which the story-teller also adheres to, look to Africa . . . we coloureds are in the majority, says Juanchi. The others have money, but we are in the majority. No matter which way you turn. We actually ought to have all the power in our hands.'

Dubbelspel is an intriguing social novel by a very gifted and interesting story-teller. Although situated in a black community, the novel has escaped the fate of many novels written by blacks, which are discarded as not being literature.

After Frank Martinus Arion's very successful debut with *Dubbelspel*, expectations were naturally high among students and critics of literature in the Netherlands when his second novel, *Afscheid van de Koningin* (*Farewell to the Queen*, 1975) was published. The novel was neatly divided into several chapters with headings which left the reader in no doubt about the tone and content of the book. These were: De Dans om Hout (The Dance for Timber); The Battle of Africa; The Battle of Holland; The Battle of South Africa; De Strijd om Orchideeën (The Struggle for Orchids).

The message was also spelt out in no uncertain terms in two epigraphs on the front title pages. The one in French was culled from *Jeune Afrique* and read: 'Whites love the black continent because it provides them with a life which they can only dream of at home.' The

From the Green Antilles

second interesting excerpt is from a poem by the doyen of Afrikaans poets, Totius – one of the totem poles of the Afrikaners in South Africa – and stressed the historical bond between Holland and South Africa:

> a Fine mystic unified bond
> binds the House of Orange, the Netherlands
> and Africa . . .

It is no accident that *Afscheid van de Koningin* is dedicated to 'women with courage', for they feature large in this second novel. In the compass of a title page and chapter headings the author succeeded in presenting a wide spectrum of motifs and issues.

The novel is political and anti-imperialist in tone. Multi-nationals, Shell, the timber industry, the SIAEE(CIA), the FBAI aid and development, apartheid – all these evils in our modern Western world are seriously taken to task. Sometimes, the author makes no attempt to disguise the names of some of the protagonists and antagonists in this evil game. Not surprisingly, the Dutch critic Reinjan Mulder wrote:

> When at the end the beautiful white South African crawls into bed with the leftist Antillean negro journalist, then they are not lying there for their pleasure – that is done by corrupt C.I.A. agents, but the entire Third World and Shell, Queen Juliana and Fidel Castro, Jan van Riebeeck and Angela Davis, are lying under the blankets. The bed too has become political.[12]

The novel unfolds through the eyes of the Antillean journalist, Sesa Lopes, the narrator of the book. In a flashback, at the very beginning, we are introduced to one of the main characters, President Wawili, who rules over an ostensibly mythical country in Africa, surrounded by very recognizable African states. Wawili, at a later stage, goes the way of all flesh in Songo in a coup d'etat aimed at correcting the situation prevailing in the state. Sesa Lopes is present at the gala ball given by Wawili in honour of the Dutch Queen who is on a state visit to Songo. Lopes removes, methodically and painstakingly, the scales from the reader's eyes. One of his first illusions which crashes occurs when he sees the Dutch Queen waltzing in the arms of the corrupt Wawili. There are constant references to his boyhood years in the Antilles. Lopes reveals a pattern of physical and mental oppression in the Antilles, finding expression in an anecdote that, when the Protestant Queen visited the islands, the Catholics were allowed to eat meat on a Friday. It was then that his mother decided to leave the Catholic Church for good. The Catholic Fathers, in particular, are heavily criticized in the novel. We are not only confronted with a process of removing the layers, but also with deception at various levels.

The reaction of the Dutch critics was varied. One referred to the 'white peril' and continued: 'He says bitter, very bitter things about whites and saddles us with a guilt complex till the third and fourth generation.'[13] The critic was, however, forced to concede that Martinus Arion was no less merciless towards the 'abuses' in Africa, in his portrayal of those big, fat black men who took over from big, fat white men and continued their oppressive practices. In rather tongue-in-cheek fashion the eminent Kees Fens[14] saw, in the novel, the average Auntie Nel also throwing her weight behind aid and development. Hugo Pos, generally a very perceptive observer of such literature, took Martinus Arion to task in the following manner: 'Frank Martinus Arion reveals himself in 'Afscheid van de Koningin' as a writer who is embroiled in a private war against a variety of institutions, for example, multi-nationals, aid and development agencies, against foreign offices etc.'[15]

For Hugo Pos the major theme in the novel is assimilation which, in his mind, is rammed down the throats of the readers with all sorts of false arguments. The writer, Gerrit Komrij, conceded the political nature of the novel, yet did not think this harmful or a detraction from the intrinsic qualities of the book:

> It is, naturally, a political novel about the grandeur and misery of Africa, about discrimination with statements such as 'racism is not a disease but a means of earning a living' and 'tolerance is a commodity which, like any other commodity, exacts its price'. And, once more, Arion knows that he is writing a novel and not a pamphlet. With the techniques of a novelist he succeeds in making his verbosity palatable.[16]

The obvious and striking feature of *Afscheid van de Koningin* is then, its political nature. Max Beloff has already pointed out that 'politics is an aspect of human relations and like other aspects of the subject (e.g. love-making) is better suited to the novel than the treatise'.[17]

Frederick Karl's observations on the political novel are also very pertinent in this respect: 'The political novel at its best . . . requires an imaginative projection in which characters are trapped, almost smothered, by the forces that remain inexplicable and subterranean.'[18] Yet, one is not aware in *Afscheid van de Koningin* that the novelist's 'social matrix will stifle his created character, this individual who is caught up in the system, and despite his efforts to the contrary, . . . is doomed to walk the night'.[19] This is partly due to the technique used in the novel. The story unfolds in a series of observations on Africa and aboard a plane en route to Paris. Sesa Lopes interviews his major characters, in particular, the Dutch woman, Mrs Prior, in a mammoth session on board the plane. Or, he discourses with others, for example, the Afro-American Professor Dadson, the young girl, Gadisha, from Mali and the blonde South African, Naomi Jobert.

The first encounter, entitled The Dance for Timber, is full of information. We realize that we are witnesses to a series of ritual dances at various levels. The Timber Dance is the Ritual Dance of Exploitation and Capitalism. Africa is stripped to the bone and this stripping process is done very methodically and systematically. The forests disappear as the timber is shipped to Europe to swell the coffers of French and Dutch companies. In between there are constant scenes within scenes, flashbacks to the Antilles and the role of the Catholic Fathers who tried their utmost to get Maria to oust Marx – that is, if the latter was ever given a chance to enter into the Antillean consciousness by the Dutch. This is a picture of psychological and historical enslavement of the Antillean by the Dutch, tempered with a neat sense of humour.

The second chapter, the Battle of Africa, starts with Sesa's meeting with the young and innocent Gadisha, barely fourteen years old. She is one of the child-like victims of Africa whose only manner of survival is prostitution. She is the Innocent personifying the brutal and irresponsible rape of Africa. Sesa refuses to sleep with Gadisha, withstanding her every attempt at seduction and, instead, emerges as the moral victor. For, as she fell asleep in his bed, with her 'warm backside against his thigh', he could console himself with the following thought: 'I could in any event say of myself, that I'd done well to walk away from the farewell ball Wawili had given for the Queen. They were accomplices. Not me.'[20]

Sesa Lopes is, however, not the disinterested, comic-ironic spec-

And Bid Him Sing

tator found in the two novels of the Ghanaian, Ayi Kwei Armah, namely, *The Beautyful Ones are not yet Born* (1968) and *Fragments* (1970). Lopes saves people with missionary zeal and Gadisha is his first convert. He simply persuades her, through his arguments and his refusal to abuse her, to return and continue her education. Gadisha, as we learn later, does better than this and becomes a guerrilla fighter in the struggle to rid Africa of its evils. In between one is constantly aware of the ritual dances being enacted in silence – the ritual dance between Lopes, the Antillean, and Africa – ancestral home of the 'middle passage man'. After all, he, Lopes, had finally never attempted to avenge his 'parents who were sold'.

The Battle of Holland is a mixture of fact and fantasy, with references to contemporaries, recognizable down to their first and second names. Once more, the narrator is busy peeling off the layers. This time the ritual dance is between Lopes and the Afro-American Professor Dadson who worked in West Africa. Dadson is the voice of conciliation, of assimilation, who waxes lyrical when he discovers that Lopes is from Amsterdam. Dadson had spent a part of his honeymoon in that marvellous city and pours superlatives on the Dutch. Systematically, clinically, his image of the Dutch is torn to shreds by Lopes. The tolerance of the Dutch becomes 'a commodity which like any other commodity exacts its price'. The myth of the clean 'cottages of Holland', where no 'spots of dust' can be seen 'even with a microscope', is annihilated and Dadson is confronted with 'dogshit' which made life a nightmare in Amsterdam. The demolition job is complete. The Battle of South Africa is about to begin.

The narrator is now confronted with his greatest proselytising attempt. The victim is the beautiful, blonde and sensuous South African girl, Naomi Jobert, who turns out to be a Dutch-born girl raised in South Africa. They move towards each other, cautiously, and their confrontation finds its consummation on Sesa's bed in Amsterdam. In the throes of sexual excitement Naomi Jobert, the South African girl, is made to shout: "I think I am going crazy Sesa!" she calls out, as I cause my millions of white children of silent pleasure to sail into her inner waters to become black children if she so desired.'

At the risk of being facetious, one is inclined to recall a passage in Frantz Fanon's, *Black Skin White Masks* by way of comment on this wonderful solution to the black-white problem: 'Some thirty years ago, a coal-black Negro, in a Paris bed with a "maddening" blonde, shouted at the moment of orgasm, "Hurrah for Schoelcher!" (it was Schoelcher who persuaded the Third Reich to adopt the decree to abolish slavery).'[21]

This chapter on South Africa, more than any other, brooks comparison with other books in respect of one phenomenon, at least – the relationship that exists, or is about to exist, when a black man and a white woman are brought together. In this respect, Martinus Arion has followed the general stereotyped pattern. Sesa's relationship with the blonde Jobert girl is typical of that which ensues when black men and white women are thrust in one another's arms. It becomes a 'kind of subjective consecration to wiping out in himself and in his own mind the colour prejudice from which he has suffered so long'.[22] As I have already observed in my work on stereotypes in South African literature: the white women are 'all pre-Raphaelites, walking straight out of the paintings of Millais, paeans of beauty, golden-haired tributes to white aestheticism'.[23] Martinus Arion's Naomi Jobert is now allowed to swell the ranks of other white heroines in fiction. Here is another proof of 'the sexual myth – the quest for white flesh perpetuated by alienated psyches'.[24] One would hate to think that the author, in the person of Sesa Lopes, shared the sentiments expressed by the Nigerian dramatist, Wole Soyinka, when the latter commented on the South African writer, Richard Rive's play, *Make Like Slaves* (1976) in unflattering terms: 'We are left to feel that, given a more sensitive white woman or a less abrasive (guilt-ridden) coloured man ... a small part of the battle would be won.'[25]

The Struggle for the Orchids brings us to the strong Dutch character in the novel, Mrs Prior. She boards the plane at Songo, during the coup, and is interviewed by Sesa, watched by Naomi, for a mammoth stretch of six hours until the plane lands in France. It is an intriguing tale and she emerges as a formidable lady of conscience who identifies herself with the struggle of the oppressed.

Mrs Prior is a principled woman whose life style and empathetic treatment of the Africans is in stark contrast to that of her daughter and son-in-law in Songo. They are typical expatriates, depicted by Martinus Arion in a very realistic manner. Mrs Prior goes against the grain and lands up in a hotel. From here she ventures into the interior and with typical business acumen – her Dutch background benefits her after all – she motivates the local inhabitants to collect the beautiful orchids which grow wild in the country, pays them well for it and then exports them to Holland. This earns her the title of Orchid

Queen. Her venture causes the inhabitants to flock to her, but it also works against the interests of the timber industry and she is, therefore, denied an export licence. But Mrs Prior is a lady of tremendous ingenuity and enterprise and it comes as no surprise to find her involved in the activities of the Food & Agricultural Organization. One gathers that this staunch Dutch lady possibly had an affair with one of the lieutenants who eventually became involved in the coup against Wawili. And, in the final dénouement, it turns out that Mrs Prior actually planted the bomb that killed President Wawili.

The novel revolves around strong women. In the first novel, *Dubbelspel*, there was Solema, the educated socialist with decidedly progressive and ideological ideas – largely absent among the men in the novel. As opposed to the educated Solema there was Nora, the personification of the proletarian 'earth mother', prepared to sell her body in order to ensure the education of her son. She represents the plight of so many women in third-world countries. Ostensibly the symbol of denigration and desecration in poor societies, she is, at the same time, a tower of strength (see Naipaul, Lamming, Selvon, Mphahlele).

Similarly, in *Afscheid van de Koningin*, the major characters are women. First, there is Gadisha, about to be crushed in Lolita-like fashion in her efforts to survive. But (and through the help of the Antillean journalist, Sesa Lopes) she rises above her situation to become a guerrilla fighter with a political cause. Gadisha symbolizes the possibilities open to youth – the rise from rot and decay. The freedom struggle offers such a noble way out.

Despite my very serious reservations about the way in which Martinus Arion handles the political section on South Africa one could state of the white girl, Jobert, that she is allowed to undergo an orphic descent in which she, unlike Eurydice, is not tempted to look back. At a more generous level one would credit her with the destruction of the 'disease of the skin', although the stereotyped fashion in which it takes place is a source of wonderment. Mrs Prior emerges as the strong person who gives of herself totally and selflessly. She is the antithesis of the multi-nationals. She symbolizes the Europe that has infinite possibilities of giving, rather than exploitation, if only the terms are spelt out by third-world countries rather than the multi-nationals. Martinus Arion refers to this courage of women in his book when Lopes is made to say:

From the Green Antilles

The most frightening thing about women with courage, or those who suddenly pluck up courage, is that they can also become reckless. Rückzichlos, yes! Their courage is namely primitive. It is impressive, awe-inspiring, frightening! Beautiful and dangerous like the pest... That servility and fear with which they live because of us men, falls away.

The author has a tendency not only to be long-winded but, also, to indulge in lengthy intellectual discussions. He has an insatiable urge to describe everything in detail. This makes his writing boring. The chapter entitled The Battle of South Africa suffers heavily from his didacticism and overwhelming desire to proselytize. The far too hasty ideological and sexual conversion of the South African girl is a glaring illustration of this defect.

Overall, it is an intriguing social and political novel which causes one to reflect on a variety of issues of fundamental importance. *Afscheid van de Koningin* is an imaginative contribution to the far too slender corpus of political novels in a country – in this case, the Netherlands – which was once the major colonial power in the world.

The main characters in Frank Martinus Arion's monumental novel, *Nobele Wilden* (1975), are three people who met each other on the barricades in Paris during the student uprisings in the late sixties. Instead of using the technique of interviews, the novelist now resorts to unfolding the first part of his novel through a series of letters which the main characters write to each other, eight years after the revolt.

One of the characters is Ursula, the daughter of a rich Swiss banker, who, ironically, has just inherited a banana plantation on Martinique, one of the places which looms large in the novel. The other central figure is Julien Bizet Constant, now elevated to the improbable status of assistant Bishop of Lourdes. The third person is Mabille, also from Martinique, and of Hindustani parentage. She is obsessed with the idea of raising money for guerrilla warfare on Martinique in order to sever all colonial ties with the mother country France.

All the critics agree (or seem to agree) that the novelist Martinus Arion is making a bold plea for the 'power of the creative imagination'[26] as opposed to the arrogance of Western society. That the novel is set in France is possibly responsible for the suspicion that the Cartesian philosophy, as embodied in the well-known maxim, 'cogito ergo sum', is not totally absent. This may well be so despite the author's attack on arrogance and the nationalism of the European. Similarly, his reference to Western civilization as *sifilisatie*, i.e., syphilization, looks remarkably like a borrowing from the Afro-American poet, Jon Eckles, who talks of 'Western syphilization'[27] in one of his poems.

The first part of the novel is called the power of the imagination. Julien, the man from Martinique, is studying to be a priest in France. His dream is interrupted when riots break out in Guadeloupe and the student revolt in Paris becomes a reality. These events turn him into an activist. Julien, one learns, has had affairs with both Ursula and Mabille. Once more, Martinus Arion confronts his readers with attempts at proselytization at various levels. Julien is disdainful of the arrogance of the whites and contemptuous, especially, of the arrogance in the hierarchically structured Catholic Church. In a sense, then, the book is also an attack on the Catholic Church as it operated in colonial territories. In this respect, Martinus Arion's numerous critical references to the Catholic Fathers in *Afscheid van de Koningin* are recalled.

Ursula, the rich banker's girl from Switzerland, is a bundle of contradictions with an aversion to everything aspired to by those with her money and background. She wants neither husband, child, family nor money. The Ursulas of this world can afford the luxury of rejection, having been born into an affluent society. Mabille, the Hindustani girl from Martinique, appears to be a classic case of someone who, initially, does not understand local culture. She is ignorant and scornful of black culture in Martinique until her lover, Julien, turns her into a convert and a revolutionary. This conversion of Mabille recalls that of Gadisha in *Afscheid van de Koningin*. Ursula, on the other hand, is not unlike Naomi Jobert; she also came from a society of privilege and sacrificed herself in order to be free. When the revolt in Martinique is suppressed in 1976 Julien Bizet Constant, after first giving up his studies for the priesthood, returns to his homeland; this act is interpreted by Mabille as one of treachery.

Julien, of course, embodies the traumas of the exile who, pulverized into helplessness in the colonial metropolis, decides to return. The South African novelist, Es'kia Mphahlele, finding himself in a similar predicament, explained in cogent terms his decision to return to his tortured and oppressive land:

We lived nine years in west, east and central Africa, two years in France, and nine years in the United States. For five years out of the nine that we have lived in the United States, my wife and I felt that we were irrelevant outside Africa. To whom was I teaching black literatures in the United States – people genuinely interested in Africa or merely students wanting to pick up an exotic grade? Should I not be where black literatures are organized and taught as a functional and organic part of African development and located, therefore, where there is a living cultural forum for them – on its own native soil? Shouldn't I be spending the rest of my life contributing to this development of the African consciousness?[28]

Julien is an exceptional human being, well versed in many languages, a man whom Mabille could admire 'as long as she could see him as the person who in the presence of thousands of Frenchmen could stand up and cause everyone to shut up, as she put it, to listen to a black Martiniquan'. She is only giving expression to that which is also greatly admired in Africa and other parts of the impoverished and colonized world. The 'man who knows book' and 'has mouth' is greatly esteemed. One need only recall the Nigerian novelist, Chinua Achebe's portrayal of the politician and populist, Nanga, in his novel, *A Man of the People* (1966) to fully understand this phenomenon.

In an interview with the columnist, Archie Sumter, however, Martinus Arion made it quite clear that he had written more than a novel about blacks, although he readily conceded that there were certain elements which were specifically black. In this respect he singled out the special brand of humour in his novel. He stated that 'unlike his two previous novels, *Dubbelspel* (1973) and *Afscheid van de Koningin* (1975), this novel, *Nobele Wilden* could 'also have been written by a white man who had lived in a developing country for some years'.[29]

The Dutch critic, Barber van de Pol, was far from lenient in her discussion of *Nobele Wilden*. Her observations about some of the major characters make interesting reading. Of Ursula she writes: 'Ursula is best described as a groupie from the period of the student revolt. She is bored when there is no action, moans to no end if confronted with obstacles, but crumbles when Julien leaves her – because of white arrogance – a theme in this novel.'[30] This same critic found Mabille someone who is 'fanatic and desperate and that is scary', while the male protagonist, Julien, is 'the person around whom everything revolves and especially when it comes to the female sex'. Van de Pol and others are not enamoured of Martinus Arion's preoccupations, that is, the imagination as opposed to what he considers the 'foul-reeking rationalism of the European'. From these critics one gathers that the alternative offered by Martinus Arion is Christian Marxism.

The second part of the book centres round Lourdes, Bernadette and the Virgin Mary. Martinus Arion's empathy for Bernadette is clear and he uses the setting to philosophize and hold forth on a variety of issues, crucial to him as a novelist and human being. Bernadette was for him 'the symbol of the poor with imagination'. His imaginary focus is very wide indeed. There is Father Maure who suffers from cancer of the throat and is engaged in a biography on Bernadette, in addition to his struggle with death. Then the reader is confronted with Cardenal 11, a tragic troubadour who loves the Virgin Mary. From him we learn that, linguistically, the Catharen (Cathars) are related to the word heretic, i.e., *ketter*, and that they were medieval Christians.

His treatise on language and the patois dialect of that part of France is a tour de force which can only be fully appreciated against the author's own cultural background, his involvement with Papiamento in the Antilles and the question of creolization. The language question is, of course, of paramount importance to the colonized, often coerced into writing and expressing himself in the language of the colonizer. Yet, the very language sometimes used by the colonized writer is tainted with colonialism and the malpractices of the colonist. Both the Nigerian Chinua Achebe and the Indian Narayan have indicated that they used English in their books to suit and express their respective African and Indian experiences. Thus, the colonizer's language has undergone, within the former colonized world, transmutations in order to give full expression to the total man or woman in the colonized world. The Indian writer R. K. Narayan puts it as follows:

> English has proved that if a language has flexibility, any experience can be communicated through it . . . We are not attempting to write Anglo-Saxon English. The English language through sheer resilience and mobility is now undergoing a process of Indianization.[31]

From the Green Antilles

In areas where a creole language is widely used as a means of communication and even literary expression, as in the Dutch Antilles and Surinam, the language question is vital in the forging of an identity. Fundamental issues such as colonialism, racism, religion, de-colonization and cultural imperialism are evident in this novel, *Nobele Wilden*. Martinus Arion sees the Caribbean and the Latin American continent as an extension of the Antillean world. Once more, the book is remarkable for its detailed descriptions. The constant attempts at proselytization jar, however. Ironically, despite his efforts to project the power of the imagination as a force, one is painfully conscious of a rational trait in the author – a quality he finds so disturbing in the European. One is left with a sneaking suspicion of the 'armies of the benighted marching to their destiny with catchwords on their lips'. One senses that the critics would have wished Frank Martinus Arion to have reversed the Cartesian 'Cogito ergo sum' into a more pliable 'Sum ergo cogito' without falling prey to the charge of exoticism. But then Frank Martinus Arion had already warned his readers in his poem 'War against Gems':

> Remember before you write man
> Writing isn't indispensable
> and writing with the wrong pen
> just like writing with the wrong hand
> can cost you your soul.[32]

Notes

1. *Literature of the Netherlands Antilles*, Drukkerij 'De Curaçaose Courant' for the Ministry of Culture and Education of the government of the Netherlands Antilles Curaçao, 1964, p. 3.
2. 'A Brief Survey on Proposals on Papiamento Orthography and Some Examples of Mixed Strategies in Papiamento Orthography as Applied by Various Dutch Antillean Authors', unpublished paper, Leiden, 1984.
3. op. cit., p. 7.
4. ibid., p. 13.
5. ibid.
6. 'Oorlog aan Edelstenen', *Gedicht*, vol. 1, no. 2, pp 3–6, April 1974. transl. by Charles McGheehan.
7. Vogelaar, 'Een Roman over de Antillen: een Dubbelspelletje Domino', *Groene Amsterdammer*, 21 November 1973.
8. 'Schrijver Frank Martinus Arion', interview with John Jansen van Galen, *Haagse Post*, 29 June 1974.

And Bid Him Sing

9. ibid.
10. 'Roman over een Spelletje Domino op Curaçao, *Volkskrant*, 25 August 1973.
11. Jos de Roo, Dubbelspel in *Kristal*, 111-1, Drukkerij Montero, Curaçao, February 1976.
12. 'De Goede Mens van Arion', *NRC Cult. Supp.*, 17 October 1975.
13. Ab Visser, 'Het Blanke Gevaar', *Leeuwaarder Courant*, 17 April 1976.
14. 'Tante Nel gaat in Ontwikkelingshulp', *Volkskrant*, 25 October 1975.
15. 'De Privé Oorlog van Arion', *Het Parool*, 1 November 1975.
16. 'Revolutionairen en Ouders van nu op Stap", *V. N. Boekenbijlage*, 22 November 1975.
17. V. A. February, *Mind Your Colour*, Kegan Paul Int., London, 1981, p. 142.
18. ibid.
19. ibid.
20. F. Martinus Arion, *Afscheid van de Koningin*, de Bezige Bij, Amsterdam, 1975, p. 60.
21. Trans. Charles Lam Markmann, Grove Press, New York, 1980; originally published as *Peau Noire Masques Blancs*, Paris, 1952, p. 63.
22. V. A. February, op. cit., p. 125.
23. ibid.
24. ibid., p. 150.
25. ibid., p. 162.
26. See Alan Hall, 'The African Novels of Joyce Cary', *Standpunte*, vol. XII, no. 2, March/April 1958, pp. 40-55.
27. See V. A. February, 'The Soweto I Love' (review), *African Literature Today*, no. 10, Heinemann, London, 1979, p. 257.
28. 'The Tyranny of Place', *African Writers Association*, vol. 1, no 3, 1982.
29. 'Verbeelding Centrale Thema in Arion's Nieuwste Roman', *Nieuwsblad van het Zuiden*, 1 December 1979.
30. 'Het Zwarte Gezicht van de Madonna', *NRC*, 23 October 1979.
31. See P. Egejuru, *Black Writers: White Audience*, Exposition Press, New York, 1978, p. 92.
32. 'Oorlog aan Edelstenen'; see above note 6.

Reviews

Novel: DUBBELSPEL De Bezige Bij, Amsterdam, 1973.

Reviewer	Magazine/Newspaper	Date	Title
1. K. Smith	Amigoe di Curaçao	14/7/73	Meesterlijke roman van Frank Martinus Arion over de hartstochten rond domino spel

From the Green Antilles

2.	J. van Doorne	Trouw	28/7/73	Curaçao... vernietigd paradijs
3.	Hugo Pos	Het Parool	11/8/73	'Dubbelspel': vol vitaliteit
4.	Sitniakowski	De Telegraaf	18/8/73	Domino gevaarlijk spel in briljante Nederlandse roman
5.	Kees Fens	De Volkskrant	25/8/73	Roman over een spelletje domino op Curaçao
6.	Hans Jonkers	Eindhovens Dagblad	18/9/73	Niet zo maar een spelletje domino
7.	J. F. Vogelaar	De Groene Amsterdammer	21/11/73	Een spelletje domino
8.	John Jansen	Haagse Post	29/6/74	'Ik wil de domme burger bereiken maar niet met een dom boek'
9.	Jos de Roo	Kristal 111	1/2/76	Dubbelspel: dubbel politiek

Novel: AFSCHEID VAN DE KONINGIN (Amsterdam, De Bezige Bij, 1975).

Reviewer	Magazine/Newspaper	Date	Title
Jan Verstappen	Amigoe di Curaçao	4/10/75	'Afscheid van de Koningin'. Frank Martinus Arion
Reinjan Mulder	NRC. Cult. Supplement	17/10/75	De goede mens van Arion
Kees Fens	De Volkskrant	25/10/75	Tante Nel gaat in ontwikkelingshulp
Hugo Pos	Het Parool	1/11/75	De privé oorlog van Arion
Gerrit Komrij	VN Boeken-Bijlage	22/11/75	Revolutionairen en ouders van nu op stap
Ab Visser	De Leeuwaarder Courant	17/4/76	Roman van Frank Martinus Arion. Het blanke gevaar

Novel: NOBELE WILDEN.

Reviewer	Magazine/Newspaper	Date	Title
Barber van de Pol	NRC	23/10/79	Het zwarte gezicht van de Madonna

And Bid Him Sing

Jos de Roo	*Trouw*	7/11/79	Frank Martinus Arions 'Nobele Wilden'. Een provocatie van blanke cultuur
Aad Nuis	*Haagse Post*	10/11/79	De bananentheorie van een nobele wilde
Hugo Pos	*Het Parool*	11/11/79	Arion zet aan het denken
Henk van Dam	*Amersfoortse Courant/Veluws Dagblad*	17/11/79	Frank Martinus Arion analyseert in boek 'Nobele wilden' het wonder van Lourdes
Archie Sumter	*Nieuwsblad van het Zuiden*	1/12/79	Verbeelding centrale thema in Arion's nieuwste roman

Bibliography

Debrot, Cola (1935): *Mijn zuster de negerin* (Rotterdam, Nijgh & van Ditmar). Originally published in two parts in: *Forum*, jrg. 3, 1934, pp. 1171-1187; again: Meulenhoff, 1955[2] and De Bezige Bij 1961[3]. Translated into English as *My Sister the Negro* (1958) and into French as *Ma Soeur noire* (1965)
Jongh, E. A. de (1953): *Guillermo*: novella (Curaçao)
Juliana, Elis (1956): *Flor di Datu*. Poësias (Willemstad, Drukkerij Scherpenheuvel)
—— (1961): *Flor di Anglo*. Poësa Y Sketch (Curaçao, Drukkerij Scherpenheuvel)
Kroon, W. E. (1956[2]): *Geambo bieuw ta bolbi na wea*. Novela intima Curazolena (Curaçao, Scherpenheuvel)
Lauffer, P. A. (1947): *Patria*. Poems in Papiamento
—— (1963): *Kantika pa Bjentu* (anthology in Papiamento) (Oranjestad, De Wit)
Lebacs, D. (1971): *Sherry* ('s-Gravenhage, Leopold)
Leeuwen, B. van (1959): *De rots der struikeling* (Amsterdam, P. N. van Kampen & Zoon)
—— (1963): *Een vreemdeling op aarde* (Amsterdam, P.N. van Kampen & Zoon)
—— (1966): *De eerste Adam* (Amsterdam, P. N. van Kampen & Zoon)
Marugg, Tip (1966[2]): *Weekend Pilgrimage* (Amsterdam, De Bezige Bij).

Martinus Arion, F. (1957): *Stemmen uit Afrika* (poems). *Antilliaanse Cahiers*, jrg. 3, no. Nov. 1957, 56 pp.
—— (1974): *Oorlog aan edelstenen* In: Journal for poetry under editorship of Remco Campert, 1e jrg. no. 2, April, 1974.
—— (1973): *Dubbelspel* (Amsterdam, De Bezige Bij)
—— (1975): *Afscheid van de koningin* (Amsterdam, De Bezige Bij)
—— (1979): *Nobele Wilden* (Amsterdam, De Bezige Bij).
Pina, N. (1962): *De ene herinnering*. Bam'i paloma poems in Dutch and Papiamento. In: *Antilliaanse Cahiers*, jrg.5, nr. 1, 1972, pp. 7–11.
Rooy, R. A. de (1954): *Juancho Picaflor*. Un tragicomedia ritmá di cinco acto, Willemstad, Paulus drukkerij
Rosario, G. E. (1969): *E raís ku no ke muri* (historical novel in Papiamento about the life of Tula, Amsterdam, de Bezige Bij

Critical Works

Debrot, Cola (1964): *Literature of the Netherlands Antilles*, Curaçao, drukkerij 'de Curaçaose Courant'
Palm, J. Ph de (1967): 'Letterkunde in de Nederlandse Antillen in het Nederlands', Schakels, NA-50, blz. 20–22
—— (1967): 'Letterkunde in de Nederlandse Antillen in het Spaans". Schakels, NA-50, blz. 17–19.
—— (1968): 'Letterkunde in de Nederlandse Antillen in het Papiamentu', *Watapana*, jrg. 1, nr. 1, juli, 1968, blz. 3–6
Roo, Jos de (1980): *Antilliaans Literair Logboek*, Zutphen, de Walburg pers
see also: *Bibliografie van de Nederlandse Antillen* issued by *Sticusa*, Viottastraat 41, Amsterdam.
also: *Cultureel Mozaïek van de Nederlandse Antillen* ed. by René Römer, Zutphen, de Walburg pers, 1980.

11

Only Connect – E. M. Forster's *A Passage to India* and Multatuli's *Max Havelaar*

The novel, *A Passage to India*, by E. M. Forster is almost compulsory reading for any student of English literature in the world. A course in Dutch literature can never be complete without Multatuli's *Max Havelaar*. The Dutch novel may be confined to a smaller readership but its impact is no less explosive. Both Forster's and Multatuli's novels have been turned into films, *A Passage to India* being highly praised and seen by a large non-English-speaking public, not necessarily students of English literature. The film *Max Havelaar* was confined to those who speak and understand Dutch and are involved with Dutch history and culture. It was no less impressive and was as much a document humain as Forster's product. The Dutch and the English were major colonial powers. The similarities are manifold. The Dutch East India Company was established in 1602 but, by 1599, the Dutch had already shown their faces in the Moluccas to trade in spices. So far as the British were concerned, Winston Churchill writes in his *History of the English-Speaking Peoples* (vol. 3):

> The English East India Company, founded simply as a trading venture, grew with increasing speed into a vast territorial Empire. About the year 1700 probably no more than fifteen hundred English people dwelt in India, including wives, children and transient seamen. . . .

And Bid Him Sing

> A hundred years later British officials and soldiers in their thousands, under a British Governor-General, were in control of extensive provinces.[1]

Churchill's vision of the British East India Company is that of an innocuous trading organization, run by businessmen in London who were only interested in dividends. In his view the complications in India were responsible for the English acquiring, by accident rather than design, a vast empire. The heroic Clive and Hastings who was appointed Governor-General in 1814, were the unwilling inheritors of India. As Churchill so charmingly puts it: 'Against its wishes and almost in spite of itself the Company was now overlord of three quarters of India.' Churchill's patriotic and uncritical viewpoint is disputed in a publication by A. L. Morton, *A People's History of England*, who boldly asserts: 'By the destruction of the village handicraft industry the peasants were thrust on to exclusive dependence on agriculture. India, like Ireland became a purely agricultural colony supplying Britain with food and raw materials.'[2]

Morton goes on to say that 'British rule in India was based, politically, on the highly trained and disciplined army of sepoys and on the support of the native princes and landowners who, in their turn, owed their own privileges to British authority.'

In this, too, the similarities with the Dutch East Indies are remarkable. The Dutch East Indies Company was a trading organization which possessed a monopoly in shipping and trading to the east of the Cape of Good Hope. The first successful expedition was in 1595 under Cornelis de Houtman.[3] The main concern of the Dutch merchants was the spices and pepper to be found in the East Indies, mainly the Indonesian archipelago. The major trading centre was Bantam and, in 1599, van Warwijck went as far as the Moluccas, Celebes and Ambon. The Dutch East Indies Company had the monopoly in nuts by 1622 and, in 1666, managed to secure the monopoly in cloves. The fleet of the Company was large, its capital enormous – all of which contributed to its being a much desired trading partner.

Like the English, the Dutch also exploited the local and indigenous rulers during the colonial occupation. Here, too, the local rulers were allowed to be corrupt and exploitative with the silent consent of the Dutch.

The difference between Forster's *A Passage to India* and Multatu-

Only Connect – A Passage to India *and* Max Havelaar

li's *Max Havelaar* lies in that Multatuli lived in the Dutch East Indies as part of the colonial apparatus. His book is, therefore, based on historical events in which he himself was one of the major actors. The Dutch, like the English, still hanker after those days in the East. In the Netherlands, articles and novels dealing with the *tempo doeloe* are still avidly read by a section of the population. The Dutch still talk of 'Ons Indië' (Our Indies) and have no qualms if their airlines advertise the Indonesian *rijst-tafel* as their national dish.

These two novels are not only memorable as works of art but important as human documents. As such, they are also excellent commentaries on colonialism in the East by the Dutch and the English.

Of E. M. Forster it was said that he was writing at the end of Victorian liberalism. At that time of fundamental changes, reforms and social upheaval a new-found liberal consciousness accompanied these industrial and social changes. This consciousness also found its reflection in a superb development of realism, humour and satire, as well as the representation of manners. In E. M. Forster's work one is confronted with this new-found liberal consciousness.

In *A Passage to India*, against the backdrop of the empire, his attitude towards the indigenous population is humane and tolerant. His treatment of the Indian problem is a belated high-water mark of the Victorian liberal conscience, concerned with what Henry James called 'the great grabbed-up British Empire'.

The setting of his novels is that of the British middle class—an affluent class carrying within itself all the inherent hypocrisies of that class. It was also the Victorian liberal's concern to check the self-interest of this class. In *Passage to India* the Ronnies of this world are the prime products of this middle class and the public-school system, so conscious of the burden of Empire resting heavily on their shoulders. They are simply incapable of coming to grips with the problems because of their 'undeveloped heart'. The Ronnies are the end products of utilitarianism, against which Carlyle warned as early as 1829 when he complained of men 'grown mechanical in head and heart.'

Of E. M. Forster, as with Swift, one could say: 'I have hated all nations, professions and communities and my love is for individuals.'

In the words of F. R. Leavis, then, *Passage to India* 'In its touch upon racial and cultural problems, its treatment of personal relations, and in prevailing ethos . . . is an expression, undeniably, of the liberal tradition; . . . it makes the achievement, the humane and decent and rational – the 'civilized' – habit of that tradition appear the invaluable thing.'[4]

Walter Allen, in *The English Novel*, commented that the 'very subject of India, with its clashes of race, religion and colour, compelled Forster to interpret his values in terms of a concrete situation taken from contemporary history.'[5]

E. M. Forster was keenly aware of the aridity of English middle-class life. Lionel Trilling stresses the theme of separateness which runs like a golden thread through *A Passage to India*. One is conscious of the barriers and the 'good fences make good neighbours', to borrow a line from the American poet, Robert Frost. Trilling observed in his study of E. M. Forster:

> Of the Anglo-Indian society it is perhaps enough to say that, 'more than it can hope to do in England', it lives by the beliefs of the English public school. It is arrogant, ignorant, insensitive – intelligent natives estimate that a year in India makes the pleasantest Englishmen rude. And of all the English it is the women who insist most strongly on their superiority, who are the rawest and crudest in their manner.[6]

Adela Quested who came out to the East to marry Ronnie and who wanted 'to know the East' discovered, to her dismay, that very few people do so. All her attempts at communication are abortive, including her sexual relationship with Ronnie. When she broached the question of love with Aziz on that fateful trip to the Marabar Caves she found out that she was only disturbed for having raised it and Dr Aziz was placed in an embarrassing position. The question only served to emphasize the great divide that existed between the English woman and the Indian Aziz— that wall of ethnicity and sex which was impenetrable in the India of those days.

The Marabar Caves, and the subsequent accusation by Adela that Aziz had raped her in a moment of hallucination, drew the lines of separation even more finely between the ruler and the ruled. Mrs Moore is sent away by her son, Ronnie, and Fielding is further alienated from his tribe for not having backed the colours. In addition, Aziz, impelled by a deep hurt, now felt a brotherhood under

Only Connect – A Passage to India *and* Max Havelaar

the skin, what I would like to call the inevitable 'epidermic anschluss' which occurs when racial insults are inflicted upon the colonized.

Adela, too, is isolated from the tribe when, after they had first backed her to the hilt, she embarrassed them by withdrawing her accusation, possibly under the influence of Mrs Moore ('Esmoor'). The separation is deeper than just colonized-colonizer, white man-man of colour, man-wo-man.

There is also the separation between Hindu and Moslem, '. . . the various branches of Indians [who] know too much about each other to surmount the unknowable easily. . . '. Aziz thinks of Das: 'I wish they did not remind me of cow-dung'; Das thought, "Some Moslems are very violent."[7]

There are numerous attempts in the novel to bridge the gap between the Indian and the English but they all fail or end in comic-tragedy (for example, the garden party). E. M. Forster attacks and attacks on all fronts. Not only are the manners and the morals of the English middle class under fire, but so also the officials and soldiers who prop up the Empire.

For E. M. Forster, English society was too steeped in convention and class prejudice. Of the English middle class he himself wrote:

> They gained wealth by the Industrial Revolution, political power by the Reform Bill of 1832; they are connected with the rise and organization of the British Empire, they are responsible for the literature of the nineteenth century. Solidity, caution, integrity, efficiency. Lack of imagination, hypocrisy.[8]

The novel was, of course, the result of his trip to India in 1912 on the invitation of some friends. This visit was, in his own words, one of 'peace and happiness'. By the time he had finished *A Passage to India* the 'peace and happiness' was gone. Forster, like so many others, found that his idealism had been dealt a severe blow by the 1914–18 war. His Indian trip had, however, awakened in him an interest in people of colour. It is important to remember that Indian nationalism reached its zenith between 1912 and 1922. For E. M. Forster, the 'undeveloped heart' was largely responsible for the inability of people to 'connect'. A prime example of the 'undeveloped heart' was Ronnie in *A Passage to India*.

In his *Notes on the English Character* E. M. Forster speaks of the public-school system as being the root of all evil in English national life. He blames the middle class which forms the very core of the public-school system. Thus, according to him, they unleash onto the world, 'whose richness and subtlety they have no conception of', a breed of men 'with well-developed bodies, fairly well-developed minds and undeveloped hearts'.[9]

The three characters in *A Passage to India* who represent a liberal consciousness (to a greater or lesser extent) are Adela Quested, Fielding and Mrs Moore. Adela is motivated more by curiosity than a direct liberal consciousness and, therefore, her attempts to break down the barriers all come to naught or have an untrue ring. Fielding, on the other hand, did act from a liberal consciousness which seemed to stem, however, from a vague dissatisfaction and emotionalism. This was probably the initial stage of E. M. Forster's own reaction. It is, in Mrs Moore, that we find the purest expression of Victorian-based liberalism. Aziz is offended when he discovers her in the mosque – a woman and white at that! He comes to the painful discovery that her transgression was marked by a great sensitivity because she had remembered to take off her shoes. Similarly, it was through her spirit, that Adela came to retract the accusation of rape against Aziz. Mrs Moore stands for the liberal spirit in the nineteenth century as opposed to her son, Ronnie, who represented 'the sterilized public school brand which never goes bad even in the tropics'.

In an article on E. M. Forster Dan Jacobson focuses on the well-known injunction used by Forster in *Howard's End*, 'only connect'. He then continues:

> 'You remember what Forster said', an American professor of history once told me earnestly – 'Only . . . only communicate.'
> To connect passion with the intellect and manners with spontaneity and ardour; the past with the present and both with a sense of the future; the life of personal relations with the external worlds of class, race and politics.[10]

Forster had most in common with his predecessor, Matthew Arnold, who maintained: 'I am a liberal, yet a liberal tempered by experience, reflection and renouncement.' Yet Forster differs from Matthew Arnold in that he did not wish to save the spirit of religious belief when its supernatural sanctions are no longer believed.

Only Connect – A Passage to India *and* Max Havelaar

Although he wrote from a more fully agnostic viewpoint, his was not barren agnosticism. He, with Matthew Arnold and George Eliot, may be placed in the category of the humanist. But, at the same time, like Matthew Arnold, he might be criticized for his emphasis on *a culture of the few*. Arnold was, however, concerned about *the education of the many*. Writing later, Forster saw too well, as some Victorian thinkers prophesied, that *the great mass is beyond art*, that *they are unthinkable*. And, to complicate matters, India was not easy to penetrate. As Forster himself wrote in that last encounter between Aziz and Fielding:

> ... the earth didn't want it, sending up rocks through which riders must pass single file; the temples ... the palace, the birds ... they didn't want it, they said in their hundred voices, 'No, not yet,' and the sky said, 'No, not there.'

Ramsaran in his article, 'An Indian Reading of E. M. Forster's Classic', conceded that the novel was about race and colonialism, about the ruler and the ruled, about the English and the Indian. But he contended that there was more to it than a commentary on race relations and colonialism.

> The conflict between individual races, classes and cultures are secondary to the main theme of the novel, and only serve as a framework for the intricate pattern of man's yearning for self-realisation ... India as the background to this quest is most suitable ... since in that sub-continent ... so many of the external diversities of human existence are quite clearly seen: the past and the present, East and West, ruler and ruled, Christian and non-Christian—all attracting or repelling one another.[11]

A Passage to India is exploration at several levels. The novel is about the abortive attempts of human beings in a colonial context to come to grips with one another. It is also a damning assessment of the English middle class and an expression of the inability of the human mind to move from the mundane in order to embrace the universal in complete harmony.

Ramsaran puts it as follows: 'To enter into Godbole's experience is to understand the Vaishnava's search for supreme bliss and unity in being – the unity of the human and the divine.'[12] For in the rhetorical question posed in the novel is contained the sheer brilliance of *A Passage to India*: 'For how can the mind take hold of such a country?' Unlike E. M. Forster's novel, *A Passage to India*, the Dutch novel, *Max Havelaar* (1860), written by Multatuli, was more directly concerned with the fortunes or misfortunes of the novelist as a civil servant in the Dutch East Indies during the years 1839–59. Interest in *Max Havelaar* was further stimulated when it was turned into a film by the Dutch producer Fons Rademaker. Thus, Dutchmen who would never have read this classic were now confronted with their colonial past in Indonesia, in a very dramatic manner. More recently, in 1985, a Dutch weekly[13] devoted almost its entire issue to the writer, Multatuli, and a Dutch book, *De Multatulianen*, was published in that year. The interest in Multatuli continues; 1987, as will become apparent, was the 'year of Multatuli'.

Max Havelaar or, to give it its full name, *Max Havelaar of de Koffieveilingen der Nederlandsche Handelsmaatschappij*, was off to a tremendous start when first published in 1860; 1300 copies were printed of which twenty went to the East Indies. According to cognoscenti, over two million copies have been sold to date. The author Multatuli (meaning, in Latin, I have suffered), was born Eduard Douwes Dekker in 1820 in Amsterdam of Frisian parents. Destined to become a minister in the Church he instead worked in a trading office and left eventually, with his brother Jan and in the company of his father, the sea captain, for the East Indies. Douwes Dekker arrived there in 1839. Unlike E. M. Forster, Douwes Dekker did not find 'peace and happiness' in the East Indies, becoming so involved with society that his entire life was shaped by the events at Lebak. His novel, *Max Havelaar*, is a consequence of those events in 1856 when he was assistant Resident.

From the start, Douwes Dekker was symbiotically involved with the Javanese whose lot he considered to be miserable and in need of serious amelioration. *Max Havelaar* is thus more directly concerned with race and colonial relationships than *A Passage to India*, reflecting the difference in style between the English and the Dutch. Events are directly traceable to real people and real occurrences. It is, therefore, not so surprising that when the film was shot in Indonesia actual houses (or the spot where these houses stood) were used. The novel was a harsh and bitter attack on colonial practices, on the abuse of power and the exploitation of the local inhabitants by the local regents, with the connivance of the Dutch authorities.

Only Connect – A Passage to India *and* Max Havelaar

During 1987 numerous commemorations in the Netherlands (even in Germany and Indonesia) marked the centenary of the passing away of Douwes Dekker in 1887. There are few novels which reflect so intimately and passionately the events which happened to a particular author. *Max Havelaar* is a superb work of fiction, relying on what Joyce Cary once called 'the power of the creative imagination'.

On arriving in the East Indies Douwes Dekker was gainfully employed within less than a month. In order to appreciate his good fortune one would have to understand the Dutch policy in the East, known as *cultuurstelsel*. This was introduced by the Dutch Governor-General, Johannes van der Bosch, in 1830 and was a policy whereby certain crops were cultivated and products manufactured solely for the European market. This system led to an expansion of society in the East Indies and necessitated a demand for Dutch civil servants. One reads that, as a consequence of *cultuurstelsel*, yields were so overwhelming that it was possible to transfer, from the East Indies to the Netherlands, 25 million guilders at a time when the national budget was only 60 million guilders.[14]

Paul van't Veer signals dual loyalties in the East Indies – between the Europeans and the indigenous administrators, as a consequence of *cultuurstelsel*. The Dutch needed the indigenous rulers to help them with the implementation of their colonial policies. Snouck Hourgonje[15] even referred to the 'act of mercy' whereby the Javanese were controlled by their own traditional chiefs, without whose help it would have been impossible to demand from the local population that they cultivate one fifth of their land with crops intended for the European market and spend one fifth of their labour for the benefit of the Dutch. Thus, a system evolved in which the indigenous regents, their subordinates, district administrators, *wedana's* (chief of a district) and *demangs* (local civil servant of middle rank), became inextricably interwoven with the Dutch colonial administration.

Douwes Dekker, according to an interim report of 10 April 1839, had made a favourable impression and was considered excellent civil-servant material. But he courted disfavour when, during a stay on the west coast of Sumatra in 1842, as a minor official, he was accused of involvement in the intrigues of local chiefs. For a period of seven years (1845–52) he was assistant Resident of Amboina. In 1846 he married Everdine van Wijnbergen, a Dutch baroness. His tryst with the East was interrupted in 1852 when he was once more in Europe. He returned in 1855. Back in the East, he caught the eye of the Governor-General, Duysmaer van Twist, who commented on him in a Cabinet missive as follows:

> At a dinner, or rather after the dinner, to which he was invited with his wife now and then, I often had occasion to speak to him, and he had gained my sympathy because he had a heart for the natives. When Lebak became available, and since I knew that the circumstances of the natives left much to be desired, I considered him to be the right man in the right place and, although the Council of the East Indies had not put forward his name as a candidate, I nevertheless nominated him as the assistant Resident.[16]

The new assistant Resident dug into old archives and unearthed more than he should have, trampling on secrets in the cesspool of corruption. Having no eye for the complexity of relationships that existed between colonizer and colonized, the ruler and the ruled, he must have appeared to the old regent, his son-in-law and Dutch officialdom like a bull in a china shop. It was a known fact that the old regent exploited his subjects – with the knowledge of the Dutch. The regents, like the chiefs in Africa under British indirect rule, did the dirty jobs for the colonialists and were richly rewarded with certain privileges.

Moralist and idealist that he was, Douwes Dekker stopped at nothing and caused the regent to suffer great loss of face when he ordered local labourers, weeding the garden of the regent in expectation of his cousin, to stop. In his probings he discovered that his predecessor had also wanted to put an end to these malpractices. The rumour circuit was responsible for *angker* (fear) and the *dukun* (medicine man) loomed large.

Douwes Dekker made some very simple miscalculations. His own kith and kin (Dutch officialdom) did not support him. He failed to understand the *adat* (Customary Law), within the East Indies context. Disillusioned he turned to the Governor-General for help but to no avail. The occurrences at Lebak may have been disastrous for Douwes Dekker, the civil servant. They were a stroke of good fortune for Multatuli and Dutch literature. The regent was eventually

Only Connect – A Passage to India and Max Havelaar

dismissed for a minor misdemeanour; despite the *adat* not even he was above the law.

The characters in *Max Havelaar* are plucked straight from history books. In Slotering one recognizes Douwes Dekker's predecessor, Carolus. Verbrugge became van Langeveld van Hemert; the unpopular General Michiels was Vandamme. The story unfolds through the eyes of Droogstoppel, the Dutch merchant par excellence, the collectivist as opposed to the idealist.

Max Havelaar is an indictment against the exploitative practices of the Dutch colonial administration in connivance with local rulers. The 1856 conflict at Lebak, where Douwes Dekker was in charge, is of importance in the shaping of the novel. He exposed the practice whereby the Dutch grabbed mineral resources and the produce of the East Indies for the benefit of their avaricious countrymen. He was appalled at what he saw and his novel is a passionate plea to put an end to these malpractices in the East. It certainly contributed to the abolition of this slave system, based on naked exploitation, despoliation and deracination. As such, the novel is also social and political in the best literary tradition.

Max Havelaar also deals with coffee cultivation in the East Indies; this is presented in such a factual manner that it is in stark contrast to the rest of the story. Max Havelaar, the chief protagonist, is the embodiment of the novelist, Douwes Dekker, who is opposed to a system which he *cannot* overcome single-handed. He is doomed to lose; he is the outsider, although not the ironic spectator who records and observes.

It is the story of a young idealistic colonial civil servant, imbued with strong moral principles and much tenacity, who is sent by the Dutch to the Javanese Lebak where he encounters despotism at various levels. The regent mercilessly exploits his poor, hapless subjects, with the tacit approval of the Dutch. After all, the Dutch thrived and prospered as a result of *cultuurstelsel*. In the end, the system proved too powerful for Max Havelaar as it also did in real life for the man, Douwes Dekker.

Three characters are of importance in the novel. First, there is the man named Droogstoppel (Dry stubble) – coffee merchant par excellence, dry, humourless, sober and hypocritical. Then there is his assistant, Stern, the incarnation of the sentimental and the poetic. One gathers that part of the information on the state of affairs in the East Indies, so it is averred, is based on the papers of the impecunious character, Sjaalman. G. Knuvelder commented on *Max Havelaar* as follows:

> Thus Dekker appears in various guises: first, from an artistic point of view, as the idealised assistant-resident Max Havelaar; next as the impoverished Sjaalman, wandering through Europe with his bundles of paper concerning certain matters at Lebak. As for the sentimental-romantic, the author Dekker hides behind Stern. The critic in Dekker, peculiar to him even in his youth, finds expression through Droogstoppel. All these men revolve around the sun Dekker who, by means of this construction, created a work of art in which he not only satirized the dull, narrow-minded, hypocritical mercantilism of the Dutch in the first half of the nineteenth century, but also left us with an indelible impression of the beauty of the East Indies.[17]

This Dutch saga strongly resembles a modern saga enacted on former territories which also belonged to the Dutch during the seventeenth century, namely South Africa. The *cultuurstelsel*, responsible for so much misery, is strongly reminiscent of the policy which eventually spawned the Bantustan leaders and Bantustans. In the Bantustan leaders, Mangope and Mantanzima, one recognises the 'Adat heads' in the East Indies, given positions of unlimited power ... which leads to corruption and exploitation of the indigenous people, with the connivance of the South African regime.

The *Max Havelaar* taught at universities in South Africa in courses known as 'Nederlands-Afrikaans', mostly at Afrikaner (and one 'coloured') universities, would serve as a very useful critical exercise for the literary critic who wants to analyse the work in terms of a. reception among white students in South Africa; b. reception among those taxonomically labelled as 'coloured' in South Africa; and c. as an excellent political novel against the backdrop of events in South Africa.

The Multatuli commemorations bring Douwes Dekker, once more, under close scrutiny. He is remembered also in Germany where, by 1875, he was living. Maria Anderson wrote a book in 1902 entitled, *Uit het Leven van Multatuli*. She met him when she was only nineteen years of age. The novelist is referred to as the 'Sufferer of Lebak'. There are many theories concerning the occurrences in

Only Connect – A Passage to India *and* Max Havelaar

Lebak during the mid-nineteenth century. Was Multatuli just a woolly-headed romantic or the civil servant who found himself up against an iniquitous colonial system which he could not defeat? Some comments by critics are laudatory, some deprecatory. Did the man Douwes Dekker finally succumb only to the dictates of his conscience?

Cyriel Offermans, the Dutch critic, writes: 'One needs only to read a few pages . . . by Multatuli to realise that he, above all, sees himself as a passionate seeker of truth . . . Getting to the truth for Multatuli always implies political unmasking.'[18]

Another critic dispels the notion that Multatuli was a revolutionary. 'He had a premonition . . . that the power of the regents and the exploitation of the Javanese would lead to a revolution . . . but Multatuli was no revolutionary . . . Even if he was not the great Che Guevara we held him to be earlier on, he was okay, he was more human.'[19]

Multatuli's novel, *Max Havelaar* will always be regarded as one of the classics of Dutch literature. As an anti-colonial novel, expressing painfully and bitterly the exploitative practices in the Dutch East Indies, it is a wonderful example of creativity.

What one critic said of *Max Havelaar* is just as applicable to that other classic, *A Passage to India*:

> He was namely strongly aware of what Herbert Marcuse would call later on, 'The affirmative character of culture', because literature, even in the most negative sense, distills the suffering of the world, makes it, at the same time, acceptable and even meaningful.[20]

Notes

1. Cassell, London, 1962, p. 171.
2. Victor Gollancz, London, 1938, p. 449.
3. For Cornelis de Houtman see Commelin, *Begin ende Voortgang van de Oost-Indische Compagne*, Jan Jansz, Amsterdam, 1646.
4. *The Common Pursuit*, Penguin Books, Harmondsworth, 1963, p. 277.
5. Pelican Books, Harmondsworth, 1980, p. 338.

And Bid Him Sing

6. E. M. *Forster*, New Directions, New York, 1964, p. 149.
7. E. M. Forster, *A Passage to India*, Penguin Books, Harmondsworth, 1950, p. 261.
8. See Rex Warner, 'E. M. Forster', *Writers and Their Work*, British Council, 1950, no. 7, p. 10.
9. See John Colmer, *E. M. Forster, The Personal Voice*, Routledge & Kegan Paul, London, 1975, p. 5.
10. 'Forster's Cave', *New Statesman*, 14 October 1966, p. 560.
11. *Ibadan Studies in English*, vol. 1, no. 1, May–June 1969.
12. ibid., p. 50.
13. *De Groene*, vol. 109, no 43, 23 October 1985.
14. See Paul van't Veer, *Het Leven van Multatuli*, De Arbeiderspers, Amsterdam, 1979, pp. 80–86.
15. Snouck Hourgonje (1857–1937), noted Dutch scholar of Islam and Arabic Studies. He was a professor of Arabic at Leiden University. Hourgonje converted to Islam. Visited Mecca 1884–85 and then went to the Dutch East Indies.
16. G. W. H.(?) 'Multatuli en zijn Max Havelaar', Rotterdam, 1958 (unable to trace author).
17. *Handleiding tot de Geschiedenis der Nederlandse Letterkunde*, L. C. G. Malmberg, 's-Hertogenbosch, 1964, pp. 375–6.
18. 'Vermoorde Broeders in Kreupelhout', *De Groene*, 23 October 1985, p. 18.
19. Theodoor Holman, 'Keizer van Insulinde', *De Groene*, 23 October 1985, p. 17.
20. Cyriel Offermans, *De Groene*, 1985, p. 19.

Bibliography

1. Allen, Walter (1980): *The English Novel*, Middlesex, Penguin/Pelican Books (first published in 1954).
2. Arnold, Matthew (1932): *Culture and Anarchy* (ed. J. Dover), Cambridge University Press.
3. Churchill, Winston, (1962): *A History of the English-speaking Peoples*, London, Cassell (first published in 1957).
4. Forster, E. M. (1910): *Howard's End*, New York, Knopf Vintage Books.
5. Forster, E. M. (1950): *A Passage to India*, London, Penguin Books (first published in 1924).
6. Forster, E. M. (1951): *Two Cheers for Democracy*, Harcourt, Brace and World.
7. Holman, Theodoor (1985): 'Keizer van Insulinde' In: *De Groene* Amsterdam, 23 Oktober.
8. Jacobson, Dan (1965): 'Forster's Cave' In: *New Statesman*, 14 October.

Only Connect – A Passage to India *and* Max Havelaar

9. Jongstra, Atte (1985): *De Multatulianen*, Joost Nijsen.
10. Knuvelder, G. (1964): *Handleiding tot de geschiedenis der Nederlandse Letterkunde*, 's-Hertogenbosch, L. C. G. Malmberg.
11. Leavis, F. R. (1963): *The Common Pursuit*, Middlesex, Peregrine Books (first published in 1952).
12. Multatuli (ps. Eduard Douwes Dekker) (1955): *Max Havelaar*, Amsterdam, Brussel (first published in 1860).
13. Offermans, Cyriel (1985): 'Vermoorde broeders in kreupelhout' In: *De Groene*, 23 Oktober.
14. Ramsaran, J. A. (1969): 'An Indian's reading of E. M. Forster's Classic' In: *Ibadan Studies in English*, vol. 1, nr. 1, May–June.
15. Trilling, Lionel (1955): *Matthew Arnold*, New York, Meridian Books.
16. Trilling, Lionel (1964): *E. M. Forster*, New York, New Directions (first published in 1943).
17. Thorpe, Michael (1969): *Matthew Arnold*, London, Evans Bros.
18. Veer van't, Paul (1979): *Het leven van Multatuli*, Amsterdam, de Arbeiderspers.
19. Warner, Rex (1950): *E. M. Forster*. Writers and their Work, British Council, No. 7, London.

See also the following *newspapers*:

Vrij Nederland, 1975, p. 23, De Max Havelaar verfilmd in Indonesië'
Vrij Nederland, jaargang 42, 29, Aug., 1981, p. 19, 'Als twee druppels water' Multatuli en Sacher Masoch; 'Herdrukken en herinneringen'
Trouw, 26 Maart, 1982, 'Multatuli handelde in Lebak als een fatsoenlijke man' *NRC Handelsblad*, 11 Nov., 1985, p. 9, 'Multatuli herdacht als schrijver die ook kon drammen en zeuren'.

INDEX

Page numbers followed by 'n' refer to notes, by 'r' to reviews.

Abasiekong, Daniel, 58
Abdurahman, Dr, 116n
Abrahams, Peter, 36
Achebe, Chinua, 103, 179, 180
Adam Kok's Griquas (Ross), 47
African National Congress, 7-8
Afrikaans, 51, 73, 88-94
    as medium in schools, 89, 107-16
    creole nature of, 89
    Fanakalo, 90-1
    Flytaal, xii-xiii, 89, 90, 91-4
    identity struggle, 88-9, 105-16
    pidginization, 90, 94
    second language movement (1903), 106
    Soweto revolts against *see* Soweto revolt against Afrikaans
    spoken by Khoi, 89-90
Afscheid van de Koningin (Farewell to the Queen) (Arion), 170-7
Allen, Walter, 190
Anansi, the spider, 33-4, 134, 155
Anderson, LF, 12, 13, 22n, 23n
Anderson, Maria, 198-9
Anglo-Saxon poetry, 2, 3
    Caedmon, 9-11
    importance of Scop, 9-11
    importance of song, 12-13
    literary devices, 13-14
    major poems, 11-14
    subject matter, 11-12
Anthony, Michael, 137
Antilles *see* French *and* Dutch Antilles

Arion, Frank Martinus, xiv, 133, 163, 165-85
    Afscheid van de Koningin, 170-7
    Dubbelspel, 165-6, 167-70
    Nobele Wilden, 177-81
Armah, Ayi Kwei, 138, 174
Arnold, Matthew, 192, 193
Asingeni see Soweto revolt against Afrikaans
assimilation, 28, 102
Auerbach, — 109

Ba Anansi (Cairo), 137, 150
Bantu Education Department, 109, 110
Bantustans, 88, 96n-97n, 104
Bastiaanse, J, 112-13
Beautiful Ones are Not Yet Born, The (Armah), 138, 174
Beloff, Max, 172
Bennett, Joan, 133
Beowulf, 11, 12, 19
Bhambatha, 15
Black Culture and Consciousness (Levine), 31, 33, 34
Black Skin, White Masks (Fanon), 31, 102, 174
Boeseken, Anna, 48
bonga, 6
Botev, Khristo, 56, 63, 64n
Bradley, David, 38
Braithwaite, Edward Kamu, 153
Brer Rabbit, 33-4
Brighter Sun, A (Selvon), 137
Brink, Andre, 35, 48, 52
British East India Company, 187-8

203

Index

'Bro' ('Repose') (Trefossa), 123
Brotherhood, 27, 30, 70
Bruma, Eddy, xiv, 150
Brusciotto, Giacinto, 80
Brutus, Dennis, 55, 56, 57–60, 64n, 169
Bryant, — 6
Bryce Ross, — 81
Bugis, Leander, 50, 51, 52
Burroughs, Edgar Rice, 26
Bushmen *see* San
Bwana Jungle, 27

Cachet, JL, 105–6, 116n
Cahier d'un retour au pays natal (Cesaire), 28
Cairo, Edgar, xiv, xv, 34, 131–61, 165
  alienation, 145, 152
  justification of exile, 136, 146–7
  obsession with blackness, 150
  overkilling, 144
  performer, 137, 140, 152
  poems, 152–5
  sensitivity to criticism, 142–3
  venomous, 146, 150–1
  see also individual works eg Temekoe
Calata, Rev, 8
Campbell, Alistair, 3, 23n
Cape of Torments (Ross), 47, 48–53
Carletonville, 166
Cary, Joyce, 25, 195
Cesaire, Aime, 28, 38
Cetshwayo, 9
Chaka (Mofolo), 81
Chaka *see* Shaka
'Child Dies, A' (Sepamla), 44
Children of Soweto (Nkosi), 43
Chocolates for My Wife (Matshikiza), 31
Christelike Nasionale Onderwys (CNO)
  see Christian National Education

Christian National Education, 89, 97n, 105, 107, 116n
Christopher (Drayton), 137
Churchill, Winston, 27, 187–8
'Civilization Aha' (Sepamla), 45
clicking, 70, 75, 79
Coleman, J, 28
Colmer, John, 200n
coloureds, 57, 107
  preferred choice of education medium, 113
  slavery, 48
Come Duze Baby (Sepamla), 91–3, 97n–98n
comedy *see* humour
Commonwealth Poetry Conference, 55–6
Cook, Mercer, 30, 39n
Cope, Trevor, 3, 4–5, 6
Coulthard, GR, 40n, 116n
creole, 29
  see also Papiamento; Surinamese creole
Creole Drum, xiii–xiv, 120, 121, 122, 133, 137, 139
Cressy, Harold, 116n
Cronje, — 110–11
Cullen, Countee, xi
Curtin, Philip, 39n

Damas, Leon, 28
Dargrati (Cairo), 149–50
Dat Vuur der Crote Drama's (Cairo), 151–2
De Groene Amsterdammer, 149
De Multatulianen, 194
De Tijd, 133, 135, 155
De Villiers Commission, 106–7
De Volkskrant, 136
De Vos Malan Commission, 106, 107
Debrot, Cola, 163, 164, 165
Dekker, Thomas, 133
demythologization, 27–30, 103, 104

Deor, 18
Dia di mas Historico, E (Jongh), 165
Die Burger, 114-15
Diop, Birago, 28
Djari (Cairo), 149
Djop (Cairo), 150
Dobru *see* Ravales, Robin
Dohne, Rev JL, 4, 71, 96n
Doke, CM, 96n
Dostoevsky, — 56
Douwes Dekker, Eduard, 194-9
Dravidian/Indian languages, 74, 94
Drayton, Geoffrey, 137
drengskapr, 17
Du Societies, 31
Dubbelspel (Arion), 165-6, 167-70
Dutch Antilles, 104, 164
  see also Arion, Frank Martinus
Dutch East India Company, 187, 188

Eckles, Jon, 45, 178
Edelstein, ML, 113, 117n
education
  Bantu, 89, 108-10
  Bantuized Higher Primary Course, 108
  English preferred language choice, 113
  forced use of Afrikaans, 107-16
  mother-tongue instruction, 107, 109, 112
  see also Christian National Education
Educational Journal, 67, 107, 111, 112
Edwards, I, 48
Eersel, Hein, xiv, 119
Eerste Adam, De (The First Adam) (van Leeuwen), 165
Egejuru, P, 182n
Eindhovens Dagblad, 144
Eiselen Commission, 106, 107

Elliot, George, 193
Ellison, Ralph, 27, 36-7
Elsenhout, Johanna Schouten, 153
emprisonment, 55-65
English *see* language
English Novel, The (Allen), 190
epic poetry, 13

FAK *see* Federasie vir Afrikaanse Kultuur, 57, 64n
Famir'man-sani (Cairo), 139-45
Fanakalo, 90-1
Fanon, Frantz, 31, 39n, 102, 135, 174
February, VA, 39n, 40n, 81, 89, 95n, 97n, 98n, 116n, 136, 156n, 168, 182n
Federasie vir Afrikaanse Kultuur, 57, 64n
Fens, Kees, 169-70, 172, 183r
Finnegan, Ruth, 1-2, 3, 22n
First, Ruth, 60-2, 64n
Forster, EM, xvi, 187, 188, 189-94
Fragments (Armah), 174
France
  assimilation, 102
  language and colonization, 102
  negritude, 27-9, 102
French Antilles, 102, 104
Frost, Robert, 190
Fulfil Thy Promise God of Truth (Soga), 81

Galant, 52
Gammatjie, 33
Garvey, Marcus Aurelius, 120
Genootskap vir Regte Afrikaners, 88, 105
Genovese, Eugene, 51
Gezelle, Guido, 135
'Giambo Bieuw ta Bolbe na Wea' (Old Love Does Not Die) (Kroon), xv, 164
Giovanni, Nikki, 45

Index

Gordimer, Nadine, 145–6
Gordon, RK, 14, 23n
Grant, EW, 3, 22n
Grattan-Guinnes, H, 80
Groene Amsterdammer, 167
'Gronmama' (Trefossa), 126–7
Group Areas Acts, 88–9

Haagse Post, 168–9
Haggard, H Rider, 26
Hahn, Dr Th, 89
Halberg, P, 3
Hall, Alan xiii–xiv, 182n, 195
Hallberg, P, 23n
Hanglip maroon community, 50, 51, 52
Harlem, 27, 29
harps, 12–13
Harris, Wilson, 68
heïti, 15
Hellinga, —— 119, 150
Helman, Albert, 119, 122, 126
Henderson, Stephen, 30, 39n, 128n
Hengherr, —— 48
heroism
 Mbongi, 16–17
 rewards for, 18
 Scop, 17
 Skald, 17
Herskovits, —— 119
Het Parool, 134
Himes, Chester, 36
'Hoemor in Elselsis' (Trefossa), 126
Holman, Theodoor, 200n
Hoogenhout, CP, 101, 115n, 116n
Hooijer, G, 96n
Hottentots *see* Khoi
Houd-Den-Bek (Brink), 48, 52
Hourgonje, Snouck, 195, 200n
Houseboy (Oyono), 37
Houtman, Cornelis de, 70, 188
Howards End (Forster), 192
Hughes, Langston, 29, 39n

Hughes, Langston G, 39n
humour
 as social control, 33–4
 minorities play comic roles, 37
Hurrah for those who have not invented anything (Cesaire), 38

'I Saw This Morning' (Sepamla), 44
If He Hollers, Let Him Go (Himes), 36
Ijzerman, WJ, 96n
Ik Ga Dood om jullie hoofd (I'd Die for You) (Cairo), 136
Imi Hobe nemi Bongo (Mqhayi), 81
Impact of the Cape Slave Trade and its Population on Demography, The (Shell), 48
In the Castle of My Skin (Lamming), 137, 145
incarceration *see* emprisonment
'Indond' Mnyama' (Mini), 8
Ingqumbo Yeminyanya (Wrath of the Ancestors), 67
Instant in the Wind, An (Brink), 48
Invisible Man, The (Ellison), 27, 36–7
Ipi Tombi, 43
isibongo, 6
Ityala Lama-Wele (Mqhayi), 81
Izibongo—Zulu Praise Poems (Cope), 4–5, 6

Jacobson, Dan, 192
Jaffe, Hosea *see* Rylate, VE
Jail Diary, The (Sachs), 62–3
Jansen, John, 181n, 183r
Jeje Disi (Cairo), 150
Johnson, James Weldon, 39n
Jones, ED, 127n
Jones, Le Roy, 125
Jongh, Edward de, 165

Jonkers, Hans, 183r
Jordan, AC, 3, 6, 22n, 67, 71, 73, 83, 90, 95, 95n, 96n
Juancho Picaflor (Rooij), 165
Juliana, Elis, 165

Karl, Frederick, 173
Kaywana, The (Mittelholzer), 48
kenning, 15-16
Kenyatta, Jomo, 30, 55, 63n
Khoi, 70-1
   Afrikaans spoken by, 89-90
   distribution of, 75, 76
   fate of people, 75
   language of, 73-5
   Korana, 73
   Nama *see* Nama
Khoi-Khoin, 75
Kitchen Kaffir *see* Fanakalo
Klerk, J de, 114
Klimpsop, R, 112, 123
Knuvelder, G, 198
Kock, Victor de, 48
Koegel, R, 23n
Koenders, Papa, xiv, 120, 121, 133, 135, 156n
Koewatra Djodjo (Cairo), 147-9
Komrij, Gerrit, 172, 183r
Kondre Sa Jere (Cairo), 153-5
'Kopenhagan' (Trefossa), 121-2, 124, 125
Krige, Eileen, 4
Kroegel, R, 3
Kroon, Willem, xv, 164
Kropf, — 81
Krune Mqhayi, SE *see* Mqhayi, SE Krune
Kunene, Daniel, 20n-22n, 43, 44
Kunene, Mazisi, xii, 5-6, 16, 17, 23n

La Guma, Alex, 35-6, 40n, 55, 56, 64n, 138
Labadie, — xv

Lamming, George, 137, 145
language, 67-99
   Afrikaans *see* Afrikaans
   as colonial instrument, 135
   English-speaking colonies, 103
   French colonies, 102
   in South Africa 104-15
   Bantu *see* indigenous
   bilinguality, 83
   clicking, 70, 75, 79
   distribution in Africa, 72, 73
   Dravidian/Indian, 74, 94
   English
      for international communication, 109
      preferred choice for education, 113
      teaching in, 110
   Hamiltic group, 73
   immigrant, 73
   indigenous (Bantu), 73-4, 79-88
      distribution of, 81, 82
      earliest publications in, 79-80
      Nguni *see* Nguni language
      not considered cultured, 71
   of Khoi, 70, 73-5
   of San, 73
   official, 73
   oral to oriture, 69-70
   spoken in Africa, 73-4
   Surinamese creole *see* Surinamese creole
   Swazi *see* Nguni language
   used by colonized writers, 180
   Xhosa *see* Nguni language
   Zulu *see* Nguni language
'Language Situation in the Netherlands Antilles' (Romer), xv
Lanham, — 109-10
Lauffer, Pierre, 165
Lauriers, Mr, 123
Leavis, FR, 189-90

Index

Lebacs, Diana, 165
Leeuwaarder Courant, 148
Legitime Defense, 121
Legitime Defense, 28
Legum, Colin, 39n
Lero, Etienne, 28
Lestrade, GP, 3, 6
Letters to Martha (Brutus), 58, 59–60, 61
Lettsom, JC, 39n
l'Etudiant Noir, 121
L'Etudiant Noir, 28
Levens, Alfons, 156n
Levine, LW, 31, 33, 34
Levsky, Vasili, 56, 64n
Lichtveld, U, 39n, 116n, 119, 127n, 128n, 133, 157n
'Like a Hippo' (Sepamla), 44
Lips, Julius, 38–9, 40n
literary devices
   Anglo-Saxon poetry, 13–14
   Nguni, 6–7
   metaphors, 8–9
   Norse poetry, 15–16
Livingstone, David, 4
lobisingi (love songs), 31
Lonely Londoners, The (Selvon), 145, 148
Lorca, Garcia, 56
Lugard, Lord, 104
Lutchman, Martinus Harridat *see* Shrinivasi
Luthuli, Albert, 19–20

MacDermott, Mercia, 64n
Machado, Antonio, 155
McKay, Claude, 27
Magolwane (Chaka's poet), 5–6
Make Like Slaves (Rive), 175
Makeba, Miriam, 8, 9, 30
Makhudu, Dennis, xiii, 73, 89, 91, 97n
Makiwane, Tennyson, 7–8, 39n
Malan, Dr, 88, 106

Maldon, battle of, 17
Malinowski, — 38
Man of the People, A (Achebe), 179–80
Mandela, Nelson, 20, 23n
Marcuse, Herbert, 199
Marks, Shula, 71
Marugg, Tip, 164
Matshikiza, Todd, 31
Matthews, James, 43, 125, 128n
Max Havelaar (Multatuli), xvi, 187, 188, 189, 194–5, 197–9
Mbogozi (follower of Shaka), 17
Meinhof, Carl, 75, 78–9, 96n
metaphor, Nguni praise poetry, 8–9
'Mi go M'ekon' (Trefossa), 125
Micere, — 70
Mi jn Zuster de Negerin (My Sister the Negress) (Debrot), 164
Mind Your Colour (February), 81, 89, 136, 168
Mini, Vuyisile, 8
Missionary Tales (Livingstone), 4
Mister Johnson (Cary), 25
Mittelholzer, Edgar, 48
Mnguni, — 48
Moeti oa Bochabela (Mofolo), 81
Mofolo, Thomas, 81
Morton, AL, 188
mother-tongue instruction, 107, 109, 112
Mpande (Zulu ruler), 8, 17
Mphahlele, Es'kia, 25, 47, 178–9
Mqhayi, SE Krune, 19, 81
Mshongweni (praise poet), 17
Mulder, Reinjan, 171, 183r
Multatuli, xvi, 187, 188, 189, 194–5, 197–9
   see also Douwes Dekker, Eduard

Nama, 73, 75
   auxiliary particles in, 78
   suffixes in, 77
'Nanga wan ai' (Trefossa), 125–6

Nangelizwe (Chief of the Thembu), 5
Narayan, RY, 180
Native Affairs Department (NAD), 107
Native Son (Wright), 36
'natives', 26
Ndaba, 15
negritude, 27-9, 70, 102
Nguni language, 73
  Xhosa, xii, 16, 80-1
    internal structure, 83
    noun classes, 84-6
    strong adjectives, 87-8
  Zulu, 86-7
Nguni praise poetry, 2, 3, 71
  functions of, 5-6
  heroism in, 16-17
  rewards, 18
  importance, 3-5
  of song, 7-8
  manner of recitation, 6-7
  meaning of 'praiser', 6
  metaphors, 8-9
  nature of poems, 6
  position of Mbongi, 8
Nienaber, PJ, 96n
Nkosi, Lewis, 43, 56, 64n, 148
Nkrumah, Kwame, 30, 63n
Nobele Wilden (Arion), 177-81
Non-European Unity Movement, 48, 49
Norse poetry, 2
  drapa and *flokkr*, 16
  kenning, 15-16
  literary devices, 15-16
  nature and subject matter, 14-15
  skald, 14
Nortje, Arthur, 55
Notes on the English Character (Forster), 191-2
Nouvelle anthologie de la Poesie negre et Malgache (Senghor)

Novib, 139
Nuis, Aad, 184r
Obja Sa Tan a Brewa (Cairo), 152, 153
Offa, 17
Offermans, Cyriel, 199, 200n
Old Man and the Medal, The (Oyono), 37
Oliver, Fanie, 115
Omer-Cooper, — 16, 23n
'On the Parade' (Small), 45
One Hundred and Seventeen Days (First), 61-2
Onions, CT, 22n, 23n
Opperman, DJ, 115n, 116n
Oral Literature in Africa (Finnegan), 3
Oyono, Ferdinand, 37

Padmore, George, 120
Palm, Jules de, 165
Papiamento, xiv-xv, 104, 164, 165
  see also Arion, Frank Martinus
Passage to India, A (Forster), xvi, 187, 188, 189-94
Pasternak, Boris, 55, 63
Path of Thunder, The (Abrahams), 36
Paton, Alan, 19-20
Peersel, Mr, 146
People's History of England, A (Morton), 188
Phillips, James Madhlope, 8
pidginization, 90, 94
Pina, Nicolas, xv, 164
Pipel, 134
Plaatje, Solomon, 81
poetry
  epic, 13
  see also praise poetry
political prisoners *see* emprisonment

Index

Pos, Hugo, 133, 138, 172, 183r, 184r
Powema Di Rutu (Cairo), 155
praise poetry, 1–23
   modern context, 18–20
   of Nguni *see* Nguni praise poetry
Price, Richard, 119, 140–1
Pringle, — 61
prison *see* emprisonment
protest writing *see* emprisonment

racism *see* stereotypes
Rais ku no ke Muri, E (The Root Won't Die) (Rosario), xv, 165
Ramsaran, JA, 193–4
Rastafarians, 34
Ravales, Robin, 136, 159n
re-tribalization, 107, 109
reggae, 34
Reve, Gerald, 166
Ritter, EA, 16, 23n
Rive, Richard, 148, 175
Romer, RG, xv
Roo, Jos de, 170, 182n, 183r, 184r
Rooij, Rene de, 165
Rosario, Guillermo, xv, 165
Ross, Robert, xiii, 39n, 47, 48–53, 97n
Rots der Struikeling, De (The Stumbling Rock) (van Leeuwen), 165
Rouffaer, GP, 96n
Rubusana, — 81
Ruku, 163
Rwanda of Burundi, 3
Rylate, VE, 67, 95n, 111

Sachs, Albie, 62–3
San, 70
   language of, 73
SANROC *see* South African Non-Racial Olympic Committee
'Santa' (Trefossa), 124
Sartre, Jean-Paul, 29, 56–7, 64n
Savage Hits Back, The (Lips), 38–9
scald *see* Nordic poetry
Schapera, — 75, 77, 86, 96n
Schuring, GK, 94, 96n, 97n
scop *see* Anglo-Saxon poetry
Seafarer, The 11–12
Selvon, Samuel, 137, 145, 148–9
Senghor, Leopold Sedar, 28, 29
Senzangakhona (Shaka's father), 9
Sepamla, Sipho, xiii, 43–5, 91–3
Shabase, 15
Shaka, 20n–22n
   heroism, 16–17
   metaphors for, 8, 9
   praise poetry and, 2
Sharpeville, 30
Shayer, Michael, 55–6
Shell, RCH, 48
Sherry (Lebacs), 165
'Shop Assistant' (Sepamla), 45
Shrinivasi, 152–3, 159n
Singane, 8
Sirens, Knuckles and Boots (Brutus), 58
Sithembiso, Mr, 110
Sitniakowski, 183r
'Sizbadubula' (Mini), 8
slavery
   absence of combined rebellion, 50, 51
   Cape of Torments, 48–53
   coloureds and, 48
   interaction between slaves and Khoisan, 51–2, 53
   literature on, 47–53
   relationship between sailors and slaves, 52
   slave-Xhosa relationships, 52
Slaves and Free Blacks at the Cape (Boeseken), 48
Slory, Michael, xvi, 153

Small, Adam, 45, 115, 117n, 136
Smeathman, Henry, 26
Smith, IK, 182r
Society for Proper Afrikaners, 88, 105
Soga, Tiyo, 81
Solzhenitsyn, — 55
songs
  freedom songs, 7-8
  importance of
    Anglo-Saxon poetry, 12-13
    Nguni, 7-8
    in Surinamese society, 137
  lobisingi (love songs), 31
  to express anger, 31-2
Sophia Town, 45
soul-brotherhood, 27, 30, 70
South African Non-Racial Olympic Committee, 57
South Street (Bradley), 38
South Western Township *see* Soweto
Soweto, cult value of, 43
'Soweto I Love, The' (Sepamla), 43-5
Soweto revolt against Afrikaans, 89, 101, 105, 110, 112-13, 114-15
Soweto Sounds, 43
Soyinka, Wole, 175
Sparrmann, — 80
Spender, Stephen, 58
Spoor, Corine, 156n, 157n
Sprache der Hamiten, Die (Meinhof), 78-9
Sranan Tongo *see* Surinamese creole
Stadler, Leon de, 22n
'Stemmen uit Afrika' (Voices from Africa) (Arion), 163
stereotypes, 25-41
  by extension, 26
  function of, 26

humour for social control, 33-4
inversion of, 34-9
negritude, 27-9, 70, 102
rationalizations, 25
rehabilitation of Africa, 28, 29, 30
songs to express anger, 31-2
Sumter, Archie, 179, 184r
Surinam, 31, 32, 104
  Anansi, the spider in, 33
  creole in *see* Surinamese creole
  Sarnami language, 94
Suriname: Spiegel der Vaderlandsche Kooplieden (Voorhoeve), 120
Surinamese creole, 104, 119, 119-29
  earliest texts, 120
  Sranan Tongo, 104
  Sranan Tongo, 134, 135, 136
    see also Cairo, Edgar
Surprise Jesus Joseph Mary, that we grabbed the missionary by the beard, 38

Teachers League of South Africa, 116n
'Teaching of South African History in Schools' (van Schoor), 49
Temekoe (Cairo), 133, 136, 137-9
Themba, Can, 45
Theodorakis, — 56
Thomas, Gladys, 128n
Those in Bondage (Kock), 48
Three Hundred Years (Mnguni), 48
Tjhaka *see* Shaka
Totius, 171
Towards Emancipation: a Study in African Slavery (Edwards), 48
Transition (Abasiekong), 58
Trefossa, xiii, xiv, 120-7, 133, 135, 151, 153, 156n

Index

Trefossa (cont.)
  later Christian poems, 123, 126
  on language and culture, 123-4
  on language and literature, 123
  poems of exile, 125-6
  see also individual poems eg 'Bro' Trefossa (Bureau Volkslectuur), 122
Treurnicht, Andries, 110-11, 114, 117n
Trilling, Lionel, 190
Trotji (Voorhoeve), 121, 125
Tsotsi-Taal see Afrikaans, Flytaal
Turville-Petre, — 3

Unity Movement, 48
'Unzima Lomthwalo' (Calata), 8

Valkhoff, Marius, 89
Valle, Susan de, 23n
van Dam, Henk, 184r
van de Pol, Barber, 148, 159n, 179-80, 183r
van der Bosch, Johannes, 195
van Doorne, J, 183r
van Houts, Catherina, 157n
van Leeuwen, Boelie, 165
van Schoor, Willem, 49
van Twist, Duysmaer, 196
van Wijnbergen, Everdine, 196
van't Veer, Paul, 195, 200n
Venetiaan, Ronald, 150
Verhael, 70
Verstappen, Jan, 183r
Vestdijk, Simon, 166
Vilakazi, Benedict Wallet, 3, 22n, 81
'Vision of the Cross, The', 20
Visser, Ab, 148, 182n, 183r
Vogelaar, JF, 149, 159n, 167-8, 181n, 183r
Voorhoeve, J, 39n, 90, 116n, 119, 120, 121-2, 124, 125, 127n, 128n, 133, 138-9, 140, 141-2, 144, 150, 151, 157n

Vreemde op Aarde, Een (Stranger on Earth) (van Leeuwen), 165
Vrij Nederland, 151
Vusmusi, Lawrence, 110

Walk in the Night, A (La Guma), 35-6, 138
Wallet Vilakazi, Benedict see Vilakazi
'Wan Bon' (Cairo), 153
'Wan enkri gado-momenti' (Trefossa), 126
Wanderer, The, 12, 18
'War against gems' (Arion), 166-7
Ward, IC, 79, 96n
Warner, Rex, 200n
Wauthier, Claude, 36, 40n
Weekendpilgrimage (Marugg), 164
Wekker, H, 156n
Westerman, D, 79, 96n
Whitelock, Dorothy, 17
Widsith (poem), 11, 13
Widsith (poet), 18
Wie Eegie Sanie (Our Own Things), 121, 150-1
Wild Conquest (Abrahams), 36
Willems, Jan Frans, 105, 116n
Wingate, Alan, 159n
winti, 137, 140-1
Wooding, Charles, 137, 140-1
Wright, Richard, 36, 156

Xhosa see Nguni language

Year in San Fernando, The (Anthony), 137
'Yu ay' (Trefossa), 126

Ziel, Henri Frans de see Trefossa
Zijderveld, Anton, 39n
Zulu language see Nguni language
Zulu Poems (Kunene), 17
Zulu-Kafir Dictionary (Dohne), 4, 71

For Product Safety Concerns and Information please contact our EU representative GPSR@taylorandfrancis.com
Taylor & Francis Verlag GmbH, Kaufingerstraße 24, 80331 München, Germany

www.ingramcontent.com/pod-product-compliance
Lightning Source LLC
Chambersburg PA
CBHW051057230426
43667CB00013B/2336